HARD TO *GRIP*

A MEMOIR OF YOUTH, BASEBALL, AND CHRONIC ILLNESS

EMIL DeANDREIS

schaffner press

Tucson, Arizona

First Edition
Trade Paperback Original

Cover Design: Evan Johnston
Interior Design: Darci Slaten

Library of Congress Cataloging-in-Publication Data

Names: DeAndreis, Emil, 1985 - author.
Title: Hard to grip: a memoir of youth, baseball, and chronic illness / by
   Emil DeAndreis.
Description: First Edition Trade Paperback Original. | Tucson, Arizona:
   Schaffner Press, 2017.
Identifiers: LCCN 2016051556| ISBN 9781943156146 (paperback) | ISBN
   9781943156177 (mobipocket) | ISBN 9781943156160 (Epub) | ISBN
   9781943156153 (pdf)
Subjects: LCSH: DeAndreis, Emil, 1985- | Baseball players--United
   States--Biography. | Rheumatoid arthritis--Patients--United
   States--Biography. | BISAC: BIOGRAPHY & AUTOBIOGRAPHY / Sports. |
   BIOGRAPHY & AUTOBIOGRAPHY / Personal Memoirs.
Classification: LCC GV865.D42 A3 2017 | DDC 796.357092 [B] --dc23
LC record available at https://lccn.loc.gov/2016051556

Printed in the United States

To Kendall

HARD TO GRIP

A MEMOIR OF YOUTH, BASEBALL, AND CHRONIC ILLNESS

CONTENTS

Prologue

WHEN BASEBALL BECAME MY ID

This may sound glaringly obvious, but: playing baseball at AT&T park as a high school student is completely different from playing there as a San Francisco Giant. Not that I have experienced both. But to draw a contrast—at Giants games, the players are big, both in the literal and figurative sense. They are idols of thousands, perhaps millions. Some of their little fans—and in odd cases full-grown fans—come in eye-black, or full uniform stirrups and all. Crowds reach 50,000. The noise at the stadium is a roar—deafening, glorious. The Jumbo-tron presents player profiles in million-pixel brilliance, like leaders of nations. Or mythical gods. And fittingly so, because after all, to many, fan and player alike at AT&T Park, Giants baseball is larger than life.

Playing there as a high school student, however? Not so much. At least in retrospect, I can attest. In a high school game at AT&T, few players are big, in any sense. Not the ace pitcher, not the cleanup hitter. Stirrups slide down because players don't have calves, pants slide down because hardly anyone has a butt. No one has fans. Probably because no one hits homers. Or throws 95. An exciting moment can constitute as a blooper that lands between the shortstop, second baseman, and pitcher. There are no vendors yelling "Hot dogs here! Get your hot dogs!" A cheering crowd sounds like a family of frightened cats.

But you couldn't have convinced me of that my sophomore year of high school. We were in the city championship. We'd made it all the way. And to add to the stakes, we'd lost the year before. A sobbing senior had taken me into his arms down the left field line and said "This won't happen again next year. You make sure of it." As a freshman, I'd found that moment to be profound, like the set-up to some Biblical saga. I thought of that player's comment as I warmed up for the championship, and I was jacked. The kind of jacked where I couldn't feel my arm, where the ball felt like a feather. So much so that I had to relearn how to throw it for a strike in the bullpen. After the national anthem, when my name was announced as the starting pitcher, I jogged to the mound as the crowd gave its meowing fanfare. There weren't thousands watching, but there were hundreds. And whatever I did in those seven innings would go down in some kind of history—even if it was an etching on a junky bronze trophy. I didn't feel like I was in an empty stadium. With no hot dogs. And no Jumbotron portraits. With shrimpy teammates all playing in a meaningless game. To a 16-year-old who'd played ball since diapers, this mattered. This felt like the world.

On a side note, it's funny, the things you end up remembering long after they've happened. The memories can be lucid or illogical or completely misshapen from years of detachment. When I think about my first memories, a few come to mind. One is eating banana popsicles at my babysitter's apartment in the Mission. Another is sitting on a swing set during the Loma Prieta earthquake in '89, seeing a girl in a wheelchair point at a blackbird and say "It was her!"

My most vivid first memory is of playing whiffle ball with Dad. We were on a dirt trail, cars parked alongside. I think it was a picnic, or birthday for someone else. There were eucalyptus trees overhead. Leaves and acorns were strewn about. I can still smell the eucalyptus trees. I had a red bat, the enormous one shaped like a turkey leg that every kid had. Dad underhanded me whiffles and when I hit them the bat went BOINK!

I loved the noise. It echoed. I giggled. Everyone cheered me on: uncles, Mom, Dad.

BOINK!

"Yayyyyyyyyyyy!"

Even strangers stopped to watch.

"Again?" I asked Dad. "Again?"

As I grew up, Dad took me out into the street after dinner to play catch. He nursed a tall can of Keystone in the bed of his sheet metal union truck, and we threw until the streetlights fluttered on. I remember the way the electrical wires crisscrossed through burning skies, and how I made sure to keep the ball low so as not to clip them.

"Hit me in the chest," Dad said. "Get your arm up, no sidearm crap."

In eighth grade my fastball broke my Dad's thumb. By the time it healed, I was throwing too hard. I'd grown, and wasn't done growing. We tried to throw again. He winced, couldn't squeeze the glove without pain. I was kind of stupid back then, so all I thought was, man this is kind of cool: I throw too hard for my own Dad. It was a source of pride, a baseball milestone. This was me becoming a man.

On my teams, kids asked, "How hard do you throw?"

I'd say, "Well, my Dad can't catch me anymore, so…"

I didn't see the other angles, anything deeper than that, such as: Dad having to learn the hard way he couldn't throw anymore, having to come to terms with his body shutting down, having to let go of a treasured pastime. All I registered as a 13-year-old was, I liked baseball a lot. Grape Big League Chew, high stirrups, the serious face that eye-black gave you, the nothing-feeling of hitting a ball on the screws. At bat I told myself a pretty girl was in the stands watching, and that if I drove in a run she would let me touch her in the parking lot after the game—and it worked. Not touching a girl, or even seeing a girl (the stands exclusively held parents and bored younger cousins and upset dogs). Perhaps more than liking baseball, I liked being good at it, staring a batter down and sending him back to his dugout. For me, no other feeling compared. I wasn't big on rollercoasters. And I didn't know drugs or videogames or even cable television.

So, what were my memories of my sophomore championship at AT&T Park? I still remember my first pitch—a strike—and the ump's call echoing across the hollow field. I remember his "ring-'im-up" call when the lead-off batter took an 0-2 fastball on the outer half. My nerves settled. I remember the middle innings when their cleanup hitter, a scary senior with full goatee (early 2000's when every real ballplayer had one), laced my changeup right at our shortstop for a one-hop groundout. Had that groundball gone one foot to the right or left, they'd have taken the lead, perhaps for good. I can't help but wonder at times how my career trajectory might have changed had that ball made it through. Because after the game, which we won in the bottom of the seventh on a walk-off double, a man approached me with his hand extended. We shook.

"Steve Ramon," he said. "I'm with the Cincinnati Reds."

Had we lost, had those sharp ground balls found holes, would the Reds' scout have introduced himself? In that moment, I felt I'd made it, like I'd already been drafted, almost like there was no further action needed. Like a Dominican, I'd be uprooted from my family and in the Bigs at 17. And I was okay with it. He gave me his business card with his number, and a questionnaire to fill out, the size of an index card. On it there were questions about my height, weight, what hand I threw with, where I was from. I filled it out and sent it back to the Reds' farm system immediately. Steve Ramon's business card went in my wallet (also immediately). I put it in the little see-through part where everyone puts their ID.

A few nights later, I was walking home from a friend's house. Poker, scavenging the dude's pantry—activities that took us into the wee hours. It was a misty night, the kind where water droplets did not fall from the sky, but hung suspended in the air—typical of San Francisco in summer. A few blocks from home, a small white pickup moved slowly, its brake lights flashing. Someone kept chucking something from the window. It became clear that it was a young boy and his dad, tossing the next day's paper. I picked one up, unsheathed it from its plastic bag, opened it to the sports section, and held it under the streetlamp. There I saw it: an enlarged picture of me, mid-pitch, with the AT&T right-field bricks as the backdrop. My face was clenched, my lips pursed. I looked like a taxidermied elf. My bent elbow had odd and gummy skin rippling like a turkey neck. Beneath the picture was an article that spoke to my prowess as a young San Francisco athlete. It recapped my strikeout total in the championship, how I'd thrown a complete game and pitched out of trouble. It also reiterated how young I was to be having this kind of success.

I could see it already, Dad driving around the Sunset District the next morning in his long-johns, coffee steam rising from his left hand, stealing everyone's papers with his right. I could see him cutting out the pictures, putting them in envelopes and slipping them into the mailbox. I could see myself in the kitchen of relatives at Thanksgiving, seeing that picture of me magneted to their fridge.

As I neared my house, I pulled out my wallet, flipped open to the ID. The card from the scout was still there. Of course it was, it had only been a few days. But I checked it constantly, like it might get stolen, or sprout legs and bolt. I pulled it out—it already had a soft, worn feel like old cloth from being handled so much. Steve Ramon, Regional Scout, Cincinnati Reds. Nothing had changed. I put it back in my wallet. Yeah, I thought. That is my ID.

And so, I guess that's as good a place as any to start my story. When baseball became my ID.

PART I:
HIGH SCHOOL

1
A PROSPECT—OF SORTS

I was right. The morning after the championship, my dad drove all around the city burglarizing people's papers. My scrunched face was framed and hung in the hallway. Then I won league MVP. It was the first time a sophomore had won since my coach, who'd been coaching for 20 years, could remember. As a junior, I threw a perfect game. I went undefeated, had a sub 1.00 ERA. More articles were written. Since covering prep high sports, as far as I could tell, was a low-man-on-the-totem-pole kind of thing for journalists, the writers seemed to treat my articles like a job interview. This resulted in their detailing my success on the mound with the drama of Custer's Last Stand. "Then with raw determination and cold-blooded resolve, DeAndreis threw the full-count pitch seemingly *through* the batter's bat," and so on.

By senior year, I started coming home from school to recruitment mail. USF and University of the Pacific invited me to tour their campus. These were the first two times I could remember tucking my shirt in. USF's pitching coach spoke with the slowness of a yoga instructor, showed the cafeteria in a whispery seductive voice that confused me. UOP's coach was thin with a mustache and crew cut—looked like the cop that gets sent out for doughnuts.

"Really shows the fall colors nicely, as you can see," he said as we walked through UOP's quad.

While on these tours, I remember thinking that the way the coaches described their campus sounded like they wanted *someone* to play for them. *State-of-the-art-library. Recently renovated dorms. Great restaurants nearby. Perfect baseball weather in the spring, a great place to spend four years, great place to be a student athlete.* But their tone, their lack of mentioning an interest in *me*, Emil DeAndreis, playing for *them*, struck me as curious. There was no specific interest in *me,* Emil Deandreis, left-handed pitcher. Just a handshake and a smile that made me wonder if they even knew my name.

Recruitment mail kept coming. Santa Clara, UC Santa Barbara, Sonoma State, St. Mary's, University of Arizona, and more. Even some small liberal arts schools on the east coast, like Tufts, which I'd previously thought was an all-girls school. I stored the mail in a shoebox, much as I had done with love notes in elementary school. Most mail began *Dear Prospect.* The letters went on to express an interest in *my proven abilities on the baseball field,* and a much more clarified interest in having me attend one of their expensive camps.

"Arm circles," I heard. "Forward ten, backwards ten."

It was 8 a.m. on a cold fall morning at a local D1 College, 45 minutes east of San Francisco. Mom and Dad had agreed to fork out the money, as a present, for one of the Prospect Camps. This was Day One. When our car slowed down at the gravel entrance, and I saw the baseball field to my right, I felt my nerves tingle. My parents let me out and I moseyed over to the left field line where the other recruits were congregating. I didn't say anything, just laced my cleats. It was a lonely feeling to be on a baseball field with complete strangers. I dreaded the moment when we were told to partner up for catch— everyone looking around clumsily, fleeting eyes, a bunch of jocks suddenly acting like it was the first day of kindergarten.

"Bend wrists back, forearm stretch."

As I looked around, some things took me by surprise. First of all, there were only about six of us, total. I'd thought this would look more like a tryout with flocks of guys at each position, ground balls and throws to home, timed sprints to first, batting practice, scrimmages. I expected there would be several coaches with clipboards and stopwatches shuffling around and barking orders. But, with only six players, that was not going to happen. One of us, I was almost certain, was in seventh grade. Another was 6'9" with the body shape of a praying mantis. When we threw our bullpens in front of the pitching coach, I expected this kid to have Randy Johnson-like velocity. He didn't. Instead, the pitching coach stood with a notepad and stared off at a distant hawk as this prospect lobbed dirt-balls. During my bullpen, the pitching coach—who was Australian, and hefty—futzed with my delivery.

"Now, how's about we tinker with your arm slight-like?"

He said my arm needed to be higher, that I needed to reach at the sky prior to my throw. His tweaks made my pitching delivery look like a tribal offering to the gods.

"It'll add years to your arm."

What it did was take the zip off my fastball. And make my shoulder hurt.

"Looking much better, mate," he said. "See the difference? Doesn't that feel better?"

"Yes."

My thoughts were, *no*. But I assumed this was standard, all part of the recruitment process. For the rest of the time, when I stood on the mound and threw in the uncomfortable way the Aussie coach had recommended, I told myself that I was doing what they wanted, putting myself in the best position to get a scholarship. After all, I *was* a recruit. I *was* a prospect. Otherwise, why would they have sent me the invitation to their camp?

Afterwards, I left them messages.

"I was at your Showcase Camp this fall. I sure had a great time. I learned a lot and improved my pitching tremendously. I'm wondering if you could see me on your roster next year?"

I never heard back. I called USF and UOP who had shown

me their cafeterias.

"Your campus was beautiful and I'd love to spend four years there as a student athlete."

No response.

I took a similar approach to other schools, essentially asking them to be interested in me. Shit. After the articles tabout me, the recruitment mails, not to mention the scout card from Steve Ramon, I had to be that good, right? So where were the scholarships? I'd always thought that, by now, fall of my senior year, I'd have at least a few offers. But with nothing yet, I was having to come to terms with the reality of my situation. I'd always felt embarrassed about it, and had always hoped it would never be a factor in my success. But it was, and I wanted to sweep it under the rug, lock it in the basement like a leprous son.

The reason I was so successful with the undefeated record, the low ERA, and treasure chest of awards and medals was that: *every other team in my league sucked.* In some cases, they sucked to the point where it almost wasn't baseball. I'd wager that less than one percent of our league's baseball players went on to play college ball. Many barely made it through high school without disqualifying themselves due to bad grades, or becoming fathers, or making the choice to bring a gun to school. I remember looking down the right field line as our opponents warmed up, and thinking they might be playing catch for the first time, somehow hitting their heads with their elbows as they threw, launching the balls thirty feet over their partners' heads. Some players insisted on sagging their baseball pants in a gesture of fashion, or allegiance to their urban roots. This made them unable to complete nearly every task of baseball. Many didn't know what a double play was, or the difference between a force and a tag play. Pitchers committed outrageous balks, and the umpires felt too bad to call them.

By the third inning our team was usually winning by 20. Our coach made us hit from the wrong side of the plate in the hope that we would *make* outs. And still we found it hard not to score. The other team would make errors, throw balls to the wrong bases, or no conceivable target whatsoever, and proceed to yell at each other as though this loss had not been anticipated.

With no money in our schools, we all played at the same lumpy public parks with no fences. I remember one year, during a playoff game, I was up with the bases loaded, hit a sharp ground ball, and wound up with a grand slam.

This wasn't baseball.

It didn't feel *good* to throw shutouts against them. For three straight years. But it was my only choice. If I was going to make it to college ball, I was going to have to do it in that league.

So I worked hard. I "played with a chip on my shoulder," as coaches suggested, though conceptually I had no idea what that meant, or looked like. Each day after school, I long-tossed, threw bullpens, hoped I was adding 1-2 mph to my fastball. I checked weekly to see if I'd grown an inch. I anticipated my senior year, hoped there would be more articles that glamorized my mediocre exploits. I wanted to believe the article about me. I wanted to stop worrying that all my accolades came with a disclaimer.

2
THE VOICE OF REASON

""There are plenty of junior colleges around here," my Mom said. "You've gotten letters from them. Why not just pick one of those?"

My mom experienced uncertainty in her childhood. She was never in the same school for more than a couple years. Money was thin. She moved out of her house at 16, hoping to create more stability for herself. And she did. She put herself through college, and was now raising a stable family. But she still harbored some of the survival tactics that aided her through her adolescence.

She remained cautious with money, insisted we live within our means. Her fight-or-flight senses seemed always ready to kick in, leaving her greatly sensitive to sound, smell, and taste. Anxiety caused insomnia, and insomnia caused anxiety.

She would toss around ideas for why she couldn't sleep—the precarious economy, political unrest in Botswana, rising cost of avocados, the Republican party, my grades, a decaffeinated tea she drank two days earlier, a particularly bright star in the cosmos. I once accused her of being able to hear a fish fart in the ocean, and she gave me a look like I was weird if I couldn't.

Before I was born, she'd been a clarinetist, a music major at San Francisco State. This was her passion and her hoped for career. Shortly after her senior recital, though, her wrists lit up with pain. This was in the '80s. Doctors didn't know what was causing the pain. She slept in hand braces. Eventually, her fingers began to deteriorate. Pressing the buttons of the clarinet, or extending a finger for a button caused wincing pain. With no strength in her wrist or fingers, she had to let go of a career, years of hard work, and a promising future in music.

She was pleasantly surprised when she learned she was expecting a child, as she would have something to focus her love and attention on. Not to mention, I would serve as a distraction to her anguish. As she raised me, her back would temporarily fall apart. I remember as a kid having to pick up her keys for her, or go to her bottom drawer in the morning to get her socks, then give them to her as she stood with her hands on her back, a 30-year-old woman with no prior history of back trauma. Sometimes, mom's neck wouldn't move, and in the car I'd look both ways for her before telling her it was OK to change lanes. Pain was worse some days, and other days, nonexistent. Like her insomnia, she was forever trying to find the causes. She like to accuse the dreary San Francisco weather. Sometimes, she suspected the wonton soup, or diesel exhaust that happened to engulf her.

When I was in middle school, Mom rented out a church to host her annual winter recital for her music students. She had some third graders playing Bach and played along as simple accompaniment. I watched from the seats, practicing my drumsticks on my lap for when I needed to accompany her jazz band for the grand finale. But then Mom pulled the clarinet out of her mouth, mid-song. She clutched her head, as if she'd had a brain freeze. She walked straight outside. Her students sort of fizzled out of the song. Heads from the audience perked up, and I stood to see whatever I could. Dad followed her out the door. She vomited on her shoes. A mother drove her to the hospital while Dad finished conducting the recital. At the hospital they did some tests on my mom, ran some colored ink through her brain and looked at it on a screen. She was having a brain aneurysm, and was rushed to UCSF for emergency brain surgery.

That week, he sat me down and told me the things Mom told him to tell me if she didn't make it. I don't remember what he said, but that it was the first time in my life that I saw him cry. Seeing her after surgery was one of those things that stick with me forever. I was used to Mom-in-an-apron, making grilled cheese after school, or Mom-with-a-scrunched-up-nose when trying to help me with math, or Einstein-hair-Mom in her robe in the mornings, blending me a breakfast smoothie. So seeing her in the wheelchair, her head half-shaved and stapled up the side, with a look like she'd been abducted by aliens—it was tough. I looked at the floor, and even in her drugged state, I saw she was embarrassed, but really wanted to see me. It was one of my first real-life moments.

It was also another ailment to add to her list.

As a high school student who'd grown up inundated in her world of woe, I'd say I handled it like a typical teenager. I had opinions on the whole thing that came and went in waves. I couldn't quite empathize, because I couldn't imagine a body riddled with mysterious pain. The only pain I'd ever felt had been caused by something. Elbow pain from too many curve balls. Lump on my thigh from getting pegged by a line drive. Gash on my shin from falling off my skateboard.

So how could someone hurt for no reason?

But I knew she'd worked hard for my life to be easier than hers had been. She peeled herself out of bed to make my lunch even mornings when anxiety attacks had kept her up all night. So who was I to get perturbed? She was just quirky, with her bloodhound senses and slight delusions. Sometimes it was even cute; other times, not so.

For instance, her opinions on how I ought to approach college:

"You should live at home. Go to College of San Mateo. It's an easy thirty-minute train ride. You bring a Tupperware lunch. Maybe sometimes Dad will let you borrow the truck. This saves the family thousands of dollars, and you still get to play baseball."

To me, that image hyper-sucked. Sometimes I felt that, since Mom had had to grind her way through life to finally achieve stability, she felt that I should have to grind through parts as well. Because to me, that's what junior college seemed like. A grind. The people I knew who went to junior college didn't *choose* to go. I believed they went because they couldn't go anywhere else—couldn't afford it, didn't have the grades. In terms of baseball, my sentiment was the same. To me, people didn't choose to play junior college baseball. They were too small, too injury prone, too undeveloped, or too dim to make grades for a proper four-year university. There wasn't much glory to that. It wasn't the image I'd been thinking of while drifting off to sleep. It wasn't what I'd envisioned when I'd been given the card from the Cincinnati Reds.

I imagined my life as a junior college baseball player waking up in the dark, taking trains for a two-hour commute, going to class, walking the campus in a haze without meeting anyone for lack of on-campus housing or college night life, sitting on a bench eating out of Tupperware, going to baseball practice, taking another sad combo of trains, eating my parents' leftovers. I would be an adult, still coming home and being asked, *What did you learn in school today?*

As an 18-year-old, all of this parental wisdom chapped my ass. It was the same common sense that had kept Mom alive in her teenage years. But I was fortunate enough that survival was not my only agenda; I was trying to be the best baseball player possible. And here I was being told to eat from Tupperware, and frugalize.

3
THE CATCHER, A PITCHER'S PARTNER IN CRIME

It was the year 2000. The scene, eighth grade All Star tryouts. Serious stuff, make no mistake. As we stretched, I scanned the others, checked the gear they were sporting, because everyone knew that kids with expensive gear were good. Shinier bats meant better hitters. Batting gloves dangling from a kid's back pockets meant: he was a baller. If he had Oakley shades, he was a future pro. Elbow guards? Hall-of-Famer. Naturally I had none of that stuff. Dad once bought me a bat at a yard sale that was so old the logo had been rubbed off. The bat wasn't even hollow, like the new aluminum bats—it was just basically a meat tenderizer, perhaps illegal.

We were told going into the tryout that 15 kids would be kept. 20 were at the tryout, and I was trying to gauge who would be sent home. Would it be the two freckled kids with the sniffles in the yellow and green jerseys? The lurchy kid in the burgundy windbreaker with the schnoz? Would it be me?

As we started to play catch, being watched by the coaches with the clipboards, in walked this new kid. We could tell he'd just taken the bus because we heard his metal spikes crunching across the street once the bus drove off. This kid was in a Big 4 Rents trucker hat, pulled over an orange-ish afro. With his freckles, flannel shirt, and exploded cleats, he looked more like some mischievous foe in *Huck Finn* than a ball player. We stopped throwing, and stared. Likely we were all wondering the same thing: How long's this kid gonna last before the coaches ask him to go home, or offer him a sandwich?

Then he hit. We watched, and collectively thought: *Jesus, one of us might end up getting the snip*. Everything he hit was on the line, and hard. I mean everything. And he hit 'em where they were pitched—rare for a middle-schooler. Pitches down the middle, he ripped right back at the L-screen, making the coach flinch. Pitches inside he shot so hard at the second baseman that he fled without even taking a stab at it. Pitches middle away were driven over the left fielder's head. His hits sounded different than anyone else's, like swords in old samurai movies. And he wasn't just flailing and miraculously connecting, like you'd expect from someone in a Big 4 Rents hat and flannel. His mechanics were smooth and explosive without trying to do too much. It was the kind of spectacle that made a budding adolescent squirm.

"Your name?" the coach asked, double-checking the clipboard for perhaps a Buck, or Elrod.

"Charlie. Charlie Cutler."

Charlie was only in seventh grade, but he quickly became our best player. He caught every pitch I threw that summer. As tends to happen between pitchers and catchers, we became friends. I learned his family was in real estate. They owned a few farms and a couple of ranches up and down California. From a young age, he'd spent weekends and summers doing farm labor, picking oranges and digging irrigation ditches, or on his ranches, wrestling lunatic baby bulls into sleeper holds in order to rubber band their balls as a form of neutering. So, as it turned out, Charlie's penchant for dressing like Annie's inbred cousin was a choice, a source of pride, not a result of his living in poverty.

Fast-forward five years, Charlie was the catcher at Lowell High. He was the best hitter in the league. Balls still flew off his bat differently than anyone else's. As he'd gotten taller and stronger, the parabolas of his bombs got steeper and more majestic. The balls shot into the air like mortars and spun with wild backspin. More balls went over fences that is, whenever we played on fields with fences. When we didn't, outfielders simply stood 400 feet away when he stepped to the plate.

Another thing Charlie continued to display in high school was his cowboy persona. He sported the boots, sometimes the hat. When he was a sophomore, his older brother Jake, a senior, and his younger brother Joe, a freshman, all sang a honkey-tonk version of "New York, New York" at the talent show. No one seemed to understand. It was like the brothers had a weird, dated energy. Which is worth mentioning here, because there was no more of a bizarre fashion statement, or identity for that matter, than a teenage cowboy-farmer-jock in San Francisco in 2003. It just didn't make sense. And it especially didn't make sense at our high school.

Lowell High School was known for its academics, ranked annually in the top 50 schools in America. 80% of the school was comprised of Asians who felt tremendous cultural and parental pressure to get into Stanford or Yale. They had no fucks to give about sports or anything unrelated to SAT preparation. The other 20% of Lowell—give or take—was a progressive crowd, with their minds wrapped up in the conflict in Iraq, and the objectification of women in pop culture. The *last* thing they were concerned with was school spirit, making Lowell the most befuddling place to try to be a standout athlete, or a Man in the traditional sense.

Yet Charlie walked around in a letterman and cowboy boots, and, chewing tobacco, he strutted about menacingly, dropping occasional slurs, outwardly supporting the Iraqi war just to spite liberals and defy the widespread political correctness.

I wasn't on the Cutler level. I was more evolved than that. But not by much. Our daily antics—they treaded the line between how-much-shit-can-I-get-away-with, to full-blown pagan. We found it hard to sit still. Farted in class, loudly. During harvest season, he came to school with boxes of oranges and tangerines from the family farms, and we cut class and sold them to nervous freshmen. On Friday nights we drank 40's at Big Rec, our home baseball field, took the empty bowling-pin-sized bottles and spelled a large "L" on the mound, for Lowell. We did this with grandiose visions of our rival high school somehow discovering our bold shenanigans, not considering that the people who were going to encounter our empty beers were disgruntled gardeners the following morning.

I slept at the Cutler house several days in a given week, opened their fridge like I was one of them. Sometimes, maybe because I was there so much, or because I had the same moppy curly hair, or because she was frazzled from raising three insatiable creatures, his mom called me Charlie. It wasn't a bro-mance, as in, I didn't pat his ass, and we didn't finish each other's sentences. But I didn't shake off his signs in games anymore, which was the baseball equivalent.

We had a sort of code. Unwritten, but formed from years of playing together.

A cornerstone bylaw of this being: no excuses. Charlie was the leader in this philosophy. He refused to sit around and listen to reasons why someone just struck out, or let the groundball go through his legs: *The umpire fucked me*, or *The sun was in my eyes*.

He found it childish.

"You fucked up," Charlie would say, lazily, but staring directly into the player's soul. "Simple as that."

In the rare cases when Charlie struck out, he'd come back to the dugout, and we'd all sit quietly, waiting to hear it. He'd grip the bat tightly, then drop it back in the pile. After a few deep breaths, Charlie would finally announce: "I fucked up."

This attitude toward baseball—it made the game for us the way it ends up being for many. More than a game. A spiritual thing. The last thing you saw behind your eyelids before falling asleep, even if it was just a sequence flashing over and over, the release point of a curve and watching it tumble into the glove for strike three, or seeing a pitch coming middle-in and opening your hips just a little to get the bat to the ball and driving it in the gap. These images lulled me to sleep at night

By fall of my senior year, when I was struggling to find a single school to recruit me, or even return my damn calls, Charlie was dominating. Colleges from around the country had started to call our coach and ask about him. I watched at school as our coach went up to him and whispered in his ear about the latest phone call from a recruiter. Charlie was swiftly becoming a national prospect. He was my best friend, and we'd grown up playing ball together, so I didn't resent it. But I couldn't help but have that feeling that family dogs must have when the first baby arrives: a bit pushed to the side.

4
MORNING STIFFNESS

It was a freezing October morning, the kind in San Francisco where the sun was out, but you still knew it was razor-tits cold and you had to layer up. My alarm sang. I reached my left arm over my head to slam it quiet, but something strange happened. My arm wouldn't move. I tried again, but all that I could muster was a shrug. It was stuck to my side.

In the kitchen, I heard the blender go off.

I sat up and I tried again to move the left. Elbow worked fine, but my shoulder was out of commission. Couldn't lift it. This was different than times when I'd slept on it, because then, my arm had been numb. This morning however, my shoulder was the opposite of numb. It was a deep pain, both dull and sharp at once. Dull and pulsing when left still, sharp and fangy whenever I tried to move it. It felt like someone had played a game of darts on it with tetanus needles.

I didn't shower. Toweling off was out of the question. Putting on pants, I had to pull up both sides with my right hand, then buckle and zip the fly with one hand as well. (Try doing that sometime, if you're ever in the mood to just get red-hot pissed.) Even walking, the natural swinging of the arms hurt, so I kept my left arm stuck to my side. In my class, we were given a pop quiz and I couldn't even write my name.

The next morning, I woke up and flinched before even moving, expecting the pain to still be there, or to have gotten worse, or for my arm to have just severed itself from the rest of my body overnight. But the pain had completely disappeared. Full range of motion had returned. I could shower, get dressed, run gel through my hair. My arms swung when I walked like the homo sapiens I was. But more importantly, I could lift weights, play catch. After school I did shoulder raises, bent over rows, dumbbell curls in the weight room. Charlie and I threw out on the football field. It was like the day before had been imagined, or just one of those anxiety dreams we all have growing up, like going to class naked, or running out of air underwater. *Never being able to pitch again.* The scariest dream ever.

A week later, the pain returned. Just long enough in between to have been almost forgotten. Again, it came overnight. It was as shocking the second time as it had been the first. The paralysis, the *tssss ow FUCK* reaction of having utter pain as the first sensation of the day. No shower, again. Walking to the bus stop, I had to sling both my backpack and jacket over my right shoulder. And this time, it stuck around for a few days.

At home, I wondered what the hell was wrong. Had I eaten anything out of the ordinary? Was I lifting too hard in the weight room? Throwing too much, too often? Was I unknowingly sleeping in a twisted shape like a figure in a Picasso painting? If this continued, how would it affect my senior season? How would it affect my college career? Or, how would I expect to have a college career if I found it challenging to put on pants?

I shrugged, which also hurt.

"I don't think I like the sound of this one bit," Mom said. She worried because, well, her worst nightmare was of passing down all of her non-winning health genes. And she wondered, with her symptoms of mysterious and unprovoked pain starting to spring up in her son, what it all meant. And more importantly, how bad would it get?

"Maybe you should take the year off from baseball." she said.

This was *Mom-throwing-shit-out-there.* Which was the exasperating cousin of *Mom-thinking-out-loud,* and a very close relative to *Mom-Debbie-Downer.*

"I'm just saying, everybody needs a rest," she said.

"Mom, please don't just throw around very upsetting ideas. I'm trying to get a baseball scholarship."

"Sure, OK, just carry on like you have been. Seems to be working out just fine."

This drove me close to the edge, and I exposed her for *Throwing Shit Out There*, to which she backfired with some mildly accurate statement that insinuated I too had no idea what I was talking about.

"Mom, no one ever gets scholarships after taking a year off from baseball."

"And no one ever gets scholarships when they're paralyzed in their throwing arm, do they?"

5
THE THEORY OF
MANNING UP

"You injured your shoulder sleeping?" Charlie asked incredulously.

"Yeah."

"You can't lift your arm?"

"Right."

"Huh."

Charlie's external confusion poorly masked his internal suspicion that I was turning into a pussy. I couldn't blame him. Remember, he had spent his childhood wrestling bulls and doing farm labor. He was a bacon and eggs guy. More specifically, a no-tofu-or-skim-milk guy. Steel-toe boots guy, not a cry-during-*Titanic* guy. So to him, taking a day off was bad enough. But on account of an injury accrued while sleeping? *Fatally* unmasculine. Clearly, at 16, he had some working theories on what made you a man. Such as like winning at all costs, not making excuses, etc.

He also maintained that, with enough will, a person could make anything happen. Think: the age old example of the woman lifting a car to save her baby. That, to Charlie, was human will at its finest. He also referred to this as manning up. If you just manned up, the world was yours. It was one of his vaguer theories, and it was forever blowing up in his face.

Exhibit A: I recall many dances in which Charlie was confident he was about to seduce a girl only to watch her swivel and gyrate frantically away from him.

Exhibit B: Once he claimed, "I'm about to go to Mr.

Culver's office and convince him to change my grade. I'm not walking out of there till he changes it." Minutes later he walked out with a lower grade, and a referral to the Dean.

Exhibit C: He thought sick people could "Man Up" their way through an illness—cold to cancer—his opinion was, the antidote was a nice dose of "Man Up." I remember late October, senior year, during the rainy season, to prove his masculinity and invincible immune system, he wore tank-tops and daisy-dukes to the batting cage while everyone else wore long johns, beanies and hoodies.

One day the wind picked up, whipped dead leaves against my skin so hard I got a papercut.

"Jesus, Charlie," I said. "Put on a fucking jacket, at least."

"Do you see me getting sick?"

"What time's your job interview at Hooters?"

The wind blew my hood off my head. It was so cold that even when you hit the ball with the barrel, it felt like you were hitting it off the handle.

"I'd go as far as to say it's crisp. This is what you call mental toughness. Marines gotta do this type of shit."

The next week he had strep throat.

As dumb as his theory was about manning up, I remember wishing that he was right. Particularly regarding my shoulder. *Wouldn't that be something,* I thought, *if all of these sporadic and unexplained pains could be gone with some Hulk Hogan vibes?*

I tried it a couple of times, telling myself there's no pain, there's no pain, be a man. I even gorilla-beat my chest a couple of afternoons to psych myself up, or to beat the pain away. I'd get about four fluffy tosses into catch and then have to quit.

That December I was invited to play on an "Elite Showcase Team," in other words, my family was invited to shell out a lot of dough for me to play baseball. Games were held at various junior colleges around the Bay Area. College coaches came to the games, looking for seniors to sign.

Everyone on the team was better than me. They were taller and bigger. Legs were trunk-like. Calves looked like socks stuffed with insulation. The pitchers threw harder. Their deliveries were smoother, their curve balls sharper. Playing out there with them, I felt like a weiner-dog racing greyhounds.

Each week, a new kid signed with a college. When that happened, their attitudes changed. They suddenly were nonchalant, chewed gum more slowly, smiled more, jogged easier, more "Baywatch"-ish. It ached to watch them. I chewed gum like a frightened mouse. I did all the little things that coaches said scouts look for (which I quietly suspected was bullshit). Things like wearing my hat the right way, sprinting on and off the mound, going out and high-fiving a pitcher as he came in after an inning. Sometimes I glanced in the stands and the scouts were oblivious to me, and busily texting. I wasn't getting approached by anyone, and clearly none of them cared how I wore my hat if I was throwing in the 70s. December passed by, and scholarships were given to over half the guys on my team.

To complicate matters, on some of those Saturdays, I would wake up with shoulder stiffness and wonder how I would get through this mess. How would I possibly go on a mound in front of scouts when I couldn't even lift my arm. Would I suddenly drop down to submarine like so many other pitchers whose shoulders blew out? Would I pioneer a new pitching strategy which entailed a whole arsenal of pitches under 40 mph? Or would I sit out—a missed opportunity in front of college scouts?

At the field on those mornings when I was ailing, I watched the scouts arrive with coffee and sunglass tans and polo shirts. They had the ex-player bodies: big forearms and chins, with intimidating I'm-Bored faces. I watched them put their equipment together, their radar guns, their charts, and told myself: *There is no way I should pitch. I can't even wave hello. There's always next time. Mom would be not just saddened, but angered, if I took the mound. It's baseball, it's just a game.* But then I thought: *Listen to me. I'm making excuses. If I make an excuse now, I'll make more. I'll have a reason why I didn't pitch, then I'll have a reason I pitched bad, and ultimately I'll have a reason why I never played college ball, why I never met my dreams. Telling Coach my arm is sore gives the impression that I'm weak. Dainty. Unready for D1 ball. Fuck that. If I'm not ready now, I won't ever be.*

During pregame, I jogged until my body was hot and my shirt was soaked. I leaned over my legs and dangled my left shoulder and did arm circles. My arm cracked, *clickety clack,* and electric pain rang out across my body. I went somewhere hidden and punched my arm, socked it so hard that, for a moment, my shoulder was numb, perhaps from shock, and I could lift my shoulder. I told myself, *all I need to do is get the ball sixty feet for a couple of innings.*

That fall my fastball ranged from 80 mph on the Saturdays I was pain-free, to 60 on the days I was hurt. 60 mph fastballs on a scout team! When I lobbed pathetic rainbows, I looked in the stands to see where the scouts were from, and told myself, *well, there goes any hope of playing at that school.*

"Everything ok out there?" Coach asked once.

"Yeah, I think I'm slipping on the mound," I said. Later that inning, I saw him in the dugout, scratching his head. Scouts had to be wondering how I'd made this team, why I was pitching alongside real college prospects. They had to be considering this a monumental waste of their Saturday. Either that or they were laughing. And I wished I had an answer for them, but instead, I was scratching my head along with them.

6
THE ISLANDS

"I want to extend a warm *aloha*," said Chad Koniri, pitching coach and recruiting coordinator of the University of Hawaii Manoa baseball team.

"Hope your guys' flight was cherry."

It was February; my senior season was now upon me. Our coach had scheduled a preseason tournament in Hilo, Hawaii. I'd never been to the Islands before, or anywhere tropical, except the aviary at the zoo. So there I was, a first-timer to Hawaii, wearing a windbreaker, and socks and sandals. Standing beside me were my teammates in similar tourist clothes. Lots of cargo shorts, bucket hats. Sunburns lurked for all of us.

We were in the middle of a seven-hour layover in Honolulu, and our coach had chosen to rent vans and take us to the University of Hawaii at Manoa to watch their baseball practice. We'd just been shuffled onto the field via the first baseline entrance.

"We're honored to have you," Koniri said. "Hopefully this gives you a sense of the way a college baseball program operates."

The muggy afternoon air glued my windbreaker to my arms. The sun's rays poured down on us molasses-thick. I scanned my teammates in our awkward teenage clump, looking like a greasy combo of the bored and lost. Personally, I was on edge. Why? Because the week before, I had called every college in the islands that had a baseball.

"Hi, Coach Koniri, my name's Emil DeAndreis and I'll be pitching in a tournament in Hawaii next week, blah blah blah." Hang up. Dial. Ring. Voicemail. "Hi, Coach Estrella, my name's Emil DeAndreis and I'll be pitching on the Big Island in a tournament next week," blah blah blah…Hang up. Dial. Ring. Voicemail. "Hi, Coach Sato, next week," etc.

I asked them to consider coming to scout me, that I was passionate about college ball, and felt I could "have an immediate impact on their program." Then I lied and told them I threw mid-80s. No coach responded.

"So, feel free to ask any questions," said Koniri. "Take mental notes. With some hard work, and a good attitude, hopefully someday you can be a Rainbow Warrior just like these guys."

Behind him, I watched a group of players jogging in black shorts and green, Underarmour shirts with the triangle-studded H logo. Some kids long-tossed down the left-field line. I observed two players throwing bullpens. A group was hitting off of tees into a net, another in the cage. The clink of aluminum bats was everywhere. Someone yelled "rotate!" and the action stopped and bodies migrated. The artificial grass was spongy; the ground balls took true bounces. What a place. I wanted to be jogging casually in H shorts, drinking cold water from the cooler after a pen, getting the ice wrapped around my arm by the trainer. I glanced at the stadium: immaculate, with waxy green seats shaded under a hulking cement overhang. Enough seats for hundreds, lights for night games in perfect 80-degree baseball weather.

Now, standing before Coach Koniri, I had the bubble guts. Racing through my mind were all those cliché phrases you hear about first impressions, how they're the most important, how they're always remembered, how your life path can be shaped by a handshake. I wondered if I should show the initiative and approach him, but worried I would stumble on words or scare him with some freakishly intense gushing like, "This place is my dream. I want to play here so *fucking* bad! You don't understand, I could cry. I brought you some Ghirardelli chocolates. I love you!"

Would he introduce himself? Would he thank me for showing assertiveness in calling him? Would he say that it's just that kind of maturity and commitment they look for in a young man? Would he grill me with pitching scenarios? Would he go drill-sergeant on me and tell me all the ways I wasn't cut out, starting with my windbreaker-in-Hawaii move? Would he have me throw a bullpen?

Had he even checked his messages?

"Ok, Lowell. I've got to get back to practice. Good luck in your tournament. Hoping you get a good taste of that *aloha* spirit!"

We clapped at the corny shit. Coach Koniri shook our coach's hand and they exchanged politician-like laughs.

Then I watched him mouth, "Which one's DeAndreis?"

It happened in slow motion. This was my chance at that first impression. It was happening. I tried to control my breath, had pre-decided to give a medium firm handshake—showing him I was a man, but not desperate to prove it—making sure to look him in the eye. I'd already come up with a cheesy line I'd say about the utopian tropical weather: "I guess I could get used to it. Ha ha!"

Our coach discreetly pointed his nose in my direction. I bulked up my chest, squared my shoulders and clenched. As I stood there, feeling like I might bust a vein in my neck, Koniri eyed me, nodded as though he'd stored data, and walked away.

Later at the airport, waiting to hop islands, our coach tapped my shoulder.

"Manoa's coach asked about you," he said.

"Oh yeah?"

"Exciting stuff, huh?"

* * *

"Get in the box, motherfucker," I growled from the mound.

It was dusk in Hilo, Hawaii. Game One of the tournament. 70 degrees with humidity, majestic, purple clouds on the horizon. The stadium lights buzzed. It was the third inning. In this weather, with adrenaline going through me, my arm was elastic. The ball was weightless. I could watch the fastball fly out of my hand, and hear it sizzle toward Charlie, watch it start in the strike zone and tail to the lower outer half.

There's nothing like being in rhythm on the mound. You feel like you're in a world you've created, and you're pulling the puppet strings. Every pitch is an opportunity to be Zeus. This was the kind of night—with the exhilaration of pitching Game One of a tournament, in perfect weather—when I knew I was going to go complete game, the beginning of a masterpiece. Hilo High was not a bad team. They had guys signed to D1's for that next year, a few guys that could easily hit a ball out of the park. They put good swings on the ball, which was why throwing past their bats, dropping in curves for called strike threes, painting the outside corner with my two-seam, felt even more empowering.

In the dugout between innings, I looked under my hat. "XIII," Roman numeral thirteen etched in permanent marker. "13" was the number I'd chosen as a sophomore. My thought had been to defy the superstitions surrounding it: *13 is unlucky? Fuck that, stack the odds against me, and I'll prove how lucky it is!* That year I won the league MVP, and I stuck with "13". Next to XIII was the graffiti: *the thrill of victory, the agony of defeat,* (from a Wu Tang Clan lyric), inscribed for the season, already blurring from the sweat of the night.

In the third inning, a lefty stepped in. Tall, skinny kid. Charlie called curve. Just a get-me-over in case he was digging in to hack at the first pitch.

Strike one dropped right in under his elbow. I backed it up with another for strike two. He rolled his eyes, looked out at me like *challenge me, you pussy.* And my thoughts were: *You don't like it? Swing.*

Strike three, fastball, down the middle, taken. He rolled his eyes, this time at the umpire like it was his fault. But there was no conviction in his glance; he knew it was a strike, and didn't want to own up. Those are the moments, as a pitcher, when you feel like a god controlling the game, feeling stronger from the pain and failure of others.

"Fuck you," I mouthed at him as he slumped back to the dugout.

In normal life, I didn't think of myself as a bully. On the contrary, I had a pretty big heart. I loved puppies. I didn't kill moths that batted senselessly against the lamp, but trapped them in my hands and released them out the window. Similarly, on dewy San Francisco nights when the snails made their sidewalk voyages, I picked them up and placed them in gardens to prevent them from turning them into escargot. I listened to classical music, emotional, pretty music, Mozart's *Requiem, Très Gymnopédies* by Erik Satie. I was an adagio kind of guy. I cried during *Lion King*, even *A League of Their Own* when Betty Spaghetti's husband dies in the war.

But on the mound, something changed. I got irrational. I approached every opposing hitter as though he'd wronged me in some unforgivable way. Each at-bat called for my revenge. I cursed at them. I spit at them. I hissed things under my breath that, if I heard myself say today, I'd have trouble not laughing at, like: "Get shit on by an elephant."

Deep down, I knew this came from a place of insecurity. I knew I wasn't as good a baseball player as I wanted to be. Being good in a shitty league, good with an asterisk, was a psychological grind. So each day on the field was a battle to prove myself. And I think that hostility, that energy gave me the extra edge I needed.

On this particular night in Hilo, there was an extra fire under my ass. I knew if a coach were there, noting first pitch strikes, and how my fastball tailed, and how I seamlessly pitched backwards (threw fastballs in off-speed counts, and off-speed in fastball counts), he'd like what he saw. But as far as I knew, no coach was there. None had returned my calls. So here I was, pitching in a tournament with real ballers, and *shoving*, with no one there to see it. And that felt like a wasted outing. So I took it out on Hilo High.

The next day at 6 a.m., our hotel phone blew up, the way all hotel phones do at six in the morning. I immediately went into a state of panic. The area around my shoulder was soaked from the melted bag of ice I'd fallen asleep on. I groaned for someone else to answer it. My roommates pretended to sleep through it. I knew they were awake; this phone was like a tsunami warning. Eventually, I caved:

"Hhhhhhhe?" I sighed into the phone.

"Emil. Good morning. Coach Estrella, University of Hawaii Hilo."

My heart attack entered stage two.

"Oh, yes, good morning, Coach, how are you today? I hope well?"

He chuckled.

"Sorry for the early call. We old people are up with the sun."

"I was already up."

"I wanted to say, I was at your game last night. I left in the fifth. Did you finish?"

"I did. We won 4-2."

"You handed it to our hometown school, ah?"

"These islands have some good pitching weather."

"Well, that's what I'm calling about."

I was clutching handfuls of bedding; heart attack stage three.

"We hope you think Hawaii would be a nice place to come and play. Division One, great strength of schedule. A bit far from home, I know. But it is Hawaii, Division One. Next year, our strength of schedule is ranked eleventh in the nation."

"Is that right?" I said knowingly; I had no idea there was such a ranking.

"We play Florida State, Nebraska, Cal. We play the teams that go on to the College World Series, Emil."

I thought about joking: "Actually Coach, I've been really holding out for Kentucky, or West Virginia. Since I was a kid, I've dreamt of freezing winters and McDonalds as the only restaurant for miles." But I chose to curb the sarcasm. This wasn't a time for jokes, not after dreaming of this moment for so long.

Hawaii. wasn't the typical setting for good old-fashioned baseball, America's pastime, with hot dogs, peanuts, American flags, Creedence Clearwater tunes in between innings. It was about as far from that as possible. But it was *Hawaii.*

I spent the day replaying the conversation in my head, and envisioned myself floating in the tropical waters of the Hilo coast among striped fish and prehistoric-looking sea turtles. *"We hope you'd like to play here."*

Despite having thrown seven innings the night before, my shoulder wasn't sore. Or maybe it was, but the soreness felt good. Everything felt good. The smell in the air was floral and salty, drowsy like a lullaby. The look everywhere of thriving foliage, knotting itself and crawling for a place in the sun, the geckos and the butterflies and the reggae in passing trucks: everything felt good.

7
THE PACT AND THE PINKIE

That phone conversation with Coach Estrella was revitalizing. It told me all the weights I'd lifted, all the long toss, all the phone calls I'd made to coaches across the country—weren't in vain. It told me that after all the recruitment mail I'd received that said "Dear Prospect," making me worry that I was anything *but* a prospect, there was finally a coach who knew my name. And he felt I was equipped for D1. Now in class, when we were allegedly learning about kinetic energy, and supply and demand, and *Madame Bovary,* my mind was checked out. I was off pitching at Wong Stadium in Hilo, wading in the warm waters, as the ocean lapped against the lava rock shore.

Fast-forward a few weeks, Charlie and I were in the Lowell batting cage. Actually—our batting cage could hardly be called a batting cage. The floor of the cage was not turf, or even level ground, but sand. Batting practice balls were heavy and potato-shaped from the elements. The L-screen, which we threw behind for protection, had holes through which line drives routinely whizzed. Really, the place hardly even looked like a batting cage; with the torn netting and sandy floor, it was more like a corny restaurant trying to pull off a pirate theme. We hit in there five days a week, and had the bruises to show for it.

Our Hawaii trip was now three weeks in the rear view. It was back to the soaking, bone-chilling, rainy months of February in San Francisco. Charlie was sitting in the dirt, stretching in what looked like a halter top and speedos.

"It's pretty far away," he said, leaning into a grotesque butterfly stretch.

"Yeah, but still, how cool would it be? College, Hawaii, baseball."

"All good things."

We were playing "The Game." "The Game" was something we invented and uncreatively named. There were no stakes in it but pride, which for me and him, was enough. You got 20 pitches, and the person with the most hits won. A hit was anything that passed the screen on a line drive. The pitcher usually did what he could to mess up the hitter. I threw screw balls and unfair heaters from 30 feet away. Charlie tried similar tactics. But while he was a much better hitter than me, he was a much worse pitcher. His curve balls sucked. Just before he threw one he always slowed his arm down and made a face like someone had farted in it. I hit the cover off his curves. If you asked me, I'd say I won The Game more. He would disagree. We played every day until it was too dark to see, then we'd get picked up by his mom.

"What if we both played in Hawaii?" I asked.

"That'd be something," Charlie allowed.

"Seriously. Think about it."

"I just said."

Charlie didn't seem too enthralled by the idea. Certainly not as enthralled as me. In that moment I realized he was better than Hawaii. Hilo *and* Manoa weren't good enough for the caliber of player he was becoming. One year from then, he expected to be getting recruited not just by D1s, but some of the best D1s in the country. I could see that, if in a year his best options were Hawaii, he'd see it as a letdown. He wasn't going to be like me, scrambling to get coaches interested; he was going to be juggling scholarship offers. He was trying to be nice about my Hawaii dreams too, all gentle and polite, which made it even worse. For his personality, and the friendship we had, it would have been easier to swallow had he said, "Hawaii's not on my radar, straight up," and then belched, and walked off.

The idea of Hawaii continued to consume me. Every weight I lifted, every mile I ran, every game I pitched, I had my eyes set on getting there, however I could. Again, college baseball hopes affected my sleep and my grades. I stopped studying. Teachers gave up stopping at my desk when it was time to turn in homework. My head was so far in the clouds with baseball dreams. I felt like one of those neurotic mathematicians who becomes so obsessed with one proof that the rest of his life crumbles as a result.

My senior season went by. We won the championship. Pitching AT&T again was a rush. It was surreal, dreamy. The kind of thing you go through and then later that night you can hardly remember the big details—how we scored, how they scored, the coach's pep talks in between innings. I remembered the little parts, the smell of the grass, the seagulls circling overhead, the noiseless moments in between pitches, the echoes. It's weird, but when you play baseball for so long, those moments are just as much a part of the game as the rest.

I won team Pitcher of the Year again. Charlie won league MVP. But if our league had taught me anything, it was that those accolades meant diddly. They were for Dad to keep in a box downstairs with the articles about me, beginning to yellow from time. What mattered was: I still didn't have a scholarship. Coach Estrella had never called back.

I settled with playing for San Mateo, a local junior college. I was going to be one of those kids I'd formerly judged, who went the JC route because nowhere else wanted him. I swallowed the idea of living at home and taking trains for hours, and getting home late.

My extended family was going to wonder: What happened? What about the articles, and the scout card? What about getting drafted?

I wasn't going to lie, say some coach promised me money and screwed me. I wasn't going to make excuses about my weak-ass shoulder, or how our screwball league drove away scouts. I was just going to tell the truth: I wasn't good enough. I wasn't who we all thought I was. I hated it. It made my stomach burn.

Signing yearbooks with all the lovey comments and nostalgia, going to graduation rehearsal, doing all the senior festivities like barbeques and scavenger hunts and water parks, where everyone snuck fruity vodka in Crystal Geyser bottles, all this stuff that was supposed to be so carefree and loose—it all felt tainted. I couldn't help but envision what all of it would be like if I'd secured that scholarship, and cemented my identity as a D1 ballplayer. Even drinking beer on Tank Hill with Charlie and other teammates on glorious evenings in May felt like being in mourning.

One afternoon, I had to go down to San Mateo to take the math placement exam. I was in this cafeteria-ish dungeon with a hundred other seniors, sitting at the hard, cold foldout tables. No one wanted to be there. Some kid next to me was talking loud to his friend so everyone could hear. He expounded on his philosophy about chicks.

"The way you do it dude? It's all about the three B's. You bang, you bust, you bounce."

The kid was a virgin, clearly. He laughed like a hyena and his friend inched away.

How would I possibly survive two years of this?

Then, at the end of May, a couple of days before graduation, I was just getting home from the senior class barbeque, when our house phone rang.

"Sure, one minute," Mom said, handing me the phone.

"Emil. Coach Estrella, University of Hawaii Hilo."

I felt like a lady in a soap opera who'd thought for years her husband was dead, only to hear his voice crackle through the receiver one afternoon: *Celeste…it's me.*

"Apologies for the radio silence. We got busy with our season," Coach Estrella said. I'd kept up with their season, checking their website a few times a week to see how they were doing: what he meant by "we got busy," was "we've been losing."

"No problem, Coach."

"I'm calling in hopes that you're still available?"

"Whoa."

"Like I said last we spoke, we'd like to have you come aboard next year. We've got a scholarship with your name on it. Full tuition, if you're interested."

I would have signed for a scholarship of Sausage McMuffins.

"Thank you, Coach."

That "Thank You" was layered. It meant thank you for the chance at D1 ball, first and foremost. It also meant thank you for fulfilling a childhood dream. But it also meant, thank you for validating a year of hard work, for diffusing a major insecurity of mine, for letting me sleep again. Not to mention, thank you for bringing me to Hawaii. So he heard thank you, but he had no idea.

I can't remember how the conversation with Coach Estrella ended—I was at a level of excitement that likely took a few years off of my life.

That summer, I played on a semi-pro team with college guys, and Charlie. Again, he was young for the team, but better than most of us. We played junior college teams in the Bay Area, much like I'd done that previous fall. Charlie and I took BART each day to warm Bay Area suburbs for night games. Diablo Valley, Laney, Santa Rosa, Ohlone, etc. The routine was glorious, vegetating on the train with baseball gear and beef jerky, talking about girls who were so hot we wouldn't last a minute with them, playing night games on well-kept college diamonds, eating postgame Taco Bell, trying our luck with the nearest liquor store, catching a buzz on the sidewalk in the warm night air before taking BART home and getting home after our parents were asleep. Nothing mattered that summer but baseball. My relationship with it was romantic. The perfect relationship. A honeymoon, no fights, no misunderstandings, nothing from the past resurfacing to ruin tender moments. The redundancy of the days was therapeutic. It was the kind of summer that could never get old, the type that you forgot would someday end, that made you feel so warm and worriless you could drool.

Except for when, a quarter of the way through the summer, my pinkie blew up.

Overnight, it looked like a traffic cone. It didn't even fit in the pinkie hole of my glove; I had to jam it in.

"You have an anteater at the end of your hand," Charlie assessed one day on the train.

As summer progressed I started having to play with my pinkie out of the glove. That summer, I began to wonder: *do other players have stuff they go through like this?* I knew teenagers "went through stuff." That was all we learned in Health Ed., that teenagers struggled and it was all normal. Maybe other players had stuff that I couldn't see. Diabetes, lupus, anxiety, bunions, or the disease where you always needed a bathroom nearby. Did they have parents who got laid off and became alcoholics and gamblers at the Indian casinos? Did they ever feel moments of vulnerability, or insecurity?

I couldn't imagine they did; they always seemed so drowsily content. They were always burping, stealing someone's protein bars, reciting favorite Dane Cook lines like "Dude, smell my eyes!" or "I will punch a bee in the *face!*" They appeared at all times completely without a care in the world, free of symptoms whatsoever. When we stayed in hotels for tournaments in So-Cal, my roommates were always asleep before me, snoring within minutes.

One night my coach came up to me during a game we were losing. He had a worn-out, sick-of-losing, I-want-to-go-home face. "DeAndreis," he said, and exhaled a balloon's-worth of air. I stood, expecting to be sent to the bullpen to warm up. I unzipped my jacket, and scanned for my glove. Soon I'd be warming up, hearing that catcher's glove pop over lazy country music. Then I'd be in the game, the moths clouding around the stadium lights in between pitches. I'd throw my change-up to a power hitter and enjoy the *whish* of his bat as he swung and missed. "Wiggle it," Coach said.

"Huh?"

"Wiggle the pinkie."

I wiggled. Coach's eyes widened, almost in terror, then he keeled over and wheezed with laughter. Phlegmy, joyous laughter. It wasn't the last time he cheered himself up this way. I didn't mind. It calmed him, kept me on his good side, even better than pitching well. And I had to admit, it looked pretty funny, the pinkie. So I laughed too. I didn't know what else to do.

Not surprisingly, Mom didn't laugh. Instead, she sent me to have it looked at, to be sure I wasn't turning into her, a walking medical mystery. She had me go to the first appointment available, even though it meant missing a summer game.

"Off to Hawaii, huh?" Dr. Young, my sports doctor asked in our first appointment. He had shaggy wet curls, looked like he'd just come from the ocean and changed out of his wet suit and into his smock.

"Yep, at the end of the summer."

"Nice, bro. Going to play some ball?"

"Yeah, pitch."

"Epic."

His demeanor relaxed me, made me feel like I was chilling with him in the back of his pickup after surfing, but his decision to call me "bro" led me to ponder how much medical school he'd passed.

"So you got a messed up pinkie? Let's have a look at that

th—WHOA—ha ha!"

He applied the stretchy opaque glove that smelled nauseously sweet, took out the gauze, the alcohol, the needle.

"Looks like a Bugle chip."

Then he did what doctors do when they're digging around in you with a needle. He tried to distract me with small-talk.

"I played some D2 hoops myself."

"Really?"

"Yeah, a small D2 out in Michigan. Point guard. Had a good career, except my knees kept giving out. Had a few surgeries, red-shirted, then med-red, until finally I was like, it's over, bro."

"Man, sorry."

"Don't get me wrong, it was a blast, apart from the knees? It just got to be a drag watching all the other bros that I was better than come in and…ha ha…*seize what was once mine.*"

"I bet."

I felt woozy. Maybe it was the talk of the blown up knees, the pain and swelling and limping that he surely had to endure. I imagined surgery after surgery and rehab after rehab, the nausea from local anesthetic.

"Oh, here it is, I think I got it," he said

I did not know what "it" was. I wasn't so sure he knew either. He pulled the syringe. I watched it fill with mucousy blood.

"Should take care of it."

I turned pale, felt a curtain of steam pass over. My armpits stung with sweat. I swallowed bile. His story made me feel cramped by the nearness of his pain, and the hard fact of a career due to and injury and surgery.

"You alright? Ha ha."

His laugh was hiccupy, stonerish.

"That's just a little fight-or-flight kicking in," he said. "Perfectly normal."

He took off his glove.

"Good luck in Hawaii, bro. Eat some raw fish. And, hey. Put that thing on a leash."

He pointed to my finger.

"I'll do my best."

PART II:
THE COLLEGE YEARS

8
FACING RUTH

I was sitting in the third base dugout of Wong Stadium. Except, I should say, the dugout wasn't really a dugout, but a few rain-warped benches, some fold-out chairs. It was the fourth inning, game two of the series. Across the field in the first base dugout, our opponents: University of San Diego. We were losing 4-0, and the night before, they'd beaten us 12-4.

I was tuning in and out of the game, as pitchers who aren't pitching tend to do. Flicking seeds in my mouth, keeping my eye on the pink lawn-chair in case my teammate got up for a Gatorade refill, knowing I would have to concede it the minute an upper classman wanted it. I looked out into the field. The same field I'd pitched on one year before, a senior in high school, in my campaign for the scholarship. The same bright green crabgrass and chocolate-brown infield dirt. The same chain-link outfield fence, buzzing stadium lights, and echo of claps in the mostly empty stands. I took my hat off, looked at it. Fitted 7 1/8, mesh material, cherry red, with the UH Hilo logo on front, to go with the cherry red jersey, home white pants, red stirrups. I turned my hat over. Under the brim read: *the thrill of victory, the agony of defeat,* graffitied with a Sharpie the night before Game One.

"DeAndreis."

My head perked up.

It was our pitching coach, "Coach Kal" Miyatake, a stout man with a Fu Manchu, and modest, yet somehow intimidating, mullet. I'd come to trust him over the fall. He instilled the faith in yourself that out of hard work came good things, and he acknowledged when he sensed you were working hard. He was skilled at getting his guys to play with a grudge and to fear no one, both helpful qualities to have on a chronically losing team.

"Get loose," he said grimly; his all-business attitude went against everything a mullet stood for. I sometimes smiled at his display. But in this moment, my nerves went haywire. Coach Kal pointed his nose down to the bullpen, in case I'd forgotten the procedure. I scattered for my cleats; I didn't even have them on. Another relief pitcher patted my ass in support.

My first college outing was materializing. I should have been excited to be sent down to get loose. It had been my hope to be an impact player as a freshman at a D1 program, and here I was getting called on in the second game of the season. That was as quick as it got. Yet, my hands were shaking. Heart hiccupping. Bending over to tie my cleats, I almost fell face-first in dirt. My fingers couldn't even control the laces. Was it excitement? Sure, but this was a lot more than excitement. It didn't feel like Christmas morning; I felt like I'd just been summoned by the Sarge for a mission everyone knew I wasn't coming back from.

The good news: my arm felt just fine. Anxiety, and the adrenaline released as a result, does an arm good, takes the pain and stiffness away. In that moment, I probably could have taken a bullet and not noticed.

I threw about eight pitches, hastily—throw ball, get the ball back and throw, no leg kicks, no deep breaths, just throw. None of my warm-ups were strikes. They were also remarkably slow—I wasn't following through for fear of losing balance and face planting.

The bullpen catcher took off his mask.

"You ok, bradda?"

I was sweating in places I didn't think could sweat. I had tunnel vision. From the dugout, a player emerged and held out his hat: the signal to ask if the pitcher in the bullpen was ready. Waving your hat meant you were ready. I waved it deliriously.

Stop waving your hat, dumbass, I told myself. *You haven't thrown a strike!* The hat trembled. I doused myself with a green Gatorade cup of ice-water.

Our starter gave up another hit, a solid one-hopper that hooked through the six hole. Our shortstop didn't dive. I remember that meaningless hit so well because, afterwards, Coach Kal opened the chain-link fence, started making his way to the mound, and tapped his left arm. He wanted the lefty.

Three months earlier, I had arrived in Hilo, Hawaii. I was one of eight other freshmen on scholarship, one of two freshman pitchers. I told myself, first things first. Do a little homework. That meant checking Hilo's roster to see what players were returning. What *left-handed pitchers,* specifically, were returning? What were their stats? Had they pitched a lot? These questions all culminated into one: who would I be competing against for playing time? I wanted to play. I wanted to report back to family and friends that I was one of the *guys.*

Hilo had a few lefties returning. I saw only one starter on the roster—a big guy with a goofball smile and the Caucasian-frizz-afro hair of Will Ferrell. He had a decent ERA from the year before, lots of innings pitched, some strikeouts. His bio also provided such pivotal information as: he liked Pearl Jam and fettuccini alfredo. The other returning lefties had pitched little the year before, which meant they were either injured, or not very good. Good news either way, I thought. Maybe I'd even have a chance at *starter.* Who knew?

After perusing the website, I noticed something else about the roster. Something a little off, and honestly spooky. Something about it looked Photoshopped. It was hard to pinpoint what was giving me the creeps, but generally, there was an outdated vibe to the photos, like the whole roster was trapped in the 80s. At first I thought it was their Hawaiian shirts: each player was in the same corny floral button-up, like a Midwestern family desperate to look like they'd been somewhere exotic for their Christmas card. But nope, it wasn't that. Then I thought, maybe it was their hats, which were nothing like modern baseball hats, but more like hats our dads wore in the 80s. Tall, stiff, pentagonal, like fireman hats.

But that wasn't it either. There was more.

After clicking through photo after photo of UH Hilo's 2004 roster, I realized what it was.

Their mustaches.

Nearly everyone had one! The mustache as a fashion was so out at that time. But not with this squad. That memo hadn't made it out to Hilo baseball. It was a whole *team* of 19-year-olds in pedophilic Aloha shirts and gold mining hats and mustaches. Some of the mustaches were thick, bold, like porn stars' from back when porn was revolutionary. Other mustaches were scraggly, sparse, giving them the look of heroin addicts who'd forgotten to shave.

I wondered, had these kids been brainwashed? Had they been abducted from their homes in the middle of the night with the promise of a "scholarship," and "paradise" and been dropped on a remote island for mind control experiments? In these team photos, their smiles—and especially their creepier *non*-smiles—were going full *Manchurian Candidate*. Would I too be brainwashed? Was this even a baseball team?

I met the ballplayers for the first time at a toga party. I wore the purple bedsheet my parents had bought for my dorm. The ballplayers I met were sans mustache. They were also sans Yosemite Sam hat. They seemed, and what a relief it was, from the 21st century.

"So I was checking out the roster, and, like, the mustaches last year?" I asked gingerly. I tried my best to leave any judgment, or horror, out of my voice. I sipped warm Pabst from a twelver my roommate and I had struggled to get someone to buy us. "I've been curious as to the origin."

The player smiled as though I'd sparked a childhood memory.

"Dude. So, last year, Coach E decided—out of nowhere—that facial hair was unacceptable on a ball club. Just to try something new. I think he watched the Yankees for the first time. So all of a sudden no one could have beards, or goatees, or whatever. Then there was a rumor that someone called Coach E a commie. I'm pretty sure he didn't even know what that was. And neither did we. But he called a big team meeting about the Cold War, and how serious commie allegations were. Then he ran us a little. Then, he revised his rule, right? He's all like, 'You can have facial hair. But only if it's a mustache. So everyone is like, 'Thanks, Coach. Not.'"

"Wow," I said, trying to decide how I felt. I had no experience in college baseball, had no idea of the rules or standards of D1, or whether or not it was communist to mandate an all-mustachio team.

"But then right before the roster photos, a bunch of guys were like: wait, let's grow them out for the picture, actually. So half the team did it as a joke. Or ironically, I think. But then with those hats and fucking shirts with the palm tree background, it was priceless. Made us look like...well you saw us, dude. This team is such a joke. You'll see. *Such* a joke."

I wasn't ready to subscribe to such a statement. I mean, this was D1. Our schedule featured the toughest teams in the nation, teams that played in the College World Series—teams that won the College World Series, with guys we'd be watching on TV *soon*. Sure, they were better than us, but so what? If we were on their schedule year after year, we had to be respectable. There was no way there were jokes at the highest level of college baseball. Right?

Jogging from the bullpen to the mound, my cleat caught and I stumbled. The inside of my mouth felt like sandpaper.

My legs were rubbery. I couldn't remember having ever felt so physically out-of-whack prior to pitching—even on the days when my left arm wouldn't move. Coach Kal smiled warmly when I reached the mound. He handed me the ball. I semi-wished I was him, handing the ball off to someone else to pitch. The San Diego players wore the cocky smirks of white collar billionaires. I couldn't believe this: the mound was where I'd always felt most invincible. And now I felt like a nerd on Freshman Friday, afraid the football players were going to stuff me in a trash can.

"Go geet em, ah?" our pitching coach said. "No worry about nawting, bra, just shove em."

I nodded.

"Shove em, bra." In case I hadn't heard.

He smacked the ball into my open hand.

"What, you nervous?"

"Nah."

He walked off. The catcher walked off.

I remembered the last time I'd stood on this mound, a senior in high school. I'd gritted my teeth, gripped the ball tight, felt capable of superpowers. As the only person on the mound, I'd felt special. Taller than everyone. Like they'd brought knives to a gunfight. The adrenaline gushing through me was drug-like, Niagara-strong. The kind of feeling that gets people addicted to baseball. But that was high school.

Now, standing on the mound, I felt alone. Friendless. I was fidgety, my mind was all over the place, far from being focused on my first at-bat. Had a doctor hooked my arm to a blood pressure gauge, he would have prescribed an ambulance and early retirement.

"Freshman, Emil DeAndreis," I heard from the PA, followed by scattered claps. There were 200 people in attendance. The walk-out song I'd chosen started playing. I immediately regretted it. It was Mexican hip hop, which was a genre of music I didn't even listen to. In that moment it sounded like an approaching ice cream truck. I'd never felt more unthreatening, or bizarre. My first warm up missed high. Then my second. I floated my last three, fastballs that probably wouldn't have registered on the radar gun.

I looked at the umps and choked:

"I'm good."

The music cut out, and aside from the hum of stadium lights, the place was noiseless: everyone knew it was my debut.

The first thing I'd discovered that fall when workouts began was, UH Hilo had…peculiar commodities. The things I assumed all D1 programs offered—practice shorts, turf shoes, unlimited Underarmour shirts—Hilo did not. I learned this at our first fall workout, when we were issued one practice shirt and told we would wear it until disintegration. Then we got one hat, which after a week was sweat-washed white and shriveled to the size of a yarmulke.

"Don't lose it. You have to pay for a new one," players warned.

I felt like the Frenchmen who joined WWI late and received bullet-holed uniforms and dented helmets.

Throughout the fall, I had also come to learn that, with regard to facilities, Hilo sadly had nada. UH Hilo's athletes did not have a separate workout facility like most colleges. So during team workouts, we shared weights with Korean and Micronesian exchange students, and learned to pantomime "Can I work in a set with you?"

This weight room was half outdoors, under a tarp, in an endlessly humid city. That meant the dumbbells had rust and, in all probability, tetanus.

It didn't bother me then and in retrospect it doesn't bother me now. I felt, and continue to feel, that if these things caused kids to not want to be there, or to transfer to a different school, they didn't deserve college baseball in the first place. But, the discrepancies between Hilo and other programs—they were worth noting.

On our first day of team practices, players rolled our helmets to the field in shopping carts with crooked wheels. Shuffling through the ball bucket, I noticed that many of our baseballs had the logos of other universities, and other conferences.

"Yeah. We steal everyone's balls," a bored senior told me.

"Oh?"

I was holding one stamped Missouri Valley Conference. The senior had just studied a Pac 10 ball, and stuffed it in his glove to use.

"When other teams hit batting practice before games, they let homers go over the fence and are too lazy to get them," he said. "We go crawling after them like gypsies. It's worth it, given our other options."

He nodded at the bottom of the bucket, which featured a gloomy cluster of deformed, black balls. They had burst seams like someone had hit grounders with them on a minefield.

"Those are Hilo balls," he said, and jogged off for warmups.

As fall progressed, I would come to find that our commodities and facilities were not the only abnormal features of the UH Hilo baseball program. There was our roster, the players themselves. We had an abundance of unique D1 ballplayers. For example, nobody threw over 90 mph. (Well, that's not exactly true. There was *one* guy humanly capable of hitting a pitch that fast, but that was only if it wasn't too humid, and he wasn't hungover—and those two stars aligned never. It's also worth noting that he once came to ab workouts tripping on acid). Two of our guys, Shiga and Kala, were 5'5" in stilettos. Shiga was this pesky Japanese squirt who banged out triples and would go on to break all the school's offensive records.

Kala, on the other hand, was legally deaf.

I remember one time, Coach Kal had us do "positive

visualization" drills. He lined as all up against the wall outside the weight room, told us to close our eyes, and pitch a complete game in our minds. Eventually, Coach whistled us into a huddle to discuss the value of this visualization. Still standing at the wall with his eyes closed was Kala, who hadn't heard the whistle.

"Leave him, Coach," one of the pitchers said. "He's in the bottom of the ninth."

Kala eventually quit to be our laundry boy.

More roster standouts: Ryan Hanopa weighed 300+ and was once a Hawaii state MVP…in volleyball. Kupe'e had redshirted for UH Manoa's football team the year before; he showed up to our first weight training in a camo bandana and shrieked when he did power cleans. We tended to avoid him, and his nickname between myself and some other terrified freshmen quietly became Alligator Rapist.

So that was what UH Hilo was putting on the field. I didn't pass judgment. I didn't subscribe to this program being a "joke" like that senior had told me at the toga party. I felt, so what if we had an enormous volleyball star? A short guy? A short *and* deaf guy? A guy who looked like one of those freakish commandos from *Predator,* who scared everyone including our coach? A player who preferred to kick back with a little acid and 'shrooms before his calisthenics? Who was I to judge? I wasn't exactly Nolan Ryan. In my opinion, you played the hand you were dealt. Which meant, in this case: you lifted rusty weights next to the Korean marine-bio major, and you did sit-ups next to the pitcher who was sweating and hallucinating Teletubbies.

Shit, I was still *excited.* First of all, how could I forget I was in Hawaii? Plus, having trainers to wrap my arm with ice, or rub down my shoulder, or stretch out my hammy—it felt so pro. Our practices were far more serious and focused than high school. Pitchers concentrated on just pitching. Flat pens. Off-speed longtoss. Towel drills. Pitch location competitions. PFPs. We had individualized throwing programs. The secret plays I had to learn were more complex than our high school plays (in high school we had one play: everyone on defense flipped out and pretended we didn't know where the ball was). On Hilo, there was always a catcher to catch your bullpen, and he was willing to catch as many as you needed to throw. The conditioning we did was hellacious—timed 100-yard sprints, 30-minute runs alternating between 10-second sprints and 30-second jogs. All in the sopping oven that was Hilo afternoon air. Nothing about any of that was a "joke." I walked into the cafeteria after fall practices, ice wrapped to my shoulder, loaded my tray with burgers and strutted like the cool guy on campus. Mr. D1.

"Pitcher, you've got a runner on first base, two outs," the umpire said. Into the batter's box stepped Shane Buschini, the 6'4" 220-pound DH for San Diego. If his stature wasn't scary enough, how about that name? Buschini. That sounded like someone who did corrupt things on Wall Street, was grandfathered into several country clubs, smoked Cubans with clients, threatened any boy that asked his daughter on a date, and back in his playing days at USD, hit towering homeruns off petrified freshmen.

While we're on the subject, let's explore a couple of other names from that San Diego roster I was going to face, like Jordan Abruzzo. Buschini, Abruzzo. These sounded like Murderer's Row names. And speaking of Murderer's Row, just get a load of this: their number two hitter's last name was Ruth. Ruth! So now we had Buschini, Abruzzo, and Ruth!

I thought, *I'm going after these guys with 80 mph? Cool story.*

Buschini stood in, giving me a look I have since named The Buschini Stare: a look of intensity with a glimmer of amusement. Amusement at the warmup pitches he'd just watched, I was sure. I dug my left foot against the rubber. Leaned over my front leg to get the sign from the catcher. My heartbeat felt like a steady drumroll, or raindrops pattering on an umbrella. It occurred to me this was one of the only times since I'd started pitching that I wasn't throwing to Charlie, my high school catcher, anymore. With Charlie behind the plate, I'd always felt like we were in the fight together. It took some of the pressure off, and gave me a person to share that exhilaration of competition. But this catcher, I hardly knew yet, and so I felt largely on my own.

I came set, let out my final breath before officially becoming a D1 pitcher, lifted my leg, and drove to the plate. My first pitch sailed up and in, just under Buschini's ribs. Ball one. It could have been interpreted as a message pitch, as in: *get the fuck off my plate, I may be a freshman, but I'm not scared of you.* Which is common enough in baseball. Ask Roger Clemens how many times he tossed at someone's ribs to back him off his plate. Pitchers need that for their psyche, for their success. The difference was, Roger Clemens threw 95. *That* was scary. *That* got a batter thinking. *My* pitch registered at 80. No one was spooked by that. And certainly, no one named Buschini. He dug his cleats in the box, and stared back out. My second pitch missed up and in again.

In a regular at-bat, falling behind 2-0 did not call for panic. It just meant, *alright fuckstick, refocus and make a pitch.* But in my *first* college appearance, I couldn't help it. The catcher tossed the ball back. Dead silence in the park. I felt faint, diabetes-weak. I twirled the ball around in my hand and took a walk around the mound. I had the worst thoughts, like what if I melt down and I can't throw a single strike? What if my next pitch bounces ten feet short of home, or soars over the catcher's head and at spectators? What if I look so bad people have to cover their mouths not to laugh? What if my college career turns into one struggle after the next to throw strikes? Until, eventually, my scholarship is gone? My panic was not just in the moment, but looking ahead, the worst kind of panic.

I peered at the catcher. He gave the sign, wiggled three fingers. A changeup. What the hell was that about? A changeup? 2-0? After two hideous pitches? What I think happened was, the catcher decided my fastball was hopeless, and we had to try something else. *Anything* else. He needed a *strike*, and he didn't care what pitch got that strike. Since my changeup had been my best pitch in the fall, he figured what the hell.

I didn't second guess. I didn't shake it off. In all likelihood, I was suffering a mini-stroke. I threw my changeup. It was perhaps the slowest pitch dispatched in D1 history. Buschini's eyes lit up. He initiated his swing, the stride, the foot plant, the twitch of the hips. But Buschini, the left-handed hitter he was, didn't count on my changeup tailing. God bless the natural tail of my pitches. Teams had no scouting report on me yet, so instead of smashing the ball into orbit like he should have, he hit the ball off his handle. It made a terrible *clink*. The ball dribbled to Shiga, our 5'5" second baseman, a seven-hopper. It almost didn't make it to him. Likely, it was the worst hit ball by Buschini in years. Shiga fielded it, tossed it to our first baseman, inning over. Buschini smiled at me as he was thrown out, a smile that said, *if you ever throw me that pitch again, I'll hit it through you.*

Coach Estrella sent me back out there after that. My adrenaline wasn't as pulpy. My arm wasn't as numb. My heart wasn't beating like a cornered animal's. I took controlled breaths between my warmup pitches. I felt balanced in my delivery. I was getting a chance at a full inning to myself. Three whole outs. It felt like possibly more than I could handle, but after getting Buschini out with that miracle changeup, I was up to the challenge. I felt like a D1 equal. Confidence—it was a crazy drug for a pitcher, a best friend, a worst enemy.

That next inning turned out to be an easy three-up-three-down. I even recorded a strike out—a swing-through on a changeup in the dirt. A wild swing. I had a strikeout. I felt like screaming like Tom Hanks in *Castaway* when he finally makes fire. *(I…have a strikeout!)*

Then, Coach E sent me back out. My third inning. It was no longer a meltdown. I began to grip the ball confidently, snapping my arm and releasing the ball the way I did when I knew the batter stood no chance, when I knew the pitch would fly past bats. I stood tall, a bit of a swaggered lean on my right foot. I hocked loogies as I stared the batters in the eyes. I cursed beneath my breath. And before I knew it, I'd thrown another 1-2-3 inning, and recorded another strikeout. Two and 1/3 shutout innings and two strikeouts in my debut.

I remember coming off the mound back to the dugout, doing this sort of clumsy gallop. It was a half-jog, half-strut. Jog because I believed in the idea of baseball gods and being punished for acting like I was bigger than the game. Strut because, in that moment, my first college outing, I felt bigger than the game. I was thinking things like: *Fuck everyone.*

Everyone being: all the coaches who thought I was too small. The scouts who thought I didn't throw hard enough. Every coach who never returned a call. All the colleges that sent recruitment mail and never followed through when I returned their stupid questionnaires. I hoped all of their recruits turned out to be prima donnas, and injury-inventors, and can't-hack-its. I also found myself thinking:

- *Ma, look what I can do.*
- *Pitching is easy.*
- *I'll be the best pitcher in the country soon.*

But the baseball gods—fickle and righteous as they can be—had other plans in store for me. Their thoughts were: *Yeah, right, kid. Here comes the storm.*

9
TAKING KANSAS BY STORM. LITERALLY.

Weather forecasters in places like Hilo had it rough. They spent their careers being, for the most part, wrong. Whenever Hilo meteorologists forecasted rain—it rained. That much they got right. But when they forecasted sun and blue skies—that's when things got tricky. They would've been more scientific on those days had they just thrown their hands up and said *flip a fucking coin*.

I don't think there was one day, in four years in Hilo, when there wasn't at least one minute of hardcore rain. The kind that makes you think your car roof might cave in, and the whole island might just mudslide down the hill into the sea. I can't tell you how many times forecasts led to tragic beach days. College students would read that the sun was to be out all day, cut school, call in sick to work, buy beer, flock to the beach, and by noon they'd be fleeing to their cars, juggling lawn chairs, soggy 12-pack cardboard, and grills.

This kind of rain, of the stealth variety, was prone to victimize more than just beach goers. I learned this in a very hands-on way my freshman year when Kansas University came to town. I was fresh off my first appearance against San Diego. I thought I was MLB-destined. And in Game Two of the series, Coach E eyed his stable of relief pitchers and called "DeAndreis." I had the jitters, but not like before. I could feel my heartbeat, but it was softer. My warmups were strikes. The bullpen catcher nodded at each pitch, an indication that my stuff was on. A little nod from a catcher always goes a long way for a pitcher. I heard the clink of the dugout fence, watched Coach Kal exit and start his walk to the mound. He looked down at me, tapped the left arm.

I grabbed the green Gatorade cup, threw ice-water down the back of my neck and felt the best kind of alive. Before jogging to the mound, I saw gentle raindrops begin to dance in the air, so light they seemed to float to the ground like feathers. There wasn't a cloud in the sky. As I began to jog toward the mound, I saw some of the locals in the bullpen forensically sniff the air, like blind dogs in the presence of a stranger. Kupe'e, who scared people when weightlifting, stuck his tongue out, perhaps gauging the volume of the drops.
"It's about to shit, bra," he said.

I swear, in the time it took for me to jog from the bullpen to the mound, massive purple clouds scooted overhead. Purple like lava lamps, and so quick it was like one of those nature shows where the sun moves across the screen in a flash, and grass spastically grows.

Then, the celestial levee broke.

Suddenly the pounding water got so loud, the announcer became inaudible. I could hardly see my catcher from the mound. I rushed through warmups to get the game going. That was a mistake. I'd never pitched in rain like this, had never been in a position in which gripping a baseball was problematic. My first pitch slipped out of my hand. When it was tossed back, it was soaked and eel-slick. I walked the first batter on four straight. I stood on the mound, being warmly pelted, waiting for a dry ball from the umpire. He wiped one off with a dripping towel and tossed it back. In its flight from home plate to the mound, it was soaked yet more with rain. This was the stuff of an anxiety dream.

I walked the next batter. Now I had two batters on, and no outs, and there were lily pads on the infield. I began to relive the hopeless, solitary-confinement feeling from my first outing.

When you're struggling and can't even record a single out, an inning—just three simple outs—can feel like being on a slowly sinking ship. The next batter sensed my weakness and swung wildly at the first pitch; the bat slipped out of his hands. Usually, games were postponed when this happened, but our umpires were out of it. It turned out good umpires in Hawaii were hard to come by. We had the same three every game for four straight years (Approximately 220 games, all officiated by Bob, Bill, and Ben. Ben was a boxer, Bob an alcoholic, and Bill was just Bill). The second pitch could have easily been called a ball, but Ben called it a strike. I had a guy 0-2. Then I made the mistake of assuming I'd already gotten him out. As a result, I didn't focus on the next pitch. I threw a curve that absolutely did not curve. The batter smashed the 0-2 pitch into left center and it skidded across the grass, shooting up water like a skipping rock, all the way to the wall for a bases-clearing triple. I had to do the ultimate Walk of Shame, the lackluster jog to back up home when you knew all runs were going to score.

At this point, I knew I only had one pitch to work with in this punishing rain. My fastball. And, me being me—that was depressing. I prayed that these corn-fed behemoths standing out there getting soaked while I threw ball after ball might get bored, or impatient, and swing, pop out, throw me some kind of bone in this nightmare.

But nope. Even in the monsoon, they stood Zen-like, taking their bases.

The umpires appeared to be enjoying the fiasco, perhaps refusing to postpone the game for fear of nonpayment, or not wanting to come back to the park for a makeup. I needed a strike of lightning somewhere. Or distant thunder. Instead, I stood on the mound, throwing my hands up at Ben, as if to ask, *why me?*

In the meantime, Kansas tagged me for five runs. Five runs, and I didn't even finish the inning. Eventually, the rain stopped. We lost by 20. My ERA shot up to 100. Just like that. The season went on. We played in 50 more games. I pitched in two of those games.

It was suspenseful to be sitting on the bench in the middle of these games against NCAA powerhouses, as Coach walked up and down, checked his notes, deciding whom to send down to warm up. Those moments were a swirling mixture of hope and dread. Hoping for a chance to repeat my USD performance, but dreading the possibility of another outing like Kansas.

But coach spent the season going with anyone but the freshman. I watched the other relievers, juniors and seniors, with pretty much the same stuff as I had, repeatedly get their names called. They racked up 16, 17, 18 appearances, ranging from clutch to train-wreck. And each time Coach called their name, vocally my reaction was: "Man, fuck." But internally, my thoughts were: *Man, fuck,* but mixed with a little bit of, *phew.* How weird it was to want something so badly yet fear it at the same time.

And I hated that I'd become that person. A "phew" person. A kid that loved baseball, who lived for the competition, who used to pitch hungry and rabid. And now sighing in relief when my name got passed, so I wouldn't have to fail again.

10
BEST PITCHER IN THE COUNTRY? YEAH, RIGHT.

Sophomore year. We were in the classroom...rain splattering outside, days before our first series of the season. Coach had canceled practice and called a team meeting to go over strategy and pitching rotation for the first series. We were playing Kansas. Again. Sitting in the room, we glanced at each other with smirks, all thinking: *we went 6-49 last year. What strategy can we have?*

"Hanopa, you'll start game three, Kupe'e you've got game four, DeAndreis game five, and we'll see what we've got for games six and seven."

(We often played seven-game series, as opposed to the standard collegiate three-to-five-game series, because teams spent a lot to come out to Hawaii and wanted to make it worth their money by beating us violently several times.)

"Any questions?" Coach E asked.

I raised my hand. He pointed at me.

"What?" I asked incredulously.

Didn't Coach remember what had happened to me *last* year? My downfall in the downpour? The outing that caused him to essentially lose faith in me for the rest of the year? Now, I was starting? Being a sophomore, with only four appearances under my belt, I hadn't ever expected to start, let alone in the first series of the year.

"What *what?*" Coach asked.

I thought about Coach's common whimsical expressions, his open mouth during odd pauses in speech, his silver hair dwindling on his head, springing from his ears. Was Coach in the early stages of dementia, or Alzheimer's? Did he think I was someone else? Perhaps a player from ten years ago?

Starting on the mound is way different than coming in for relief. A starter is expected to go six strong innings; a relief pitcher needs only six strong outs to have what constitutes as a successful outing. Starters get the glory, with their names recorded in the win, but they also absorb the stress of expectation. If you look at pitching like a piece of art, which it certainly is: a relief pitcher enters the game with the framework of the painting done; all he has to do is add some color here, some shade there, and perhaps a few unmemorable details. A starter is given a blank canvas, and it falls upon him whether the painting turns out to be a Mona Lisa, or a mound of shit.

I couldn't sleep that night before the game.

Anxiety attacks rolled through me like swells through a dinky boat. My shins sweat through my bedsheets, and when I threw the covers off, I shivered. It seemed I had forgotten that baseball was supposed to be fun. I couldn't step outside myself for a moment and tell myself: *Bro, you're lucky, you love this game, and you've earned a chance to start. No one expects you to go out there and put the team on your back. It's Kansas. They're going to beat you, and it's ok. Just have fun and let the moment happen.*

I just couldn't take a few deep breaths and convince myself. I was suffocated by "What Ifs." Stupid "What Ifs." Like, what if I couldn't sleep? What if I lose the strike zone, can't hit the broad side of a barn? They were the kinds of "What Ifs" that become realities if worried about enough. The kinds of "What Ifs" that make you wish the human brain wasn't such a complex and ironic and volatile piece of machinery. Next to me, my roommate Robby snored like the worriless left fielder he was. Tomorrow, he got to stand out there and tan. What a life. I ached to be in left field. Our hotel room was filled with bluish light from the TV. *Ocean's Eleven* was on: scene after scene of

George Clooney and Brad Pitt being so preposterously suave.

My start was at our field in Kona, on the sunnier, more touristy side of the island. We played there whenever heavy rain was predicted for Hilo, which—considering Hilo received more inches of rain per year than any other city in America—was often enough. The air in Kona was drier, and the faucet water tasted like Los Angeles water, which is to say, it was a liquid fart. Demi Moore had a vacation home essentially in the backyard of the ballpark. Her atrium was constantly getting ambushed by foul balls. But, she was never there. She might not have known she had it.

The field was in pretty bad shape. Speedbumpy. Bullpen mounds were glorified anthills. No shade, anywhere. The infield dirt was so loose in some places that you could step and be ankle deep. Truthfully, playing there wasn't all that different than playing at the underfunded ballfields back in San Francisco where people did crack and slept half-naked in the stands while gophers carved tunnels that crisscrossed the outfield.

The morning of my start, I was light-sensitive. This was my body's way of telling me it yearned for drawn shades, air conditioning, and REM sleep. I ate very few items featured in Uncle Billy's Hotel breakfast buffet, which was known to cause unstoppable diarrhea. The Hawaiians, on the other hand, ate plate after plate of Vienna sausages and eggs and rice and chili. Literally everything I could think of that gave heartburn, they inhaled. I chewed a banana slowly, and felt like a towel that had been wrung dry. I was sitting by myself, in sunglasses. It was a tradition, and a sign of respect, that the pitcher was left alone on mornings of his start. At breakfast, he had his own table. On the bus, his own row. In warmups, he was off solo-stretching, on his own clock. I remember feeling honored, and presidential, sitting there eating breakfast in sunglasses by myself. But I also felt alone. Left to my own thoughts.

Kansas didn't score in the first inning.

And then my luck ran out.

In the second they scored four. I gave up a homerun that no one saw land. Basically the batter swung and immediately there was a comet that left earth. Then the next guy drag-bunted for a hit. Which was the type of thing that gave coaches semi-boners. They thought it was the ultimate baseball move. Humble, poetic, yet deeply tactical. It re-started the rally. Re-flustered the pitcher. Got him back in the stretch. Caught the enemy completely off guard. To me—and probably every pitcher ever victimized by this strategy—it was overrated, not to mention soft. I was just thinking, *cool bro, you can bunt.*

In the third, Kansas scored three, and I didn't make it out of the fourth. They were winning by seven. It was just one of those days when every kind of contact, even the weak kind, found some open grass to roll on forever. Even ground balls—perfect candidates for inning-ending double plays—hit divots and dodged fielders. Kansas's rallies were so long and miserable I could sense my defense getting annoyed. Not necessarily at me, but just at having to stand out there interminably, wondering if they might ever get back in the dugout. And there I was, coming set, throwing meatball after meatball. It felt more like I'd been hired to entertain some sluggers on their birthday. I imagined the Kansas players in their dugout snickering, saying things like *my dad's got more zip on his fastball.* When Coach came out and pulled me, I swear I saw steam rise from my forearms.

The team filed in front of the entrance to greet me, slap my hand. It was standard procedure, one of those things in baseball everyone hated. They didn't want to congratulate me because they knew I *didn't* want to be congratulated. Because seriously, what had I done to deserve it?

I wanted to throw chairs, pound walls, curse at things, but our Kona field offered no sanctuary. All we had was a chicken wire dugout and some tin bleachers with a capacity of eight people. There was no locker-room or clubhouse where I could blow off steam. Everyone could see everything. So when I sat down, seething, I felt like I was under a microscope. Everyone gave me space, but they also mouse-glanced at me, trying not to stare, observing just how exactly I was dealing with my failure. I pulled handfuls of my hair until I looked like a Troll doll. I briefly gnawed my forearm. I poured a cup of ice-cold Kona fart-water down my neck, and when that didn't cool me down, I stormed out of the dugout, no particular destination in mind. The nearby beach? The liquor store? Demi Moore's porch? Wherever I was going, I was headed there in a hurry.

Then I felt a hand on my shoulder, the hand of Mikey Riggs, our ace, a senior.

"C'mon, man," he said.

He'd observed my furious walk. I'd hoped it looked bad-ass, like Henry in *Goodfellas* when he's about to pistol whip the guy working on his car across the street. But I knew I'd looked more like a runway model who feverishly had to piss.

With his hand on my shoulder, I could tell Vinny relished this moment. I stopped to listen because he was a senior, and ace, but nothing was more incensing than someone trying to calm me with a calming touch. It would have calmed me more to be in a fistfight with someone.

"There's nothing to be upset about. How many kids get their first start against Kansas? As a sophomore, no less. That's pretty big time."

I didn't consider anything that had just transpired to be "big time."

At least you got through a *few* innings, right?"

"Funny guy."

It was odd that Mikey had decided to counsel me, because though he was the team ace, he was also the team *prima donna*. He often argued with Coach E, bickered with teammates. He called out the team when they didn't get up to shake his hand after a bad game, stating "Oh thanks, guys, for all the support!"

He also yelled at us when we *did* try to shake his hand after a bad game, saying "You all know I pitched like shit, so stop pretending."

At parties, he wore pink polo-shirts, and popped the collar. Sometimes, he wore two polos, one on top of the other, and popped *both* collars (!). He also wore mocha-tint sunglasses, like he was walking down the Hollywood strip being blitzed by paparazzi. He shaved his chest. And—sorry, Mikey, if you're reading this—he also had nipple rings.

So, standing there with his hand on me, I found it odd that this guy was showing an underclassman like me empathy. But he was, and I was letting it happen.

He reached over and took my glove out of my mouth, where I'd been gnawing on it. It was bent backwards like a wilted flower. I'd never owned an adequate piece of baseball equipment. Everything came from yard sales and used sporting goods stores. No Rawlings Heart of the Hides, no A2000s. To be frank, I had never heard of either of those very commonly used gloves. My college glove was one of those with a pro's signature stamped in the palm, the kind with a lot of glue, and very little leather. The kind normal people stopped using after middle school, when they've decided to play for real.

"Pleather?" Mikey asked, fake-intrigued.

"Fuck you."

I punted the glove. We both watched it sail into Demi Moore's atrium.

"Alright," he said, patted my ass, and walked back to the dugout. A couple of teammates who had seen us from the dugout had their faces buried in their hands, they were laughing so hard. I snuck onto Demi's property for the glove.

"Fuck Kansas!" I yelled.

"That's right. Fuck Kansas," Mikey called back, loud enough for the entire field, and umpires, to hear. Coach E looked at us in horror from the third base line. Perhaps it was true, what I'd been told as a freshman. That we were a joke. I sure felt like one.

After Kansas, I was happy to be demoted back to relief pitcher/lefty specialist, a role which lasted only one or two innings at a time. It felt safe to know I could always flee the game just before my opposition made the necessary adjustment against me (which was: wait, wait, and wait some more). I'd already accepted, at least for the time being, that I was most effective as a relief pitcher. The role gave me security, like someone who moves away from the excitement of the big city for the quiet and safety of the 'burbs.

Later in my sophomore season, I was again concerned that Coach might be entering some pre-stage of dementia when he announced:

"Emil, you got game four against San Jose State."

I knew better than to raise my hand and ask dumbly "what?" again. I'd heard him correctly.

A few days before the game, I lay awake into the wee hours, bathed in TV light, watching the same cycle of Sportscenter, the same college hoops dunks, the same jokes from Scott Van Pelt over and over, until by 1, then 2 in the morning, his jokes were making me depressed. I prayed for a hurricane to come wash my start away. Usually, every baseball season at Hilo featured one red-alert hurricane warning. None had yet materialized, and I was thinking this would be a good time.

We had a senior left-handed pitcher named Cadian whose career had been haunted by elbow injuries. Just before the season opener, his father had been killed in a car accident back in Washington. The tragedy left him eerily calm. He nearly decided to sit his senior year out, but said his dad would have wanted him to finish strong. Now, in the twilight of his career, he was running out of chances to pitch, so a couple of days before my scheduled start against San Jose State, I approached

Coach E and asked if I might be able to offer my start to him, in the name of kindness and sportsmanship. I kept my real reason to myself—that I was fucking scared. Coach E was touched by my gesture, and allowed it.

"No, thanks," Cadian said, "You earned it."

Fuck me, I thought.

I also thought: *Exactly how have I earned this?*

Leading up to the game, I told myself, O*k, I've still got twenty-four hours for a storm to hit.* Then when that day passed, I thought: *Ok, I've still got a full night and morning for some rogue rain.* Then a sleepless night passed, and I thought: *Ok, I still have all morning. Come on, Hilo, do what you do.* I spent the morning of my start in bed, blanket pulled over my head, Westside Connection and G-Unit playing from my computer in an attempt to pump me up.

By the fifth inning of my start against San Jose, something unprecedented was unfolding. We were winning. I couldn't tell you the details of my start, only that I remember it was going by very fast. I wasn't out there for very long each inning. Ground balls went right to a defender, and the defender made the play.

To a normal person, this might sound like regular baseball. But for me, for UH Hilo, this was a phenomenon. In one inning I gave up a two-out double, and instead of giving up another double and surrendering a rally like I half-expected to, the next batter hit a lazy pop-up to our third baseman. I had a feeling like I was cheating death.

Coach took me out in the fifth. My pitch count was in the 70s, and coach sensed that I was on borrowed time, that San Jose State would MacGyver a rally in no time. I respected that very real danger, and didn't put up a fight when he pulled me out. Since this was the first game of a double header, it was only a seven inning game. All we had to do was hold on for two more innings, and I would have my first win. To be on a team that averaged under ten wins a season, that really was a special thing.

Sitting down, I saw my jersey jump like a popped kernel with each excited heartbeat. I felt sweat, still fresh from pitching, switchback from my sideburns down my cheek. Air had never tasted better. I went to the locker-room, rummaged through a teammate's gear for a sock where I knew he kept his Copenhagen. Dug out a pinch, carved it into a pocket in my cheek, went and sat back out in the dugout, occasionally receiving the congratulatory pat on the shoulder. I wondered if game one starters of big time schools always felt like this. Completely elated, filled with purpose and validation, after a five-inning start.

I laughed at myself, got philosophical for a moment. I thought, in the big picture, considering the cosmos and whatnot, this would go down as one of the more irrelevant events in history, to be archived and buried on some unvisited website. In essence, this game, this coming win, barely even existed. But it was mine, in just two more innings.

Our ace Mikey Riggs was talking to Coach E. I could tell he was lobbying to close the game. I knew what he was saying: *My arm is on two days rest, that's plenty! Why save my arm? I'm a goddamned senior. I'm our best chance at this win. We'd do anything for the feeling of a win.*

And Coach E went with it. He didn't stick with the throwing schedule, or worry about arm health, or fair playing time, as had been done in the past. Faces lit up when Mikey headed to the pen. No one who was scheduled to pitch looked sour for getting passed up. I remember thinking, this is what a team feels like.

In the pen, Mikey threw rapidly with arm circles in between. As soon as he got the ball from the catcher, he was firing it right back. I watched from the dugout, hearing him pop his glove—*clap, clap, clap*—thinking *this is a goddamned masterpiece, a Mona Lisa.* When the bottom of the sixth ended, we were winning 4-2. Mikey jogged to the mound for his save. The approximately 20 diehard fans clapped, knowing that with Mikey coming in, they were about to witness a rare Hilo win.

And wouldn't you know it, Mikey came in and blew the lead. Pretty quickly, too. Sharp grounder in the six hole for a single. Double right center, suddenly second and third, no outs. It wasn't like he was making bad pitches. The batters were just better trained for 88 mph fastballs from a righty, than odd, funky 79 mph fastballs from me. Next batter: ground-out up the middle. One out, but they scored. Now we were only winning 4-3. One more run and my win was gone. Next batter, deep fly, runner tagged. Tie game.

When Mikey got the third out, he blasted through all our limp high-fives, and declared a calamitous war against the locker room. Folding chairs and cleats and equipment were being tomahawked into the lockers, denting and disabling them. It sounded like two vending machines having sex with each other.

I felt like I needed to walk in there. Especially in light of earlier in the season, when he had tried to talk me off the cliff.

He was sweating, heaving for air. There were possible tears in his eyes. His left knuckles were bloody and swollen. Like Crash says in *Bull Durham*, a pitcher never punches with his pitching hand. Mikey came up to me in the doorway, having heard the unmistakable crunch of metal spikes on concrete.

"Don't come here fishing for a fucking apology," he said, clenching fists and then releasing them, clenching them then releasing them.

I knew the feeling. I hated it. Losing a lead was like swallowing nails for relief pitchers. It made us feel so useless. So blatantly inadequate. A starter would bust his ass for five plus innings, pitch his heart out, then hand off the baton, and the reliever would not even be able to record an out. How pathetic. It could make a man wonder, how are these two people on the same team, or even in the same league, if one can throw five shutout innings, and another can't throw one shutout *out?*

I could not console him—he was the senior, the old wise one. Anything I said would have been counterfeit. We both knew it. By now, the bottom of the seventh had begun—our chance to retake the lead, and seal the victory in walk-off fashion.

"I know the feeling," I said.

I left him alone in his agony, just as he had done for me earlier in the year. For pitchers truly in that pit of despair, there are no words. Mikey, likely worn out from trashing the locker room, sat there for the remainder of the game, which we ended up winning 5-4 in the bottom of the seventh, a win that was credited to him, a win he was not proud of.

I drank that night with a couple of relievers in the parking lot overlooking Honali'i Beach. Down on the beach a high school bonfire was blazing. The waves took on a glacial blue under the moonlight, barreling subtle two-footers. I gulped my green Mickey's 40, the only beer in college I could ever afford. Poor Mikey, I kept thinking. It didn't make sense how the day had played out. That I'd succeeded, and Mikey had failed. In what rational world was that possible? Maybe if Coach had left me in, I would've shut them down. Or, maybe if Coach had enlisted one of our enthusiastic, elderly Japanese fans in the bleachers to come close the game? Possibly, San Jose would've been stumped! Who knew? That was the mystique of baseball. So much went into the preparation, the fundamentals, the coaching, the strategy, and still, the worst pitcher could strike out Mighty Casey. Hilo could win. Baseball was a bitch, and it was a savior. I stretched my shoulder against the car hood, finished my beer. I felt the angst, the serenity, and the splendor of the game swirl warmly in me like being in the eye of a hurricane.

11
LEFT-HANDED PITCHER

Other than playing baseball, I was a pretty typical college student. Half-crooked SF hat, XL white tees or other urban paraphernalia that broadcasted my Bay Area allegiance provided my off-the-field uniform. I wore pink flip-flops to be eccentric, to draw attention, to go out of my way to show I was secure enough to wear pink, just like any insecure late-adolescent. I listened to hip hop and gangsta rap. I was a sucker for a good orchestral sample in a beat and an angry rapper. That combo made me want to lift weights, or pitch, or fight. I drank a lot of protein shakes, because everyone was trying to bulk up, and I thought it would make me feel stronger, throw harder, look tougher.

I was a hybrid class clown and don't-fuck-with-me tough guy, depending on the day, or the hour, or moment. And I drank, which amplified all of this dual personality, because that's what college athletes did. It was a rite of passage. Indeed, its own fraternity. And the consequences that started to come with drinking—heavy, blackout, binge-drinking—I went along with these after-effects as though they were rites of passage as well.

Toward the end of my sophomore year, I got evicted from the dorms. My stack of write-ups had grown so thick I needed something bigger than a manila envelope to store them: drunk-in-publics, accidentally walking into RAs' rooms with cheap vodka duct-taped to my hand. I racked up more than a few indecent exposures. I always pushed the RAs until they were about to tell Coach, then I'd blubber apologies. Finally, they were just like, go away and never come back.

I moved into the Baseball House, a two-story a few miles up the hill from school that had been the residence for white guys from the mainland for eras of Hilo baseball teams. It was an eighth wonder of the world that the owner of the house had never once evicted anyone. I did not use this life-change, however, as an opportunity to turn my act around, or mature. On the contrary, I now lived in a completely unmonitored environment. I became the occasional apocalypse. I bought a car, for $175, and picked up where I left off.

Promptly, I was driving the car drunk. One night, 90% blacked out, I drove home from a party on the wrong side of the road, the entire way, while my roommate rode his moped in front of me, standing, and naked. Another night I was a fifth of rum deep and found myself weaving through a maze of cop cars, who had all decided to be present for one prostitute's arrest. They motioned me through their lane of flashing lights, and my world was spinning. Then I got home, told my roommates, and we all thought it was a real knee-slapper.

When the Baseball House wasn't playing baseball, or at morning conditioning, or evening weights, or study hall, we hung at home. We got stoned on our porch and watched the bug-zapper and got philosophical. We split Hamburger Helpers, showed up to parties as the Baseball House and left as the Baseball House, nursed Sunday hangovers and watched "Sopranos" DVDs or walked up the street to Boiling Pots and dove off the waterfalls. We played wingman for all our failures. We went "camping" on the other side of the island, which meant packing Saff's Rav 4 with teammates and the softball team and handles of rum, body surfing during a mind-melting sunset, and draining the car battery all night while dancing on the beach and finally sleeping in a pile of sand using an economy-sized bag of Honey Nut Cheerios for a pillow—the kinds of nights that made you desperate for a toothbrush the next morning.

Hilo had a block party on the bay-front each year called Ho'o'laule'a. I pronounced it incorrectly for four years. There were multiple stages with live reggae, kiosks with beaded jewelry, Korean spare ribs, and shave ice. College kids felt that this cultural event existed solely to host them drunk. I was one of them.

Junior year, I went with the Baseball House. I drove down with Saff, a fellow left-handed reliever who'd become my closest friend in Hawaii. He was a year older than me. His fastball was electric, but he often struggled to get it to the strike zone. He probably had the best slider on our team as well, but wasn't always confident enough to throw it. So he didn't pitch all that much. Out of high school, he'd been looked at by a couple D2 and junior colleges for football as a cornerback, but an ankle injury killed their interest.

At games, we sat in the dugout, and made fun of opposing batters.

We also barked at the umpires.

"You're terrible, Bill/Bob/Ben!" we'd cry, and try to keep straight faces when Bill/Bob/Ben glared in to see who the hell it was yelling at him. Once, we were in the bullpen warming up for a game against Navy that looked like it was going to go extras. Our left fielder Robby hit a walk-off double in the ninth and everyone dogpiled at home. Me and the likes of a couple other relievers, including a stumpy catcher in all his catcher's gear, were about three minutes late to the celebration because we had preemptively decided that if we won, we would cartwheel from the bullpen to the dogpile. By the time the catcher got there he was nearly dead from exhaustion, all his gear sideways. Coach looked at Saff and our ilk, knowing who'd been behind this. In baseball, there is a term for the likes of Saff and myself: Left-Handed Pitchers. It means you're eccentric, inexplicably goofy, and sure, a little bush-league. The type to be superstitious and blink exactly four times before a pitch. The type to be late to practice, thinking practice was at a different time, though it's never at a different time. The type to prank-call their coach, or wear pink floaties to a team meeting.

That night at the Ho'o'laule'a, Saff and I drank vodka from Nalgene bottles. Wandering and squinty, we were separated. Vodka had dissolved my concern for anyone's personal space. Laughing, I stumbled unapologetically into Hawaiians. Saff found me and followed as I walked around, pushing through crowds. People started to push me back. Hard. Into other people. Everyone was pissed off. I was a drunken pinball. One of my last memories was looking into a man's eyes and seeing fiery hate, as if seeing me reminded him of hundreds of years of people like me: immature and oblivious and entitled light-skinned douche-bags infiltrating his home, bleaching his culture.

I leaned into Saff with a dumb grin.

"I think there's gonna be a fight," I said.

"Ok," Saff said.

"I'm so ready," I said.

Which I wasn't.

My face bounced like a balloon from all the uppercuts that angry man dished out. I made no attempt to break free; I was too busy laughing. Legit giggling, as this man pummeled my face. Saff rushed over and socked the guy in his ear. He fractured his hand as a result, and had to sit out the next month of baseball. Saff told the trainers he'd fallen off a ladder, which they did not believe. He wasn't the least bit upset that he had to sit out baseball, or that he couldn't use his hand. For weeks after the incident, he was most disturbed by my reaction while my face was getting pounded into ground chuck.

"It was like you couldn't get enough, dude."

On Halloween that year, I dressed as a ballerina. I also

bought a young girl leotard and tutu (pink) and squeezed into it. I bought a pink and orange tiara. My finishing touch was a thong I borrowed from a girl on the tennis team, who would later become Saff's wife. She said, as she handed it to me that night: "Just keep it."

Saff and I split a gallon jug of Carlo Rossi though neither of us liked wine. We drove to a house party hammered. The first thing I did when I got out of the car—with my ass fully exposed—was go up to a stranger, and ask:

"Who the *fuck* are you?"

"This is my house," he said, clearly wondering who the fuck I was.

In my state, and my attire, I decided the best course of action was to punch him in the face, then go home and make a protein shake.

One morning, toward the beginning of the baseball season that year, I woke up next to Band-Aid wrappers. I rolled off my bed and moaned. My stomach felt like it was digesting old pennies. In the living room, I felt a draft. Our window, which offered a panoramic view of the Pacific, was shattered. Crushed beer cans and Solo cups lay in the shards of glass on the floor. The TV was on a Madden game, paused. A faded poster from the 90s of a hot chick in a one-piece bathing suit had fallen to the floor. The microwave door was open, full of thawed taquitos. Evidently, someone in his stupor had wanted taquitos, but could not figure out how to push the buttons. Quite possibly, that person had been me. Our house smelled sour, like a recycling bin. I found Saff sprawled across his bed in a kimono and wearing two different socks. Some bird feathers floated eerily around him.

"What happened to the window?" I asked.

"You don't remember?" he murmured into his pillow.

He tried to sit up, but couldn't.

"I have no memories."

"You threw Lars through it."

Lars was one of our pitchers. He was the only guy that got drafted when I was at Hilo. He pitched in slip-on shoes, refusing cleats. Coaches allowed this, because he threw upper eighties with a pro slider and had scouts coming to our games for one of the first times in school history.

"You guys were open-hand slugging each other in the face. Like, taking turns. Politely and shit. Here."

Saff tossed me his camera. I moved my jaw. It clicked. I watched a video of Lars and me, which was like watching a video of two strangers. Hours of the night were but a blank screen. I watched on the video as one of us braced for the blow, and the other delivered. Over and over. Then, in the video, I did a pitching wind up and slugged Lars to the floor. It was the deadened sound of meat being tenderized. Lars was kind enough to return the favor. I flinched. Some of my teammates were off to the side laughing in discomfort, or putting their hands over their face like "oooooooooh!"

"You guys were hugging it out afterward. Dude, you kissed him by the way," Saff said. "Not sure if I got that on camera. Then it became like, wrestling, and not hugging. It was like, a gorilla-retard hug, and you guys went through the window."

The window was $200, something I hadn't had in college since I emptied my bank account earlier that year to buy a car. My account was eternally hovering in the 20$ range—there was often so little I always had to check my balance before making the minimum withdrawal. I couldn't have asked my parents for an extra 200 bones to repair a window I'd destroyed in a moment of homo-erotic team-bonding violence; that, I knew, had not been figured into their monthly budget. But I had to get it fixed, and soon. There was only so much of this shit our landlord would tolerate.

A couple of weeks later, UH Hilo had a road trip to New

Mexico, where we played NMS and UNM. On that trip, I stayed locked in our hotel eating ramen and continental pastries and drinking water from the bathroom faucet while watching *World Series of Poker*. All of the NCAA per-diem money went in my pocket for the window. $25 a day, for eight days. And I was in desperate need of some filtered water, and a vegetable.

Charlie and I spoke on the phone a couple times a month, chatted on AOL Instant Messenger. He'd spent his senior year getting flown around the country by top baseball universities. He'd had several scholarships on the table, and ultimately chose Cal, to continue to represent the Bay Area. He was now their starting catcher. Whenever I checked my stats, I checked his too. He had good stories, teammate ones, party ones, girl ones. He had a braggart's way of talking of his failures that invited hearty laughter at his expense. When we were in New Mexico, and I was paying off the window by eating ramen, I called Charlie and filled him in about how stupid I'd been.

"Let me tell you stupid," he said. "This wasn't me, but I heard this story from a teammate who played with this guy last summer in the South."

We were supposed to be going to the hotel's conference room for study hall, which was an hour of our entire team in one room watching YouTube while Coach E stared out a window.

"This guy was a reputed drunkard," Charlie said. "He'd been booted off a couple teams before. He really had a problem."

He said the last part as if it was an insight that had just come to him, a provocative side-thought.

"So one night, his team's shacked up in Myrtle Beach for a series. And I guess there's some lake out there, or bay? Maybe it's just the straight up ocean. Anyways, tourist water where they rent out canoes in the day. So this guy just blacks himself out in his room off some Seagrams and is suddenly determined to steal one of those canoes and take it out. Mind you, this is the middle of the night. He heads out, wrangles a canoe loose from its chains, pushes into the water, and paddles out into the middle of this bay, or whatever. No paddle, by the way, just hands."

"Don't tell me he drowned."

"Worse."

"Hmmm."

"In the middle of the lake, in the middle of the summer night, by himself with no paddle, this guy decides to take all his clothes off. So he's sitting in a canoe naked. Then he decides to throw all his clothes overboard. Of course, he wakes up getting his tits beat in by the morning sun. No idea where he is, or where all of his clothes went, or which part of the shore he came from."

Charlie paused now.

"You know where this is going?" he asked.

"Not really," I said. "If it's not just killing himself."

"Worse. He had to paddle in, return the canoe to the tour shop, and walk back to his hotel, into the lobby, ask for a key replacement, take an elevator back to his floor, walk down the hall and let himself back into his room…naked."

"That man's got one proud mom," I said.

"Can you imagine some of the phone calls that poor lady's gotten over the years?"

What else could two 20-year-old college athletes say about someone like this? This mythical dingleberry whose misadventures were making their way through the baseball underbelly of America? Whose stories made people cringe, and laugh, but also intrigued—and in a way, made my failures feel harmless by comparison.

Charlie and I reminisced about our summers with the Oakland Oaks, when we'd get picked up from the BART station in our coach's Geo Metro, out of the kindness of his heart, share the car with all of the gear, and then pick up two

6' 5"-tall black kids from Oakland who also didn't have rides, and scrape along the freeway to the glorious East Bay fields for dusk games.

"Worry free," we always said of those times.

"For the love of baseball, nothing else."

"Brotherhood."

That summer, I knew Charlie would go play in Cape Cod. Few things on earth were more certain at the time than me *not* playing in Cape Cod. Our baseball paths were ever-diverging: his toward the pros, and mine toward the end of a career. So we both, for separate reasons, indulged in reminiscing in the days of coming up together, me on the mound, him in the crouch on a field in the Bay Area, the afternoons in the batting cage when we tried to strike each other out, and afterward, speculated about our futures.

12
A GAMBLING MAN

That's how pitching in college came to feel for me: a gamble. That is, if the gambler was just a normal guy, not a card counter, or a math whiz, or even a guy with money to blow. What I mean is, I sometimes felt like I had no control over my fate. Not in a religious, higher power sense. I just felt, sometimes I made good pitches—low changeups, sharp curves, inside corner fastballs—and they got hit hard for doubles in the gap or homeruns even. It was a brutal feeling to make a quality pitch, the exact pitch and speed and location I was going for, and to have some guy pulverize it. It made me think, *shit, if these guys crush my good pitches, God only knows what'll happen to my bad ones.*

Plenty of times, I made bad pitches—hung changeups, curve-less curves—and batters swung and missed foolishly or hit into double plays. It didn't make sense. And that was baseball. Sure, preparation, mental toughness, focus, all the recycled blather that coaches told you—that all played a big role. But there was other stuff that no one told you: umpires, weather, the quality of the ball field, the distance to the homerun fence, positioning of your defense, how much sleep your shortstop got, the focus of the opposing batter. For that reason, pitching was like gambling, in that no matter what the odds said, you just never knew. And it was a hell of a rush, as gambling can be.

I was addicted to freezing someone with an inside fastball for strike three, or getting them to chase a low changeup for a sky-high pop-out to shortstop. I felt qualified to talk shit to the other team. I rewarded myself a chew, iced my shoulder, went home and looked at my new stats online, reveled in how many points my ERA had dropped, and imagined friends and family back home, getting up the next day, checking the website over coffee and saying:

"Emil pitched again. Oh look, even got himself a couple strikeouts."

When I had bad outings, my rage and disorientation were uncontrollable. Not dissimilar to gamblers after a rough night at blackjack. I made fists and released like a hyperventilation bag filling in and out with air. I didn't allow myself a chew. I didn't ice my arm, told myself *you don't deserve ice*. I thought maybe I didn't truly belong in D1, maybe I'd conned my way in, duped kind old Coach E into giving me his scholarship money. I lost sleep worrying, what if my next outing was just as bad or worse, and people back home saw that I only pitched one and a third innings and gave up four runs, including two homers?

I thought about Charlie, whose career at Cal was taking off. He was now a sophomore, having enjoyed a very successful freshman season. He was a *real* D1 player in my eyes, in a *real* conference, the Pac 10, playing a part in many wins. His games constantly had pro scouts attending. Guys were always getting drafted off Charlie's team. Brandon Morrow had just been taken fifth overall by the Mariners. Brennan Boesch had gone in the third round, Allen Craig in the eighth. Cal was a team of *ballers*, and Charlie was the young buck, starting in that star-studded lineup. He was always hitting over .300. There were often short articles about how his clutch hit late in the game sparked a comeback. He was the hometown hero.

At the time, Cal had a lefty on their roster who I compared myself to: Craig Bennigson. I'd never met him, had no idea what he looked like other than his roster photo. Didn't know his personality. Didn't know what pitches he threw, how hard he threw, nothing. All I knew was that he was Cal's lefty reliever, their specialist, their spot starter. He was their me. When I checked Charlie's stats, I always checked Craig's too, to see if he'd gotten in that night's game. I checked how many innings he'd pitched in his appearance, and whether his ERA went up or down. When his ERA went up, and mine went down, I felt validated. On occasion, my ERA was lower than his, and, looking at the screen, thought, *I could've pitched at Cal. I'm just as good as any other lefty reliever. I belong.* Then sometimes I'd check and he'd have started a game against USC and gone five shutout innings. I'd think, *Yeah, I can't do that.* And I'd feel bad for sitting in my room alone on my computer rooting against a complete stranger. I probably knew this kid's stats better than he did.

The good news was, as a junior, I was pitching in more games than anyone else on our team. As I passed the halfway point of my college career, I realized I had a shot at the school record for appearances. The record was 46. I discovered it at our annual preseason baseball fundraiser when leafing through the school records pamphlet. I sat at 35 appearances. My math skills narrowly enabled me to deduce that I needed 11 more, in a season and a half. That was more than doable, barring injury. So I started to push myself to pitch even more.

Once, against Santa Clara, I pitched in both games of a double header. If I said that to old timers, they would say, so what? And rightfully so. People back in the day used to pitch 16 innings. Then they'd come back and pitch the next day. But these days, usually once you pitched, even if it was just an inning, you iced, and you were done. Well that day, I pitched, iced, then told Coach I could pitch in the second game. Possibly, bless his heart, he did not remember that I had pitched the first. My arm felt gummy and powerless when I warmed up for the second game, but I didn't care.

Another time, we played University of Washington at their purple field. Tim Lincecum had been drafted from there 10th overall by the Giants just a year before, and his number was already retired on the wall in right field. It was February and snowing in Washington. In the dugouts, they provided space heaters, which our guys held their bats to when they were on deck so that in the event that they made contact, their hands wouldn't shatter. Our Hawaiians hit with beanies under their helmets. Muscle-bound with tribal tattoos and usually prison-serious mugs, those guys got obscenely giddy when they caught snowflakes on their tongues for the first time.

That series was a hands-on class in why pitching in snow sucks. One, muscles are cold and bloodless. Two, the leathery texture of the ball freezes and becomes like sleet. The traction of fingerprints also is lost. So, in essence, you can't move or throw. I figured, the best thing to do in such conditions was tell Coach I wanted to pitch. In the bullpen, my warmups were looking like the pitches I had seen when I was a little league umpire.

I held out my hat when Coach held out his to see if I was ready; I couldn't feel my fingers.

What I remember most from that outing is this one pitch. I threw a curve ball that was so slow that while the ball was *in the air,* the batter started laughing, and dropped his bat and stepped out of the batter's box. *Then* the ball was caught. Our catcher was laughing too. He took off his mask and almost keeled over. Then, the umpire called it a strike! And *he* took off his mask, and was laughing.

In Texas against Dallas Baptist, there was something about the air, something more than just "the air was thin." It was really like the sky was a vacuum, and anything that went up there just got sucked away. Before I came into that game, our starter gave up two grand slams in one inning. A cool eight spot. "Oh..." people on the bench reacted mournfully. Again, I felt compelled to tell coach, "I'm good to go."

When I entered the game as reliever in the later innings, it was entirely out of hand; I proceeded to surrender two *three-run homers* in the same inning. That's 14 runs, in four pitches. And I swear, those balls left the bat and got sucked away, like the kind of thing that would get investigated on *The X-Files*.

It happened again in New Mexico, junior year. The air was very "thin." We played at the Albuquerque Isotopes stadium, the AAA stadium for the Dodgers. It was immaculate. Me and Saff took a bunch of bro pics, posing in left field with the gargantuan scoreboard as the backdrop. The bullpen was behind left field, so far that they had phones to communicate with the dugout. All pregame we were crank-calling the dugout, until our trainer answered the phone and said the next guy who called was getting his ass beat, by him; he was possibly 65 years old. And named Dick Koch (We pronounced his last name as Cock, of which he approved). He called everyone "big guy," though, standing at 6'5", he was the biggest guy. He often went on golf excursions with our players. His handshake could liquefy your hand. Everyone loved Dick. And he was sick of us fake-ordering pepperoni pizzas and prostitutes from the bullpen phone.

In the fourth inning, our starter gave up back to back…to back…homers. Three straight dings. One flew over us in the bullpen, landing possibly 450 ft. It was the kind of thing that made the crowd forget they were watching a game and think they were watching a spectacle, like The Harlem Globetrotters. "Ahhhhhhh," they gasped after the third one. We watched from the bullpen like soldiers in the trenches seeing their buddies get mowed down on the front line. Sorrowfully, fearfully. Except, in contrast to the military analogy, we were also laughing.

In the bullpen, I picked up the phone. Coach answered, probably because he needed a distraction from the horror.

"Hey Coach, it's Emil."

"What."

"I'm good to go," I said.

"That's not how it works," he snapped. "If I want you to get loose, *I* tell *you*."

He hung up. One of the bullpen catchers had his pants

pulled down, with his ass pushed up against the mesh fence, which the whole stadium could have seen, should they have found themselves looking in the left field bullpen. Pitchers were rolling around, laughing. I decided it wouldn't be all that bad to spend the evening out in the bullpen with this bunch. Moments later, the phone rang.

"Dominoes," the catcher answered.

"Get Emil loose," our pitching coach said. I didn't hear this, but I saw the catcher's eyes dart to me. My stomach nerves activated. I tied on my cleats and started throwing. Before our pitcher could give up another homer, and before I was completely loose, Coach went to the mound and signaled for me. He looked a hundred miles away.

The first kid I faced check-swung at the first pitch. The ball shot like a torpedo off the right field wall for a triple. The kid had tried to *not* hit the ball, and that was the result. Before I continue this story, let me paint a picture as to the technology of baseball in 2007, when this happened. Back then, Easton made these things called Stealth bats. They were the rave. Why? Because they had *ludicrous* pop. You could be a terrible hitter, make bad contact (i.e. that kid's check swing), and still hit a bomb. Naturally, everyone wanted one. And everyone had one. Power numbers were through the roof. It was a brutal time to be a college pitcher. I would liken it to the Steroid Era in the 90s. Then, some pitchers got essentially decapitated from line drives. People decided that perhaps these bats were *fatally* good, and so they stopped making them, and suddenly the rave of baseball technology was to *deaden* aluminum bats to be more like wood bats. But by then, the damage had been done to my ERA.

After the check swing triple, I hit a guy in the calf with a changeup. Which wasn't just a clear lack of focus, but *the* most embarrassing way to plunk a guy. If you were going to give him a free base, you at least wanted it to *hurt*. A changeup in the calf may have actually felt *good* to the kid. Then Coach E called a trick play which we'd done hundreds of times in practice, but I was so rattled at that point that the play confused me, and I balked in a run. Then I got pulled. As I walked from the mound, the stadium played "I've Seen Better Days," which was the softest, corniest alternative rock jam ever, made perhaps solely for these moments, and never to be taken seriously. New Mexico's home crowd gave me a standing ovation and I wanted to flip them off and call them all hicks though I was pretty sure that wasn't what they were.

So I pitched in snow and rain and wind and a whole lot of sun. In dry air and heavy-quilt humidity. From sea level to high altitude. In empty stadiums and packed houses of hecklers, who ranged from frat boys to mid-life crisis dads. I pitched against the best of the best, future major leaguers, future World Series champions, and plenty of regular old D1 guys like me.

Even when my arm hurt, when it really could have used a day off, I went to the trainers before games, hooked my arm up to stem-therapy, pumped it with electricity to relieve some of the pain, or shock the pain away. (I was never really sure what the science was behind all those pads and wires). After that, I lathered my arm in Icy Hot, wore the tube of a tube sock around my elbow, all in blazing Hilo sun to keep the body hot. Uncomfortably hot. Sometimes in warmups I dropped down a little sidearm to give my shoulder a break. Other times, I slung the ball like a catapult to rest the elbow. In the fifth and sixth innings, I typically got up and walked around in front of Coach E, just so an image of me was fresh in his mind when he started to think of who would pitch next. Or I'd flat out tell him "I'm good to go," even when I wasn't.

13
LEFT-HANDED PITCHER II

*C*ome to my office tomorrow between 11-12. We need to talk. -MP

This popped into my inbox one Sunday afternoon toward the middle of Fall semester, senior year. MP—Dr. Mark Panek—was my English professor. Before him, high school had been four years of getting essays returned blood-red with comments like "awk sentence," "WC?" "Sp.," and the-ever explanatory "No." So many sentences and ideas of mine had been deemed "No."

I met Dr. Panek for the first time in English 100, sophomore year. In that class, he told me I was a strong writer. I squinted at him. Then I laughed. He kept a straight face. Dr. Panek turned out to be vehement, and somewhat neurotic, about making writing fun, especially for kids like me who'd been trained to have no faith in their literary skills. Dr. Panek structured his class so that you could really do anything—use run-on sentences, curse words, whatever—as long as your stance was clear, as long as you backed your ideas, and as long as you weren't some Sparknotes derelict. After English 100, which was my first A in English in a very long time, I took Intro Creative Writing with him, and Fiction Writing, and Nonfiction Writing, until I had over half the credits for the English major. I declared English as my second major. Figured I might as well. My other major was Communications. That major taught such monumental concepts as: eye contact means someone is paying attention to you, and laughter can sometimes reduce stress.

A year before, on my 21st birthday, one of Dr. Panek's friends, an award-winning novelist, had been in town. Dr. Panek had given me a draft of the guy's latest novel-in-the-works and entrusted me to edit it. Then, he told me to meet him at Bamboo Garden, a Korean bar on a side street of downtown Hilo (which is not a regular downtown; no building is taller than two stories and restaurants close at 6). At this meeting we were going to discuss his friend's draft. I really didn't know how to react, or prepare. Very seldom in my life had my input been requested in any intellectual capacity.

That night after the meeting I drank too much at a party, passed out, and lost my glasses in a giant fern. When I came to and got home, I joined Saff and the rest of the Baseball House and smoked on the porch and giggled at the bug-zapper until I was un-blacked out, and desperate for pork rinds. We smoked until sunrise, by which time my IQ was that of an earthworm. I dug around our backyard in my boxers and tried to pick bananas from our tree, which left us with a partly felled banana tree, no bananas, and me looking like a connect-the-dots drawing of mosquito bites. When I finally got into bed at six, I called Dr. Panek. I remembered him saying at the bar earlier that his wife was due to go into labor any minute with his first child. He didn't answer. I mumbled something in his voicemail asking whether his wife had given birth. He called back seconds later.

"What're you doing up?" he asked. "Actually, don't answer that."

"I was just wondering if you have a son," I said.

"I do."

"That means your son and I have the same birthday," I said.

"That you do."

"You gonna be one of those dads that carries his kid in the frontal backpack?"

"Get some sleep," he said.

I wasn't sure what Dr. Panek had called me into his office for. But I knew better than to ask; he liked to maintain an aura of mystery about things.

I drove my Dodge Colt to Dr. Panek's office, knocked on his door, holding the latest draft of what I was working on, in case that was what he wanted to discuss.

Dr. Panek's bookshelf was crammed with everything from Pat Conroy and Kurt Vonnegut and Joan Didion to Polynesian history, grammar books, and contributor copies of his own books—a heaping collage of colors and thicknesses, paperbacks, hardbacks, not appearing to be organized by genre or author or anything. The room had the fossilizing paper smell of a grandfather's study. Outside his window was a crabgrass meadow where students walked, or played Frisbee, or napped.

"What's up, Doc?" I asked.

He paused a moment before speaking.

"Have a seat."

Typical.

I'd spent three years in this office, being posed open-ended questions to which all of my answers seemed to have both lots of merit and no merit at all. We'd met so many times over drafts of essays and stories. He'd helped me sculpt story arcs, pushed me to identify the real argument in my papers, despite the argument I *thought* I was making. I'd learned basic rhetoric, how to identify logical fallacies in our readings, as well as fallacies in my own logic. I'd realized that this class not only made me feel like I had a brain, but it gave my brain needed stimulation. (My other waking hours consisted of long runs, watching roommates play Madden tournaments, beer pong, and even-more brain-mushing: Communications classes.) In the book he had just released that year called *Big Happiness*—a biography of a Hawaiian sumo-wrestler turned drug addict who was murdered—Dr. Panek listed me in the acknowledgments for having helped edit it. This catapulted my image of myself to undeserved heights. I felt I was on my way to giving the commencement speech at graduation, writing the next great

American novel, having a leathery cigar den in my house in the Hamptons.

"How you feeling?" he asked.

"Good," I said.

His eyebrows furrowed.

"Good," he said, as if the word had many definitions, and he was unsure which one I meant.

"Should I not be?" I asked.

"We've got a problem," he said.

"I see…"

"What time is class on Thursdays?"

Where could this possibly be going?, I wondered.

"What do you mean?" I asked.

"Simple question."

"Two?"

"That's right. Class is at two. A.m. or p.m.?"

"P.m. Am I coming late again or something?"

"Two in the afternoon. And you're coming to my class drunk."

I adjusted myself. Looked out the window. Didn't reply.

"And it's not just me who notices. It's getting old. Not to mention, you know, dangerous."

His class was on Thursdays, the day after College Night at the local club, Uncle Mikey's, and I was drinking to the point where by two in the afternoon the next day, I was barely alive, hardly able to talk, still too drunk to drive, and apparently I wasn't hiding it very well with my teary and sunken eyes, my scabbed knuckles, and the smells of nail polish remover emanating from my pores.

"It was cute, maybe once," Dr. Panek said. "But this is every Thursday. I can be professional about it and say don't show up to my class drunk again, or I'll fail you. Which is true, by the way. Or I can be a human and ask if everything is alright?"

"Yeah, man," I answered quick, feeling uncomfortable

beneath his stare. "Everything's fine."

"You sure?"

"Yeah." I laughed, to ensure that this was a laughing matter, to release some tension. I was used to laughing these nights away anyway. Like the guy who paddled himself into the middle of a lake to get naked and lost. To a 21-year-old, all that stuff *was* funny.

"I know you've got your boys, and this is what you do in college," he said. "But you come to my class in shape from here on out, or you can explain to Coach E that you drank your grades away, which will lead you to explaining to your parents how your scholarship was taken away."

I could tell from his face that it pained him to get serious with me. It pained him to threaten me, and I hated that I had put him in such a position. It was humiliating at my age to be causing people to worry as if I was a toddler again. This meeting did not reinforce my image of myself as a tough, invulnerable college athlete, which was sometimes how I rationalized my nights. This meeting flipped that image upside down. It gave a glimpse of myself I preferred not to see. I left Dr. Panek's office with a brittle, broken down feeling, not much different than a hangover.

14
ONE WEEK LATER

I woke up in a room darkened by the drawn curtains. Outside I heard footsteps and carts rolling around with people speaking pidgin. A couple of tropical birds chirped. I discovered I was shirtless with a long diagonal scratch across my body. Next to me was another lifeless being, a man. It occurred to me that this was the exact scenario of low-grade horror movies when tourists wake up and realize their kidneys have been stolen. I looked closer to find it was Coach Clark, our pitching coach. He opened his eyes, grumbled some form of a laugh, slowly pawed the bedside table. He hit his keys, knocked over a glass, then stopped once he'd cupped the tin of chew. He raised it to me; I puked in my mouth.

"Hangin'?" he asked, thwacking the tin.

I looked across in the other bed, saw Saff and our other assistant coach, Watson. The room smelled like the parking lot after a Niners game.

"Breakfast?" Clark asked.

"Shut up," Saff moaned from across the room.

The night before, the four of us—Saff, our two assistant coaches, and I—drove across the island and got a hotel room for my birthday.

"Happy birthday," they cheered from our balcony, the smell of tourist cigarettes rising from Ali'i Drive. We watched the ocean change from auburn to deep blue as we took down a handle of Smirnoff.

I barely remembered leaving the hotel. I closed my eyes and saw flashes of me walking into a beach bar, sitting at a picnic table under an umbrella. I remembered leafing through a menu, looking at the prices, and giving up on the idea of dinner. Saff, Coach Watson, and Coach Clark got short ribs, and I ate their garnish cabbage that wasn't meant to be eaten. Then they bought me shots. We sat there and listened to the "live" band, which was one man strumming Eagles covers on a ukulele to a pre-processed beat.

My memory provided snapshots of me getting escorted out by the bouncer.

"What happened at that first bar?" I asked, rubbing my eyes.

"You were putting in work with this huge lady. In front of her husband. She was like fifty. You asked her husband if he wanted to step outside. Even though, the whole restaurant was outside."

Saff made a noise into his pillow.

I sighed.

"Then we lost you, dude. You were gone for like two hours. By the way…"

Coach Clark reached to turn on the light.

"Yep. You have a black eye."

I got up and fell into the wall, then walked into the bathroom. I shrieked at seeing my face in the mirror, and discovered half my front tooth missing. We went to breakfast and I couldn't hold down water. My head pulsed so bad I could see my heartbeat in my vision, blipping like submarine sonar. My eye socket ripened to an eggplant-purple. I had no strength.

When we got home, I sat in bed, sickly. I couldn't lie down due to the spins. At midnight I walked out my screen door and onto the patio. There was a placid sound of coqui frogs, a calm breeze. The patio had a Supersoaker, a bong, a Frisbee, some running shoes, dip spit in cat food cans, and a couch that looked like it had been through the war in Kosovo.

I leaned over the rail, puked. Saff heard me retching from his room upstairs and AOL messaged me:

Yikes.

I typed back, *I'm not right.*

Concussion?

Prolly.

Want me to take you to the ER?

Nah, thanks.

That night, I sat in bed for hours, too dizzy to sleep, the taste of puke and toothpaste in my throat. The next morning, not feeling any better, I skipped class and went to the trainers, and told them I'd been jumped in Kona for being a *haole*. They did concussion tests, had me follow their finger with my eyes, had me stand on one foot with my eyes closed and try to balance. I fell.

"Your blood pressure's through the roof. That's got to calm down before I clear you."

I felt like I was back in Dr. Panek's office being admonished. Being exposed. Being told, *bro, you're weaker than you think, and everyone can see it.*

"Second, you have a concussion."

"I don't *feel* like I have a concussion," I lied.

The trainer sighed.

"Two weeks off from baseball," he sentenced. "At least. You need a reset. Then we'll talk."

When I told Coach E I'd been jumped for being a *haole*, he felt terrible, as if it were somehow his fault.

"Take as much time off as you need, Emil. To heal physically, as *well* as emotionally," he said, and nodded slowly while holding my eyes, as though referring to secret information only he and I knew. I felt so guilty for taking advantage of his kindness, I almost came clean. I wanted to cry, I remember, and it was the most I'd ever hated myself, or alcohol, or both.

During my recovery, as a form of self-punishment, I quit drinking for a month, which was a milestone. Also as self-punishment, I grew out my beard for the first time in my life.

My goal with the beard was to be as uncomfortable and ugly on the outside as I felt on the inside. It worked. My beard was itchy with little hairs that curled into themselves and pissed each other off. I scratched myself bloody at one point. After a month, I looked like some kind of scraggly auto mechanic looking to rip everyone off. Our team photos were taken during this beard phase, so this version of myself was published on our team website, and seen by the tens of people worldwide who kept up on UH Hilo baseball. It was my self-prescribed Scarlet Letter, and I felt cleansed to be suffering through this publicly. Of course, those who saw my photo likely did not fully grasp its profundity; they probably just saw it and thought that a creepy hitchhiker had somehow made it onto a roster of normal looking athletes. But that was fine. I needed this, whatever it was.

Had I known who was about to enter my life, however, I probably would have taken the old razor to my face.

15
SOUTH

She wore faded salmon jeans, had tawny skin and the thighs of a gymnast. There was a Vaseline shine to her lips from an over-application of gloss, but I could tell from the way she sat, a mix between proper and aloof, that she'd overshined her lips not for attention, but from clumsiness. They were pretty lips, in a bug-bitten sort of way.

It was the beginning of spring semester, senior year. I was at a UH Hilo basketball game with Moon, another pitcher. His full name was Jesse Moon, but people called him Moonpie, because he looked like he ate his fair share. I was fresh off a month of sobriety, enjoying a chew with Moon in the gym bleachers, half-watching the game, half-watching the girl a few rows over. This much I knew about her: we had Fiction Writing with Dr. Panek. She'd told me her name a week ago in class, but I hadn't heard her correctly through her syrupy southern drawl.

"Haa, A'm Keyimball," she'd said. Exchange student, I diagnosed. There'd been several in my years at Hilo. Mostly from the Deep South.

"I'm sorry?" I asked.

"Keyimball."

"Kimball?"

"Yep!"

And I was thinking, *No. That's not actually your name, because that is nobody's name.* But I left it at that, because I didn't want to come off as an idiot, and I was fixed on the beauty mark on her right cheek. So that was where things stood.

"That girl's in my English class," I told Moon. He looked, noted the same things. The thighs, the skin. The natural, unavoidable things of a woman.

"Why are you sitting next to me?" he asked.

He spit in his bottle. I spit.

"Huh?"

He nodded his head at the open seat next to her.

"I don't have anything to say."

"Talk about English."

"But I'm not even drunk."

Moon rolled his eyes, though he understood.

To her right was presumably a friend, thin but pear-shaped with a bowlcut. She looked like a mom that had just given up. The two clapped politely when Hilo scored, as if watching a well-executed routine at a dog show. Kimball's hair was long, and silky, and pecan-colored. It looked yet to be de-virginized by product. I crept down the few rows, as if trying not to wake someone.

"Can I sit here?" I asked.

"Sure!" she said, the way a young boy might respond to his father asking, "Say, son, how'd you feel about going fishin' this weekend?" It gave the impression that she'd never considered sexual attraction, or flirting, or puberty, as things that existed outside of soap operas. We sat, awkward and wordless for a few Hilo possessions. She introduced me to her friend and we shook hands. I looked back at Moon, who was laughing, flashing a sarcastic thumbs up.

"Where are you from?" I asked.

"Sath Carolana."

"On exchange?"

"Mhmmm."

Her skin smelled good. Not in a manufactured way, but natural. Like the smell when you swim in a fresh water hole. Her teeth were ivory white and almost impossibly straight.

"What're you doin'? Is that chew?" she asked.

"Yeah."

"Gosh. Ew."

But I could tell she wasn't grossed out. Not fully grossed out at least. I'd seen girls get full-blown grossed out, offended even, as if by chewing tobacco I was also insinuating that I did not support women's suffrage. Kimball simply shrugged at the discovery.

"Must be a baseball boy."

"Guilty."

"What position?"

"I pitch. Do you like baseball?"

"Of course."

"Who's your team?"

"Braves, dummy."

My gut feeling was that she didn't know a single thing about them. I presumed her dad had been a fan and taken her to some games as a girl, before she inevitably devoted herself to EZ Bake Oven.

"Who's your favorite player?" I asked.

"Chipper."

"What position's he play?"

"You askin' cause you don't know? Or quizzin'? Cause either one's unacceptable."

I raised my hands, showing that I came in peace. A silence came over us that terrified me. I couldn't let the conversation end, especially there. This was a baseball girl, I could tell. She leaned over and said something to her Beatles-look-alike friend.

"What's your favorite Disney movie?" I blurted, interrupting her friend in mid-sentence. I was like a child tugging at his mom's pant leg for attention. Respectfully, after her friend finished her response, she turned to me: *"Beauty and the Beast."* She asked me back and I said *"Jungle Book, Lady and the Tramp* a close second." I moved right along and asked what her favorite music was. "Led Zeppelin, Bob Dylan, Eric Clapton." I couldn't name a single song of theirs; I'd been raised in a house where Coltrane was king. I was possibly the only college athlete in America likelier to recognize a Chopin nocturne over a Zeppelin anthem. On my iTunes there were thousands of songs. All kinds of hip-hop, reggae, classical, 90s punk. But search Led Zeppelin, or Eric Clapton, and you'd get squat. I asked her what her favorite food was, then her favorite place on the island, her favorite movie. I was paying attention to her answers, but just enough to ask follow-ups.

"What is this, twenty questions?" she asked at one point, only half joking. "Didn't you come here to watch the game?"

I laughed at that. Hell no, I did not come to watch the game; this was UH Hilo sports. At that point, all I wanted was the game to go into overtime. Triple overtime. When the buzzer ended the game, and people slowly descended the metal bleachers, I panicked.

"So…my buddy Moon and I are going to a party later."

Her clothes implied she was not a big partier. A chain around her neck marked an allegiance to Jesus.

"Not a big party," I clarified. "More like a…potluck? A gathering?"

This was my attempt to use vaguely churchy words.

"Maybe I could have your number, in case you decided you wanted to continue this conversation?"

"Sure!" she said, once again, seeming oblivious to the existence of courtship, or sexual intercourse. I entered her number, then I got stumped as to what to put for her name, knowing it couldn't possibly be Kimball. So I saved her as South.

"I'll be in touch a little later," I said.

"OK, but just to let you know, I'm probably staying in, playing Yahtzee and watching 'Monk' with my Church friends tonight."

Who the hell was this girl? And what the hell was I doing? These questions butted heads with my other thoughts, which were: *the girl is beautiful without trying, and I love the ease with which we converse, and the lack of ulterior motives in her tone.*

"I saw you got that number," Moon said, walking to my car.

"I did."

"She's pretty."

"I know, she really is."

"What's her name?"

"Dude, not sure. Kimball?"

"That's not possible."

"I know."

"She coming out tonight?"

"She, uh...she's playing board games? With church friends?"

"Abort mission."

10:04 pm

Hi it's Emil. We're headed to the party soon if you have a change of heart. Let me know. I liked talking to you.

No response.

1:17 am

The party was lonely without you.

I stared at my phone for five minutes before sending that.

No response.

8:05 am from "South"

Haha...I'm sure you held up just fine.

Not the response to my flattery I was hoping for, so I called upon a spineless defense:

10:46 am

That was actually my friend Moon texting you, he stole my phone while I was in the bathroom.

In class, she was all business, arrived five minutes early, volunteered her ideas about *The Things They Carried* from her copy rainbowed with Post-Its. Our eye contact led on to nothing, as if our conversation at the basketball game had been in my imagination.

Another kid in our reading group, Brandon, quite obviously took an interest in her as well. It made me want to punch him in the throat. Luckily, he had tiny hands and early-onset gray hair. He showed up to class with squinty arrogance and no completed work and tried to smooth-talk Dr. Panek for a good grade, which was like flashing tits to a blind person. Brandon's whole existence made me look chivalrous and hunky. One day, Dr. Panek passed back a quiz to Kimball, and I snuck a look at her name: *Kendall*. Kendall Pope. The church girl's last name was Pope. How rich. And possibly, a bad idea.

I went home and looked her up on Facebook, scrolled her profile pics. One was of her kissing a girlfriend's cheek, back when her hair was shorter. Another was of her hugging a tree. Another was of her playing acoustic guitar, and in another she was wearing a very asexual camo hat and a Led Zeppelin t-shirt, eating a pancake. No kissy faces, no pictures of her in a bathing suit, nothing with a beer anywhere, no picture suggesting she had ever had hormones, or gone somewhere at night. Her interests were listed as: Peanut Butter and Jesus.

This was hopeless.

I feared the farthest I would get with her was Scrabble. And yet, I couldn't stop thinking about her. I even thought, *so what if we only play Scrabble?* I'd spent a lot of nights feeling alone in the past months, and ever since I'd met her, thoughts of her had crowded out other thoughts. Worries about baseball. Thoughts about drinking.

If you wrote a story about a jolly 60-year-old school bus driver with a club foot and a tooth that doubled as a can opener, what would you name him?

One Friday, I texted that question to her. I was lonely and she was consistently on my mind. I really wished she was a part of my life, but couldn't figure out how to make that happen without being cliché, or creepy. And somehow I decided this was the way to not be creepy.

Saff and the other roommates were invested in a videogame saga upstairs; MLB The Show. I heard them exchanging caveman shit-talk and coughing.

I awaited the vibration and blinking light and unopened-envelope icon of my phone. But it stayed dark, connected to my charger.

I'm an idiot! I thought. *Why the hell did I text her that? Of all things. I'm 21 years old and I'm texting that?* She probably thinks I'm a fucking psycho, or worse, desperate.

Then my phone vibrated. I reached for it.

Get stoned on the porch in ten?

The text was decidedly not from her, but from upstairs; they were evidently having an intermission.

One day went by. Then a whole weekend. Then finally, on Sunday night:

Crusty Pelvis.

I fell in love. It was a *brilliant* name, I thought. Something to even consider for my first-born son. I kept looking at the text, rereading it over and over like an acceptance letter to a prestigious school. Then, in came another:

How about a nearly retired yoga instructor with a brown fro and saggy boobs that are so big she is on disability?

I needed to marry this girl. Not the fictional yoga instructor, but Kendall. I considered her query for some time. I also felt relieved, and tantalized, to learn this girl *did* know what boobs were. I replied:

Geraldine Flavanga

Then:

How about a tollbooth guy who steals money from the booth and then loses it betting on crooked boxing matches?

South:

Good one. I say Gerbille Malvinski

Me:

Can we hang out sometime?

We were slated to hang out that Saturday night. On Friday, I texted to confirm. What exactly we'd be doing, I had no idea. I made sure our board games had all of the pieces. I stacked a bunch of DVDs that I figured she'd enjoy—*The Sandlot, Ferris Bueller's Day Off, The Fast and the Furious*—movies that did not feature stressful amounts of drugs or sex. I put together a playlist that contained no gangster rap or curse words or offensive concepts, just old-fashioned jazz: Benny Goodman, Count Basie, Billie Holiday. I got some hot chocolate together, also ingredients for s'mores. I felt like I was preparing for a snowed-in winter with my grandmother.

Come Saturday, she hadn't responded. I waited, did not go out with Saff and the rest of my roommates. Nothing. I just sat around, convincing myself that I wanted to stay in and save money. I kept looking at my phone, hoping. Sunday night, she got back to me saying:

So sorry, was on a weekend camping retreat with Church.

I had this weird feeling upon getting that text. Like I wanted to talk shit about Jesus and blame him for getting blown off.

That Wednesday in class we confirmed, again, to hang out that weekend. Friday went by. On Saturday:

What time should I swing by to pick you up?

4 PM passed, 5, 6. No response. This wasn't going to happen to me again. Who the hell did she think she was?

I knocked on a roommate's door.

"What you doin' tonight, Vitale?"

At that moment, he appeared to have been sitting in tighty-whities, staring at his wall. His room forever had the skunky smell of weed that had been smoked 30 minutes before. He was the same guy who'd driven his moped naked on my birthday the year before.

"Not a lot," he confessed.

"I'll tell you what you're doing. You and me are going to 7-11 to get a bottle, and we're taking it somewhere where there are girls, and we're drinking."

"I thought you had a date."

"She's standing me up, again."

At 7-11, we were going back and forth between the cheapest vodka and the cheapest rum available, when my phone vibrated:

South:

Just showered, wanna come get me?

I got jittery. I paced up and down the aisles of 7-11, if only to make her wait for a reply. She waited about 30 seconds.

Certainly.

I put back the rum and vodka and picked up a decent bottle of wine to have just in case I could convince her it was for religious purposes. Then I dropped off Vitale and replaced him with Kendall. She wore tight jeans and a purple blouse. She also had glittery makeup and I could see she'd colored in the beauty mark on her cheek. We went to Sak 'N Save where I let her choose what we ate for dinner, and when she brought the ingredients—pasta, basil, parmesan, garlic—and dropped them in the cart, she got so close that our chests touched, and I could smell her, and we both knew what was happening. I had about $20 in my checking account, per usual, and I was prepared to overdraft my account, go bankrupt even, for this night.

By midnight—next to the $200 window that I once shattered in a blackout, after the pesto I botched, after the bottle of wine that tinted our teeth crimson, and talking on the porch on the Kosovo couch—Kendall and I slow-danced to Benny Goodman, watching a full moon drift across the Pacific, in just our underwear.

16
THE SEASON OPENER

"Hiya, Doc," I said into the phone.

"What's going on?" Dr. Panek said.

I clutched my trembling index finger over a half-opened can of Hearty Skillet Sirloin, one of the only dinners college students can afford when not on a meal plan.

"Oh, not much. Just bleeding everywhere. I think I need, like, an actual doctor."

"Which hand?"

"Left."

"Shit. You drunk?"

"No, sir."

"Come see Noriko."

Noriko was Dr. Panek's wife, a nurse. I'd been to his house a few times to drop off papers. It was ten minutes up the hill.

"Come on in. Be quiet," he whispered. "Ken-Ken's asleep." His son was four months old now. I briefly thought how cool it would be someday to be calling him and wishing him happy birthday, maybe giving pitching lessons when I visited the islands.

Panek's house had a remarkably clean hardwood floor that creaked under bare feet. There was a grand piano in his living room, two conga drums, a snorting Rottweiler mutt, and no television. On his kitchen table was a baby monitor, and I could hear the raspy gurgles of their son from the other room.

"Oh, sssssssssss, ouch," Noriko whispered at the sight of my finger. The cut was slit like a snake eye. "What did you do?"

"Stupid soup can."

"You slotted to pitch in Game One?" Dr. Panek asked, not

in a whisper, but a low voice. He was in non-professor apparel: a plain white shirt and flannel pants, which tripped me out.

"I'm always slotted to pitch."

Noriko washed the cut, applied Neosporin, pinched the wound closed and wrapped it with a butterfly Band-Aid so tight that the tip of my finger poked out, ghost-white.

She told me that when I replaced the Band-Aid, to go to the trainer and get some Krazy Glue.

The next day, our team flew to Oahu for our season opener against Manoa. Game One was under the lights. During pre-game I tried throwing without a Band-Aid but the wound kept opening, staining the ball red. Saff got more and more uncomfortable as our ball got continually bloodier.

Come game time, the stadium was buzzing. This was a real D1 program, with over a thousand fans, TV and radio coverage, pre-game interviews, everything. In the third inning I was sent to the bullpen to warm up. Then told to shut down. Then I was told again in the fifth. Then, again in the seventh. I reached a point, which happens to relief pitchers sometimes, when they are made to warm up so many times that they run out of gas.

Drunken surfer types leaned over the bleachers and heckled.

"Yo, my beagle throws harder than you, bra"

"Dude, I feel bad. Can you even get *laid* throwing like that?"

Saff was next to me, warming up to close the game. He threw much harder than me, but was wilder, with a spastic delivery at times.

"Whoa, hey, easy tough guy," they told Saff. His next pitch sailed completely out of the bullpen.

"Uh, Coach? Attention Coach of UH Hilo, do NOT bring him in!"

Saff came in and did well aside from hitting a guy in the wrist. From the mound, he could not hear the hecklers as clearly. We were winning when he came out in the ninth, but we lost in the eleventh. Everyone on our team went back and forth between being angry that we'd lost, and enthralled that we'd almost won.

Many players on our team felt a deep grudge against Manoa. Manoa got all the attention, they got all the cool gear, they got the turf field and the stadium and the publicity. All of the Hawaiians on our team had tried to play for Manoa, and some had been strung along by their head coach only to get dumped at the last minute. So this wasn't just any other series. And I remembered being a high school senior, visiting this stadium on that muggy February day, watching the practice, seeing their coach mouth, "Which one's DeAndreis," and then never hearing from them again.

The next day I was sent to the bullpen.

"You'll be first in, no matter what," I was told.

I didn't want to risk my cut opening up mid-inning; I'd get taken out of the game immediately. So I pitched with my Band-Aid. I had a slight case of nerves, knowing that this game was on live TV. In my one inning of work, I didn't do so well. Throwing with a Band-Aid felt like trying to race barefoot on an ice rink. I gave up a homerun that hit the tip of the left field fence and bounced over with cartoon-like slowness. Later in the hotel, watching the nightly news with my elbow in the bucket, I learned that the kid who'd hit it was a fifth year senior, with zero prior homeruns. Saff, on his bed, eating a whole Papa John's pizza choked at this.

"Sorry man. That's harsh."

He was trying to stifle more laughter. I was too.

Kendall texted:

That dang fence was cheatin!

Dr. Panek was reading the sports section that Monday when Kendall and I walked into class together.

"Nice outing," he said drily.

"Band-Aid."

"Please," he said, taking his eyes off the paper.

I watched him register that Kendall and I had walked in together. He saw that we both looked to have just rolled out of bed, that she and I were eating apple bananas from the same cluster. His face was Sherlock Holmes-ian. I looked at him to find he was giving me a paternally stern frown, as in, *be good to her, you little fuck.*

17
HILO'S FIRST SERIES WIN SINCE THE FORMATION OF THE ISLANDS

It came against Kansas, the team who'd been coming over to the Islands and bullying us, for the past three years. But now, things were different. We had a solid core of seniors—eight total, mostly locals, some transplants like Saff and myself—who had spent years together losing dehumanizingly to everyone. And all that losing had calcified us into a bitter clan, and more importantly, we knew what we were up against, and with *nothing* to lose.

On the bus over to Kona, Kendall texted, *I miss you already.* She then made this claim official with the stamp of: ☹. It was her first time confessing, in words, or I guess words *and* emojis, feelings for me. Leading up to this, she'd seemed to guard this information, to hold onto the option of saying, "I'm not trying to make this thing more than it is." I had noticed how sometimes she seemed to be enjoying a conversation, and then sort of drew back. Or she'd be looking at me deeply, and then blink, and have a different expression altogether, as if some voice had told her: *this isn't what you think it is, you don't know this guy, you're from different worlds, and ultimately this will hurt.*

But with the unhappy face, she'd let go of that.

Her text sent a surge of vitality through me. Sitting on the bus as jungle and ocean passed, I romanticized this moment, pictured myself as a prisoner of war, receiving this letter and suddenly finding the strength to make it home.

I responded: *I feel the same.*

South:

Bring back a win!

Me:

Don't get ahead of yourself.

We lost our first game 4-3. Like our first game of the season, many of us were conflicted. Sure, we'd lost, but: we'd only lost by *one!*

"We got to stay competitive," Coach E said in the postgame huddle. "Good things happen if we stay focused."

We tuned out Coach's proverbs and instead listened as Kansas' coach laid into his team down the right field sideline. He screamed, as if by beating us by one, they'd lost.

After the game I iced my arm, feeling a sense of reserved bliss; I had pitched three innings without giving up a hit, and the job of a relief pitcher on a habitually losing team was just not to contribute to the loss. There was no better night's sleep than a pitcher's after a scoreless outing. The roommate's weed you smoke leads to no paranoia, only giggles and thoughts you find to be deeply philosophical. The pork rinds from 7-11 that accompany your philosophies taste gourmet. The Kona sunset is euphoric. You watch late-night "Popeye" and crack up. The world makes total sense. You wake up with drool on your pillow. The birds are chirping outside: they are your friends.

The next day, in our double header, we beat Kansas. Twice, to be exact, extra innings in the first game, then in dominating fashion in the second. As we pulled away with the lead in the second game, as their third baseman committed Hilo-ish errors, as their outfielders neglected to communicate and allowed balls to drop between them, as their pitchers walked us with the bases loaded, we looked at each other quizzically. Was Kansas University really getting behind 3-0 with bases loaded, then laying some unconfident cock-shots? Were we really punching clutch line-drives up the gut with guys in scoring position, among other things UH Hilo never did? And in the later innings, when we were up by eight, and we all assumed at any minute that Kansas would turn it on, hit double after double and put us in our place—they didn't. They hit routine popups and threw their bats in disgust. They hit easy two hoppers to us and got thrown out by ten feet. We had no idea how to act, like peasants at a royal feast unsure of what fork to grab. We were leading the series two games to one.

The following day, the seventh inning of a tie game:

"I'm good," I told Coach Clark. Late in this tie game, they needed strikes. And if there was one thing I could do, it was throw them. As bad as they sometimes were, they would be strikes. Coach Clark went over and told Coach E that I was ready. Then he walked back over.

"Then go get hot," he said.

When I took the mound in the eighth, there was no fear of failure. There was only the hunger I used to have in high school. Maybe it was being a senior, a veteran, having the freshmen hang onto my jokes and stories, bring me water, get out of chairs when I motioned them away with a wave. A whole year of that perhaps had inflated my ego. Maybe it was the fact that Kansas was on their heels, and I hated them from years of abuse. I smelled blood.

Maybe I was feeling more whole since I'd met Kendall.

Maybe I'd eaten the perfect breakfast.

Maybe it was all of these things.

That's baseball.

I got us through the eighth unharmed. Then in the bottom of the eighth, we took the lead from an error by Kansas's third baseman.

In the ninth, I mouthed "fuck you" to the first batter as he stepped up to the plate; he struck out—it was a called third on a floating curve that he tried to throw his elbow into. The next batter, a large lefty, lobster-red from the week of being white in

Kona, swung at a terrible slider; strike three. I mouthed at him, "fuck you" as he walked away. The next guy came up and should have just conceded. Our dugout was coming undone. The team was ripping the chain-link fence apart, the same chain-link which two years earlier had prevented me from hiding from my failed outing against this very team.

The guys were banging ball buckets with fungoes, hats on sideways. They were quite possibly frothing at the mouth, making noise that was ruthless, cannibalistic, wretched… borderline horny? We were one out from the series win. Crystal clear "fuck you's" were screamed directly into the batter's earhole. It was probably the least fun at-bat of this guy's career. Coach E was blushing and pacing outside the dugout.

The batter fell down a quick two strikes. He was so flustered that I threw an 0-2 fastball right down Broadway and he whiffed. His swing was so half-assed, he was possibly walking back to the dugout mid-swing. I'd struck out the side. I'd recorded the win. And the save. We dogpiled. Coach E shrieked, "act like you've *been* here before!" which made us fall apart with laughter. Seeing the writing on the wall, he decided not to travel with the team back to Hilo.

"Salud!" I cried on the back of the bus from Kona back to Hilo, beer in hand. The bus driver had heard the unmistakable *schlick* CRACK of cans being opened, but he also knew we'd won the series, and anyone on the Big Island knew it was a once-in-a-lifetime thing. He knew too that, had he attempted to put an end to our beer, we would have kicked him off into some lava rock field, and forced a freshman to drive the rest of the way while we partied our first series win.

I sat drowsily, a couple of cold cans icing my shoulder, a pinch of Skoal in my cheek. I found myself feeling nostalgic. For what, I wasn't sure. Baseball, friends, partying, things that made college what it was—this was the homestretch. Even the bad stuff—the lonely nights, the hangovers, I felt nostalgia for that too. It was all part of what had led me to this moment on the bus. Outside, the sky across the Pacific was the pigment of a bruise—a patch of yellow where the ocean ended and the sun had just died, and purple and blue insulating it.

That night, we got dropped off at the athletic department and convened in the locker room, where for a brief moment 70 testicles were sagging in a small space. By now we were all used to the smell of the locker room, the eye-tearing combo of Axe spray and sour socks.

Plans were made to celebrate.

"Meet in da apartments at dakine o' clock."

"Chee hoo!"

"Shoots!"

I felt love for my team, the kind of love when years of struggle yield a glimmer of success. It was a feeling so strong that, in the moment, it made all the losing seem worth it, as ridiculous as that sounds. We'd gone 6-49 my freshman year; that's a whole lot of fucking losing. Whatever this feeling was, it was bubbling over, and I wanted to share it, so I drove from the locker room directly to Kendall and picked her up. That night, I introduced her to the team. I had never brought a girl to a party, never had anyone serious enough to introduce. The freshmen and sophomores, as was their duty, went out of their way to be kind. They stood from their lawn chairs and took off their sunglasses to kiss her on the cheek, the proper Hawaiian greeting. The juniors and the seniors, who had seen me in my worst moments, my sloppy nights of plummeting knee-first onto pavement from the beds of pickup trucks, and punching undeserving strangers—they kissed Kendall's cheek a little gentler, in more of an embrace, as if conveying: *he needed this.*

By the next morning, none of us had slept. Kendall and I were both haggard from celebrating. My car's radiator blew up on the way home. We had to push the Colt to the side of the road and abandon it. From there, in blazing Sunday heat, shielding ourselves like vampires, we trekked to the only nearby eatery, an L&L. Our morning mouths already tasted like roadkill, and this was not going to improve things. With the combustion of my radiator, our morning had morphed into an extended moment of seeing each other at our ugliest, our grumpiest, our stinkiest, and poorest. It was the kind of experience that no couple should endure until they've been together for at least a year, and are hostel-hopping through foreign countries. We split an L&L combo meal, which made us feel more dead. Then we walked back to my car, with no plan. We chuckled at how few options I had with this corpse vehicle (I had no money for repairs, and my parents didn't even know I owned a car).

I stuck the keys in the ignition and said a prayer. Kendall was busting up in her seat. My engine gargled—in its own language—"I hate you," and came to life. I drove at seven miles an hour with steam shooting from the hood like a plummeting fighter jet, while Kendall and I shrieked with laughter into my driveway, holding hands.

A storm hit Hilo that February like nothing I'd ever seen. School was cancelled. A lake formed downtown. Pictures on the news showed cars being swallowed up to their rear-views. Shelters opened up for residents whose houses were sinking. I lived on a hill, and the rain rolled down, so I wasn't affected apart from the endless spattering of water that sounded at times like it would shatter our windows. This went on for a week. With my car out of commission, I borrowed Vitale's moped, poked my head through a garbage bag for a poncho, and picked Kendall up to stay with us through the storm.

She and I sat on the porch and watched the deluge. When it let up we walked to the top of the hill where there were ponds and waterfalls that we swam in on occasion. Because Hilo was taking upwards of 20 inches each day, the waterfall at Boiling Pots had become like a ceaseless tidal wave, or "God running a bath," in Kendall's words. We let ourselves be stunned. A UH Hilo cross-country runner had died up there the week before, diving off a rock into the bubbling abyss in an effort to prove something. I thought, that could've been me on any drunken night. I was glad to be up there, watching the power of nature, accepting my place in it. I was thankful for Kendall. We talked a little bit about death, and we felt deep.

Once, Kendall was asleep in my bed while I stayed up late working on a story. An earthquake struck, brief but fierce, and she rose in my bed, wide-eyed yet still in some state of sleep.

"Yikes!" she peeped. First I laughed, then realized she was serious. I rushed over and held her. Her heart was racing and she was absent, spooked. I welled with emotion to be with someone whose involuntary response to true panic was, "Yikes." Not "Is this house earthquake proof?" or "Get over here and protect me!"

Just, "Yikes!"

I was the happiest I'd ever been in college.

We slept in on the weekends, tickling ourselves awake and then doing homework in our underwear while taking fondle breaks. On Sundays, if she didn't have me drive her to early worship, we went onto the porch while tropical birds had their morning freakouts. I went into the yard and picked oranges and apple bananas and got violated by mosquitos while she called her parents and with a thick southern dialect detailed her week—how her classes went, how church was, the weather. Her language was alien compared to how she spoke to me. It almost sounded like a kindergarten teacher addressing her students, full of enthusiasm, simplicity, deliberate pronunciation.

"And I tell you Daddy it just *rained* and *rained* and it seemed it wud'n eva gawna stop!"

And:

"Mmhmm, yes sir, just like back home with the afternoon showers, but I tell you whut, I sure do miss me some thunder.

Yes, sir. And how's Me-Ma?"

I'd call up to her "Do I *know you?*" and in her panties, she'd kindly flip me the bird from the Kosovo couch.

Here's what she'd told me about her family: her older brother had played in the 2004 College World Series for the University of South Carolina. Her dad was a high school baseball coach. Her stepdad played in a competitive men's baseball league. In other words, baseball was in her DNA. The more we hung out, the more it became clear that she possibly knew more about the game than me.

Here's what Kendall told her family about me: there was a boy from English class in her reading group who played baseball. Details about sleepovers were omitted. The first thing her baseball family did when she mentioned me was check my roster bio on the UH Hilo website. They wanted to see who I was, where I was from, my stats, etc. They also wanted to see what I looked like. And the picture on our site had been taken when I'd grown out my punishment beard. So their first impression of me was that I looked like a pedophilic elementary school teacher turned runaway Alaskan fisherman.

Eventually, by April, when school was winding down, she mustered the will to announce she liked that "baseball boy from English class," but by then we were in deep.

"You still awake?" I asked.

I was short of breath.

"Yes," she said, a yes that showed she knew something was different, something was off.

"You still want to get together?"

"Yes."

There was a silence. I was clutching my phone so hard I thought it might break. I wanted to feel the satisfaction of cracking something hard in my hands.

"Is everything all right?" she asked.

"I'm headed over."

Unshowered, I went to her apartment from my game—basketball shorts, sandals, tank top. The first time I'd done that. When she appeared at her door, I attempted a smile, but it was mangled, I could tell. I sat on her couch, looked straight ahead at the turned-off TV screen.

"What's the matter?" she asked.

"I'm embarrassed," I said. Still, I was out of breath. The game had ended close to an hour ago. The last thing I'd wanted to do was to see Kendall after. I did not want to feel obligated to act happy around anyone. I did not want her to see me like this, because I knew how ridiculous it was.

It was just a game. And it was childish to let it carry over like this, and I didn't expect her to understand. It was unreasonable to ask anyone to understand.

"Did something happen in the game?" she asked. It was her first time dealing with this, and I could see her wheels spinning. Should she come smother me in whispery, tender support, or go to her room and let me handle whatever this was on my own, or treat me like a coach would and tell me to buck up and flush it? My fists were balled, veins in my forearms pumping richly, still wet from fury-sweat. I couldn't look her in the eye, and it was beginning to scare her. I hated that all this was the result of a baseball game.

"Something happened, yeah."

It was supposed to be an easy five wins. Patten University, out of Oakland, California. They weren't even D1, perhaps the most unlikely team ever to come over to play us. Their players were short, and bird-chested. They wore their hats sideways. We'd just come off successful series against Hawaii, Kansas, UAB—our record was floating right around 500. Aside from coughing up that peewee homer to Hawaii in the first series, my senior season was unfolding nicely. And after beating Patten in the first game of the series, I expected my appearance against them, whenever it came, to be a a great opportunity to pad my stats.

I got two quick outs when I entered the seventh inning of Game Two. Then, almost thoughtlessly, I sent in a get-me-over first pitch fastball to the third batter. The kid punched a chopper just out of the reach of our first baseman. It was such a pesky hit. Two outs, guy on first. Up stepped a lefty. A white guy, some tattoos, gaudy Jesus chain, an East Bay kid, no doubt. He appeared to be trying to cock his helmet sideways. He didn't strike me as the most poised hitter; he looked easily defeated by curves. I dug into the rubber, started the kid off with a curve. Strike one. He nodded at his bat, then nodded at me, mouthed something. This fucking clown. At what point did a bench player at Patten earn the right to mouth anything? (The irony being, I'd spent a whole career mouthing preposterous, unspeakable things.) I came set, lifted my leg, and the runner at first bluffed a steal. I picked over. *That* guy mouthed something at me. As if his bluffing and my picking skills were another competition taking place. I was thinking, *bro, you suck, you chopped a ground ball. Nobody cares.* Next pitch, curve ball, strike two. Baserunner stole second.

Maybe there was a lot suddenly aggravating me about these guys, their unwarranted swagger. Maybe I felt they were personally challenging me and I needed to be the one to remind them who they were. Maybe I thought I was bigger than I was, as a pitcher, as a person—enough to let my guard down.

Catcher called curve ball in the dirt. That was the smart call: this player was amped and obviously illiterate when it came to off-speed. I shook it off; I wanted to embarrass this kid. I wanted to go the man route and blow him away. Fastball inside, that's what I wanted. Had I been a freshman, I'd never have thought to shake, but being a senior was different. I shook until I got my pitch. The batter called time, and stared at me the whole time, and I held his stare, unblinking. Suddenly—

and manifested from nothing—this had become a high stakes showdown.

I came set, and put everything I had into the fastball. I watched it tail up and in, likely to drill the kid in his wrists. I didn't care. I hoped it hurt.

But then he swung. As hard as he could, and he was on time, pulled his hands through the zone and got extended nicely.

The ball sailed into the night in a hurry, toward the palm trees lining right center. Home run. Unsurprisingly, this kid milked every moment, walked a third of the way up the line, then finally started jogging slowly, his chain bouncing off his chest. He clapped his hands like he'd just sent his team to regionals. I watched our first baseman, a 6' 4" Hawaiian who was in an eternal state of hoping a white person would piss him off, point at the kid and tell him to start moving.

The kid started moving.

Coach came out and pulled me.

I walked back to the dugout with the burden of two things. One, I'd lost a showdown to some rodent who'd probably just hit his first homer. And two, someone else acted on my behalf, like I needed our big strong tough guys to handle my beefs while I sniveled on the mound.

And here I was, sitting in Kendall's apartment, gnawing holes in my Underarmour, an hour later. I told her what happened. The abbreviated version.

"I gave up a two run ding to a bad team."

"Why don't you take off that shirt," she said.

I took it out of my mouth, like a guilty dog told to "drop it."

She didn't act perturbed by my melodrama. She also didn't come over and get all gentle, which, she must've sensed, would've made things worse. She seemed to understand that this was like any other Hilo storm that needed to run its course. Suddenly, my legs cramped on me, both of them at once. It was a mix of anger, and lifting heavy legs earlier that day in the weight room, and not drinking any water in the Hilo air. So I screamed and alternated one straight leg on her sofa at a time, stretching just long enough before having to switch to the other. I was doing a slower, less jolly, Russian dance.

"Can I stretch you out?" she asked. Her tone didn't assume any authority on the matter, didn't baby, just merely threw something out there. In that moment, it seemed like the only thing I'd be able to tolerate, psychologically, and physically. I went to her room and lay on my back, and she stretched me, and I mean really stretched me. Straightened one leg on the bed by straddling it, straightened my other into the air and pushed, leaning forward slowly. At my knee joint, I felt the initial tingle of blood rush. Then, this sensation spread, into the meat of my hamstring, and my calf. The tingles boiled. My leg trembled, then outright quaked the further she pushed. She stretched longer than I'd ever had the patience to do myself, more intimate than I'd ever felt like getting with Dick, our enormous trainer. I felt the bundles of muscle fibers, like knotted spaghetti, untying and letting go, filling with deeply rich oxygen. I could not remember such an intense feeling. It bordered on orgasm, or clawing a terrible itch. I'd thank her on occasion, and she'd *shhsh* me. I showered afterward, came out and from the tips of my toes all the way through my legs I was blissful jelly. I held Kendall that night. I'd never met anyone before, not even another baseball player, who got it, whatever "it" was, how she did.

18
ENTERING THE
RECORD BOOKS

The air was dry and cloudless and smelled like hot dogs. The song on the speakers of the Sacramento State baseball diamond was "Flashing Lights" by Kanye West. I had some butterflies, some relief knowing that after this outing, I'd hold a record for UH Hilo. My arm, simply, felt like crap. I watched our catcher raise his hands, signifying to the middle infield that he was about to throw down. Before I took my last warm-up, I saw a flurry of kids arrive and fill up the stands, all in UH Hilo caps; my little cousins, ten of them. My aunts and uncles followed, then my parents, then my grandpa. Two friends from high school anchored the group. They wore UH Hilo baseball shirts which I'd bestowed upon them and which they'd cut into college day-drinking tank tops. I watched in the periphery as my aunts and uncles drew their kids' attention to me, pointing, saying "Look! Emil's in the game! He's setting his school record!" They were too intrigued by hot dogs to take notice. Which was probably for the better.

In my appearance, I hit a guy. Then I walked a guy. I only recorded one out before Coach Clark was emerging from the dugout. It was the most inglorious making of history possible. I laughed as I was taken from the game, handed the ball over to Coach Clark, who also laughed. My parents had seen me pitch twice in college, and both times I'd desecrated the game of baseball. As I neared the dugout, I wanted to give a dramatic bow to my family, who'd driven from all over California to see this, as if to say, "Yes...*this* is my life's work."

I stayed in San Francisco with my parents while the rest of the team were booked in a hotel in Sacramento. Charlie was now a junior at Cal. He was their captain, and starting catcher. He took BART up to stay with his parents for the weekend, and we met in a dingy bar in the Haight to play pool and drink Pabst. It felt surreal to be seeing him during baseball season; this hadn't happened since high school.

"I wish I could've been there to see it," Charlie said about my un-historical pitching performance. He had a way of being funny by not laughing. His statements were often purely observational, with an implication of humor that he either deliberately ignored, or was oblivious to.

"Glad you didn't," I said.

"You want to talk embarrassing? Two years ago, Long Beach State Regionals?"

"When you dropped the fly ball?"

"That lost the game, and eliminated us from postseason, yes."

When Charlie was a freshman, Cal had had a senior catcher. But, they wanted Charlie's bat, so they plugged him in left field, a position he had never played.

"What I did was far worse than drop a fly. Some kid from Irvine hit a missile basically right at me but a little over my head, with top spin. So I kind of jumped to catch it and it hit the palm of my glove, which literally trampolined it to the wall. Like, the ricochet off my glove added another seventy feet to the hit, and I think it ended up one-hopping the left field fence."

Charlie in left field, swatting a ball further away from him instead of catching it—that image was priceless.

"It was a national embarrassment."

He spoke with gloating self-deprecation. He had the tone of someone who'd recovered just fine. He still had a curly mop of hair and a tangle of forearm foliage. To me, he looked like an Arabian jewel peddler, though I was not sure I'd ever seen one. He was stronger, with more meat on the wrist, more width to the back, more neck, than when we'd played in high school. He looked like a ballplayer, like all the other D1 guys I'd faced over the years. His average was over .310. The Cardinals, the Rockies, the Blue Jays, and the Braves were talking to him. He was going to get drafted at the end of the year, it was just a matter of by whom, and in his voice I could tell he knew this.

I felt jealous, which made me feel ashamed. He was my best friend, and I was 22 years old. I didn't resent him, as in, I didn't want to be there instead of him. I just wanted to be there. I thought about sitting on the bus after the Kansas win, icing my shoulder just a little over a month before. That was a deeply *good* feeling. Charlie was going to get to keep having that feeling, and there, I wondered, *why shouldn't I?*

The reality was, my arm was getting to be toast. I thought of my shoulder like old brake pads, squeaking at the stop sign. There was no cushion left, just metal on metal, bone on bone. But, technically, my arm still *worked*, and as long as I could lift it, and throw an 80 mph fastball with movement, a good changeup and a 50 mph curve ball—essentially a mythical *ephus*—I figured I could play. *Every team needs someone like that, I thought. Even just for one batter, once in a while.*

"How's the arm?" Charlie asked at the bar.

"It's hanging in."

"That's so tight you broke a school record."

He didn't ask about pro ball, if I was going to try out for a ball club, what my plans were beyond college ball, if any. He assumed my road was near its end: I hadn't mentioned scouts. I hadn't mentioned prospective teams. And it wasn't as though being a relief pitcher for Hilo would lead to pro ball anyway. As we played pool, I had a miserable vision of myself one year later, living at home, working a boring job as a copywriter, or having no job, checking Charlie's stats online, reading minor league articles, wondering what could have been.

* * *

Senior day was against Hawaii Pacific. My last day as a ballplayer. We had six senior pitchers. Each went an inning, then as they came out, the announcer gave their career stats, and the crowd cheered. Many of us laughed, because our careers were so bad. Saff pitched just before me, so we warmed up together in the bullpen, which consisted of one warped bench. It had been the same splintering driftwood for four years.

"I'm not going to miss this piece of shit," Saff said, nearly breaking it as he sat down to drink water.

"I think I am."

When Saff's inning ended, Coach Clark picked him up from the mound in the golf cart. It was ultimate bush-league. Coach E shrieked and paced from the dugout "In my thirty years of coaching, never! This is an embarrassment to the program!"

And our unanimous thoughts were: *Coach, how could our program get more embarrassing?* But deep down, we all loved Coach, and at the very least appreciated him. We seldom said it, but each and every one of us owed it to him that we ever set foot on a D1 diamond. No one—and I mean no one—on our team had been juggling scholarship offers before choosing Hilo. Hilo was all we had.

In my last outing, I pitched one hitless inning. Kendall snapped hundreds of pictures in the stands, likely to send to her parents to prove that I was *not* the man they'd seen in the roster photo. As my inning ended, I got emotional; it was going too quick. The first kid swung at the first pitch, infield pop out. Next kid showed bunt, took a strike. Took another strike, grounded out to the second baseman. Next kid hit it hard but right at the shortstop. Three outs. That's all, folks.

I thought about my first memories, playing whiffle ball with Dad. I thought about going to A's games to see Mark McGwire and José Canseco. I thought about meeting Charlie and becoming best friends from the simple repeated action of pitching and catching. I thought about high school ball, college ball, and how people's hobbies turn into passions, which then become the focal points in their lives. The path here had been as glorious as it had been mundane, as life-changing as it had been routine, as rewarding as it had been defeat-filled. Three small steps, and I would descend the perch of the mound, enter the clubhouse, take off my cleats, and cease to be a ballplayer.

I was distracted from these melodramatic thoughts when I heard a small engine that sounded like a lawnmower.

In foul territory the golf cart was staring me down, grumbling in idle. It felt like a standoff. In the cart sat Saff and Coach Clark, grinning. Saff had a beer in his hand. His grin was the same one he'd had one of the first nights I moved into the Baseball House, when he snuck stool softeners onto my DiGiorno pizza. I had flashes of our four years at Hilo, falling asleep on beaches, coming up with nicknames for opponents, standing beside one another during our several drunk confrontations, laughing at our bloopers on our porch.

Coach Clark pressed the gas. Coach Estrella attempted to lunge in front like a secret serviceman to prevent this. He was nearly run over. The cart reached me. The crowd applauded. I was carted off and away from the mound at UH Hilo. I waved like a president embarking on Air Force One for the last time.

PART III:
THE REAL WORLD

19
THREE B'S: BELGIUM, BASEBALL, BEER

Throughout my career, I'd tracked who had gotten drafted from the teams we'd played; most teams had a handful. Some went on to excel, become aces of staffs, win Gold Gloves, become All Stars, and win World Series games. Alex Gordon and Joba Chamberlain of Nebraska, Allen Craig, Brandon Morrow, Josh Satin, and Brennan Boesch of Cal, Mike Pelfrey and Conor Gillaspie from Wichita State, Darwin Barney of Oregon State, and plenty more had made it to the Bigs shortly after I played against them. To watch them on TV in the summers gave me a rush, made me feel like I was back on the mound at Wong Stadium.

"I played against them," I'd say to whomever I was watching the game with.

"Was he really good?" was a typical follow up.

"Yes."

"You keep him in the yard?" they'd ask.

"Nope," I'd usually be forced to say.

But what about all of the other guys we played? Guys like Keoni Ruth and Shane Buschini and Jordan Abruzzo from San Diego, and dozens more. They all got drafted too, and I was sure I'd see them on TV someday. But when I researched them, most never made it out of single A. They played a couple of years in the minors, then for whatever reason, disappeared. Some of them even had good careers. Then…poof.

As much as I liked watching the guys that made it, I couldn't help but wonder what happened to those that didn't. Injuries were a safe bet. Maybe a pregnancy; maybe religion. I knew a kid who'd played at Utah and had a lot of pro buzz, but hung 'em up after college to go on a Christian mission. Maybe some of these kids secretly loathed baseball and resented the fact that they were superstars, and the grind of the minor leagues was where they drew the line.

Maybe they got some rare disease when they were least expecting it.

Anyway, as senior year wound down, and I had no more practices or games to take up my late afternoon, I found myself sappy for baseball, anxious about the future. I'd never thought about actually having a job, or normal life. So privately, during the time I was supposed to be writing senior papers and theses, as my days before graduation dwindled, I started researching international pro ball as a pipedream. All through the night, as coqui frogs chirped through my screen door, I surfed websites all around the world, Iceland to Singapore, in search of baseball. Coach Clark had recorded one of my bullpens toward the end of the season, and I uploaded it to YouTube, hoping it might be intercepted by some coach out in the great beyond.

First, I reached out to Italy, but their teams only allowed one American, and that American either had to be really good or really Italian; I was neither. I looked next to Belgium, Germany, Sweden, the Netherlands, who all had leagues with openings for Americans. I joined a forum for players looking to play overseas, and provided a link to my bullpen. Some teams from the Netherlands and Belgium responded with interest. Their English was off in a way that was hard to pinpoint. I kept my replies brief and simple, molding my speech around the kind of English they sent to me. Our correspondence looked somewhat as follows:

> *Dear Dirk Hoffbrauer,*
> *I am Emil DeAndreis, of America! I play baseball for Division*

One University of Hawaii. For you, I am interested to play professional. Please watch my baseball video below, and tell me you want me.

http://www.youtube.com/watch?v=Tg3hV77JKtk

Thank you, and when you call, I will be ready,

Emil DeAndreis.

Coaches from Denmark, Holland, and Belgium all had equally cryptic replies:

Dear Emille,

Thank you for the greeting. We are loving the option of your fitness. Your cinema is pleasing. Please be humane and tell us your height and density of grams when possible.

Your answer is coming,

Christof Dietger

Head Coach.

My pursuit of pro ball brought me back four years, when I was a senior at Lowell High, desperate for D1 ball, writing eloquent messages about my average baseball abilities to college coaches.

I assumed pro ball in Europe wasn't anything like American pros, nothing like what Charlie would go on to do: midnight bus rides playing cards and sipping whiskey through unknown American cities, country music and 4th of July fireworks, pretty Southern and Midwestern girls in shorts filling up the seats for the 85-degree first pitch. There was something simple about that, if a bit lonely, but also there was an American romance to that life that had been tugging at the hearts of American boys for over 100 years. Because for every one of those pros on that simple, lonely path, there was a chance it'd end in some 50,000-fan cathedral.

Belgium, decidedly, was not that.

But I figured, shit: if they're paying me, it's professional. I didn't care if it was Egyptian baseball and I rode to games on a camel.

When a coach from Belgium replied a month later, I had my doubts. All correspondence thus far had fallen through. Some clubs had been interested, but their season started before I graduated, and they needed me to ship out literally that day to be eligible. I assumed this team was no different. The coach's first question was: are you still available; I said yes. "Yes" was also my answer to his question, "have you played baseball in the last five years?" That question kind of raised my eyebrows. What kind of pro ball was this? Did they actually have players who *hadn't?* Did they have guys who'd seen their glove collecting cobwebs in the garage and decided, *you know what? Fuck it. It's been five years since I played baseball. I think I'll go pro now.*

In the follow-up emails, the coach explained their American pitcher had spontaneously retired, or disappeared—it was unclear—and that they'd watched my bullpen on YouTube. The better news was, for whatever reason, they didn't need me until August, 2009, over one year from then. So if all went as planned, I could graduate, sign the contract, move home, stay in shape, then head out for my professional baseball career.

This development still struck me as gloriously far-fetched, until I started receiving phone calls at 4 A.M. from numbers like "000-456-29056-45-000-12693…" accompanied by voicemails saying "Hello, this is *Ay-meele?* I call about baseball team to play the Merchtem Cats in Belgium. This is your number? I call back again soon."

I looked further into their team, and discovered they played such fearsome teams as the Zottegem Bebops, and the Borgerhout Squirrels. In our first phone discussion, I was told about the contract, how I would stay with a host family, be given a car, some meals, and a monthly stipend. Off the phone I converted my salary from euros. $1,200 a month, an underwhelming sum, but that was fine. This wasn't about making millions (or even thousands, apparently). Baseball dreams stopped being about that in sixth grade when I realized my dad was 5'6" and my mom was 5'3," and that having them as parents was only exciting if I was an aspiring horse jockey.

This pursuit was about those moments on the bus after Kansas. The feeling of freezing someone with an inside fastball, inducing an inning-ending double play, or getting them to chase that low and away changeup. The rush and then delicious fatigue of victory. The feeling that I was worthwhile.

In one of the conversations leading to my contract, the coach said:

"Oh, Emille, ehh, I hope this is naht so much a prowblem, but, after we practice, ehh, many of the playairs, like to have a glass of lager, or more."

And so my thoughts were, onward and upward! I was set to ship out in August, 2009.

20
HERE COMES THAT PAIN AGAIN

"Vietnamese sandwiches are good!" Kendall said. On her first trip to visit me in San Francisco, she was introduced to my friends, and Sriracha, both of which were overwhelming in large doses, but necessary to have around at all times.

"I wanna go check out all the spots from when you were a kid."

So we did. We went to Big Rec in Golden Gate Park which was our home field in high school. We went to the beach where I ran to stay in shape. We went to Polly Anne's, the ice cream spot by my middle school. She got cookie dough and I got pralines and cream.

"That's a senior citizen flavor," she said.

We played catch. She made me teach her my changeup, which didn't quite work in her little hand. On the very street where my dad and I used to play catch, I caught her "bullpen."

"My dad used to make me throw ten strikes before we went in, usually for ice cream."

"We're not going in until I throw ten strikes then," she said, and hocked a dramatic loogie.

Kendall and I had been doing the long distance thing and hadn't seen each other for a few months. The last time I'd seen her was when I left her sobbing in the security line at the Hilo Airport. For three months we'd skyped each other. The conversations were static-y, her movements choppy and blurred. She'd say "I'm going to get some water," and the next frame, there'd be an empty chair. I got to know what her South Carolina room looked like behind her computer, the backboard of her bed, the purple poster of Widespread Panic. I missed her smell. Her southern accent, hollowed by the computer speakers, felt so far away, when in person it was like a warm bath. At night before I slept, I called her. No matter how late it was for her, she answered and chirped in indecipherable puppy languages. I'd tell her I loved her and she would murmur something along those lines, and in the morning she would accuse me of having forgotten to call and I'd have to recount our sleepy rendezvous from the night before. I wrote her poems that she cherished and folded into her wallet and read at night when she was lonely, which I refused to hear her recite due to the cringing embarrassment of *I wrote that?*

I wasn't sure how we would handle Belgium. She said she would visit, and that if I even considered not pursuing pro ball, she would leave me. I was overwhelmed by her selflessness, how she made things easier for me by essentially not giving me a choice; I *had* to go. She *actually* lived as Jesus told people to live, which, in my experience, never happened. She understood what baseball was for me, and could never live with herself for being the reason I didn't go. You couldn't ask for a better girl than her, and that created a paradox: the best girl in the world wanted me to follow my dreams, which might have led to the loss of the best girl in the world. I could really kick myself for losing Kendall. That thought gave me that despairing feeling in the sternum that usually precedes a good cry. I felt any girl I ever met after her would, at *best*, be second best. But losing baseball, at that time: I would never forgive myself. Well into my old age, I would think about it. It would make me absentminded. I'd become a broken record. I'd be delusional.

One night when Kendall was in town, my grandpa Carlos called.

"*Aye,* Emiliano. Whatchoo say, man?"

"Grandpa, how we living?"

"Alright, alright. Say, watch'oo got going on next week?"

He ran a business in HVAC, which dealt with ventilation. He had Jerry Garcia hair and squinty eyes from decades of working on roofs in the sun, and always being stoned. His language was the near-extinct dialect of beatniks. Rarely was he not sporting a full denim suit and straw hat. When I was in high school, he'd come to games; he was a high school pitcher himself, and had a roster spot at a college in Los Angeles but had to hang 'em up because he had kids.

As an HVAC technician, his job was to go around the Bay Area where new buildings were being built, or old, crumbling buildings were being renovated, and ensure the ventilation systems were pushing out and sucking in the right amounts of air and at the right temperatures. Since coming home from college, I'd been working as Grandpa's assistant. It was only to be a summer job until I left for Belgium.

Mostly, I chauffeured him around because he hated traffic and preferred sitting in the passenger seat smoking a joint, listening to Charlie Parker. He also had me carry tools and hand them to him while he was on the ladder, adjusting fans. Many of our days ended earlier than planned, not because we were efficient or skilled, but because we'd driven to the wrong jobsite, or my grandpa had brought the wrong tools.

"Fuck a duck," he would say whenever something went wrong, which was always.

Once he was on a scissor ladder, raised 30 feet in the air. He had just reached the top of a dome ceiling when he realized he'd forgotten the screwdriver. *Fuck a duck.* Another time we drove all the way to Manteca, a two-hour jaunt, only to learn he wasn't supposed to come until next week. *Fuck a duck.* Grandpa then figured, since we'd driven all that way, he might as well go to the nearest Lowes to buy a screwdriver and take a dump. Then we drove home, and golfed.

We worked at private mansions, convalescent homes, schools, department stores, city buildings. Sometimes we crawled through ducts, sometimes we got on our knees underneath houses. For the most part, I thought the job was brutal. *Especially* as a career. I had to wake up hours earlier than I'd ever woken up before, and drive in gridlock traffic. Workers at the jobsite had tattoos of their kids but constantly bitched about them. They smoked cigarettes in a manner that made them look pensive, yet ready to strangle someone at the drop of a hat.

Sure, I too was offended to be awake, but *their* bitterness came from the fact that this was inescapably their lives. I, on the other hand, was not trapped. In no time I would be in Belgium, paving my way to hometown hero-dom, getting paid to travel the world and play baseball. Working the job with Grandpa, I had the feeling of a white collar man serving an unfairly short prison sentence, knowing soon I'd be in fresh air while the grunts remained caged.

"Kendall is visiting right now, Grandpa. So we've been pretty much playing it by ear."

"I dig, I dig. See, I got this gig next week," he said. "Out of town."

He was puffing a joint—I could hear in his pauses. I could talk all day to him about anything.

"Where?"

"Back down in *Manteca*. It's the time I'm *actually* supposed to be there this time, ya dig? Three-day gig, type 'a thing, they're building an old person home, was checking if you wanted to make the trip down. Five hundred bucks, three days. You can bring the missus, man, how's that sound? Get out of town a while, kick back in a hotel. Shit you know what, if she *wants*, she can work."

"Let me call you back tomorrow."

Manteca was a flat, hot suburb with some poverty, some

drug problems, and a water park. My gut answer was no, being that I didn't think Kendall wanted to "kick back" in Manteca, let alone to do manual labor.

"Uh. It's just mostly handing Grandpa wrenches and him getting stoned," I explained.

"Sure!" she said. "I love hotels!"

During those few days we wore our hard hats periodically, did some undemanding labor involving reading back numbers and retrieving tools, smoked weed in our hotel room while Grandpa smoked in his, then cross paths with him in the nearby taqueria, all of us giggling in sunglasses. This was also the time when Grandpa got 30 feet in the air without a screwdriver and echoed across the dome ceiling:

Fuck a duck!

"Poor bastard," a plumber muttered.

And I looked at the plumber and felt: *Poor bastard.* Sunburnt, varicose veins, crumbs on his cheek, cigarette voice, worn look on his face. It put into perspective the career I was about to have.

I did pushups and sit-ups in the hotel to stay in shape. Four sets of 50 pushups, four sets of a 100 sit-ups, kissing Kendall on the hotel bed in between sets, feeling incredibly lucky to have her in my life. She was really down for anything, which apparently included going to a hot and dingy city to wear a hard hat. And if she could see the bright side of Manteca, I thought she and I just might make it through my pro ball stint. She'd visit, we'd travel. When alone, I'd write short stories, and letters, and poems to her on a bar stool in a pub.

It was during these pushups in the hotel with Kendall that I began to feel a slight twinge in my elbow. It wasn't pain, just a twinge. The kind of thing that almost felt like it wasn't there, like it was hidden. I thought maybe I was even imagining it. I had experienced this kind of thing often in college. The feeling would burn away with a little adrenaline and sweat in the bullpen. I would pitch through it, go on a run, ice the elbow and shoulder, and wake up the next morning feeling fresh. It was the kind of symptom for which doctors gave a vague diagnosis of rest. I knew whatever this was, it wasn't worth a visit to my doctor. These were just tweaks. The kinds of things where, even if you went to the doctor, they would have some vague prescription of rest, then say they're almost positive it's nothing to worry about. The human body is a mystery, they'd say, but also a constantly healing organism. I'd heard this forever.

Charlie had just been drafted by the Cardinals in the fourteenth round. He was already in Batavia, New York, playing rookie ball. We talked once a week or so.

"Dude, there's nothing like the fans. I thought Cal was nice. These people? You gotta remember, this is Batavia, New York. They have *nothing* out here. So they're all about their 'Muckdogs.' I would say the majority of the clientele is old people and special ed., but dude, they get fired up."

"I love it."

"Even the bus rides, the downtime. I don't mind. It's *Bull Durham*, an adventure. There're some Dominicans who wear literally bellbottoms. They blast *reggaeton* in the clubhouse and hump couches as they sing along. We've got a couple hicks who buck-hunt on off-days then go to church, some preppy boys with earrings who think they're ghetto until they're around actual ghetto people. Then they just stand off to the side and text their girlfriends. Some dudes have two different phones, for their two baby mamas—to eliminate the paper trail, I guess. Their thighs are forever buzzing. There's this big black guy from Tennessee, like 6'6", 270, who doesn't go to sleep without his stuffed bear. The bus rides get raucous. Dudes gamble whole paychecks over a poker hand. I'll tell you what, that's a long bus ride when you lose that hand. We've got a guy on our team who doesn't know the alphabet. There's lots of work for a sociologist on a minor league team, I'll tell you that."

Charlie sounded wide-eyed, giddy. He only got this way about certain things, like fishing, and playing cribbage with his grandma.

As the conversation moved along to my exciting developments. I took the phone off my left ear and straightened my elbow. It was inflamed. It felt tight, constricted.

"I just found out I'm going pro too."

"What?"

"Yep."

"You sneaky bastard. Indy ball?"

"Nope. Belgium. Contract is in the mail right now."

"This is insane. That exists?"

"They've got pro ball. I researched it, put a bullpen up on YouTube. A team took the bait. The Merchtem Cats."

"The *who?* This is *crazy!*"

"I'd been looking into it for a while. Ever since that night we talked in the bar in Haight. Didn't tell anyone because there was nothing to tell, not unless I got the contract."

"Our journeys continue," he said.

"Talk in a few days," I said.

"Hey, man. Seriously. You and me are some of the luckiest guys in this world."

I played catch that afternoon with Kendall. It was one of her last days before going back home. I pretended I didn't feel anything in my elbow. We promised to see each other at least once before I left. Promised this wasn't goodbye. She cried anyway.

When she left, I kept up with pushups, ignoring the needle-like prick in my joint. After a week, my elbow felt like someone was holding a small flame to it. The feeling started to spread around my elbow, not just the inside of my forearm, but now the little tendons around my tricep. It became a challenge to pinpoint the exact location of the burning, and the feeling began to show up even when I wasn't doing pushups or throwing. I would just be sitting around, watching TV, and realize my elbow was burning, and had been burning for some time.

By June—a month and a half since my last pitch—flexibility was affected. I couldn't straighten my arm. My elbow was bruise-tender, and stiff, especially in the mornings. Whatever was happening was burrowing deeper into my joints. It was active; it had a pulse. Instead of 200 pushups a day, I was down to 50. Instead of lengthening the distance of my long toss, increasing the number of pitches in my bullpens, I was shortening everything. There were stretches of days when I was so inactive that I forgot I was a professional pitcher, that I had a job to do in the coming months.

Fuck a duck, I thought.

21
CORTISONE

"I remember you," said Dr. Young. It was my first visit to the sports medicine department since high school, and my sumo-pinkie. "Baseball, right?"

"Yeah, pitcher."

"That's right. What was up with you again? Something weird, right?"

I wiggled the pinkie.

"Oh, man," he said. "That was classic. I told my friends."

Dr. Young hadn't aged much, still had the surfer look, but with a few new grays. His face suggested he knew just the cure. He didn't ask any further questions about my elbow, or the swelling. He applied his gloves, got out the gauze, picked up some syringes and formulas casually, the way a cook might pick up ingredients for a dish he's cooked many times.

"Belgium, huh?" he asked. "Nice, bro."

Dr. Young lacquered my elbow in alcohol and my bowels activated. After numbing me, he inserted the needle, and slowly dug around. I felt the miraculous nothingness of having a needle in numbed flesh. Then I felt the needle hit resistance: bone. Dr. Young sloshed through more of the blubbery swelling. As he did this, he looked up as if thinking of a word for something. Then I felt the needle pause. Then jerk, locking itself somewhere in my elbow. Then I watched his thumb push the syringe down. Modern medicine. I was nauseous.

"Voilà," he said.

I couldn't be out of there quick enough—the hospital, where mortality was so close and everything so white and sanitary and pungent. I just needed it for a shot, then I'd be out of there, immortal again. In a few days, my elbow would be shrunken back to size, just as my pinkie had years ago. I'd throw, at first tentatively, and then I'd gradually start humping it up to 80 when I was painless. Probably, these couple weeks off from throwing had done my arm good, allowing all the other ligaments and over-worn tendons to recuperate some.

Except, within days of the appointment, my elbow enlarged. I tried throwing, stopped after two throws. I tried pushups, went down, but couldn't get back up. I pushed, felt ringing pain in the elbow, and fell face down into carpet. I even began to notice swelling in the knuckles of my throwing hand.

I was back in Dr. Young's office two weeks after the shot. This time, he lacked Bro-Enthusiasm. He was more of Somber Bro now, like Spiccoli in *Fast Times at Ridgemont High* when his pizza gets handed out to the history class.

"Looks like I need a thicker dose of cortisone," I said. But Dr. Young wasn't ready to agree.

"Here's the thing," he said.

This sucked. Right off the bat, I didn't like his tone.

"This is no good, what I'm hearing."

I thought about my future in Belgium, pitching in a town with old architecture, going to jazz clubs in a beret and trying beers, getting to tell my kids that baseball took me around the world.

"It's one thing if the cortisone doesn't work. That happens sometimes, and that's cool. You just come back in for another dose. But when it doesn't work, and the swelling just keeps getting worse, and starts showing up in other places?"

I felt like he was straining for the best way to tell me to kiss it all goodbye.

"I just want you to consider something. I'm going to put you in touch with a doctor. In a different department. I'm sure it's nothing, but you always want to be sure. Gotta rule it out. She's in rheumatology."

"Rheumatology?"

"Are you familiar with it? Rheumatoid Arthritis?"

I laughed, because: what a funny question. Why would I be familiar with any arthritis? I was an athlete, in his physical prime. All I knew was that my friend's mom had it. Growing up, when she drove us to our baseball games, she parked in the handicapped zone. We would go to the field, and she'd appear minutes later, having walked with dreary slowness. Her kids and husband carried things for her—groceries, lawn chairs. She was always gripping a handrail. She was quiet, and always had this look like she was waiting for a bus in a blizzard. And, as kids we just copped this expression up to her being old. (To kids, 34 meant gray-haired and ancient. And even when we were told she had a disease, that sounded old to us as well).

I was also familiar with Rheumatoid Arthritis through the medicine commercials, which were starting to appear more and more during baseball games. It seemed like they all began with a variation of a woman in great pain.

Ssssss ow! she'd grimace, having just picked up a newspaper. Everything would suddenly go black and white.

Then a voice would say:

"Don't let moderate to severe Rheumatoid Arthritis control your life. With **BRAND NAME** *you can have your life back. Get back to the things that* **really** *matter. Ask your rheumatologist about getting started…***today.***"*

At this point in the commercial, color would return. Flowers would be in full bloom. The previously afflicted woman would appear intoxicated with joy and hope. The commercial then would pan to her being getting back to do the things that "*really* matter," things like: tying her shoe lace, digging in her pockets for loose change, picking berries.

I used to watch these commercials and think: *picking berries? What good are those meds if that's all she can do? It would be one thing if, at the end of the commercial, Granny was doing flawless cartwheels and shooting bullseyes with her heavy archery set. But picking berries?*

"My friend's mom has it," I told Dr. Young. "My familiarity

is that moms, and moms of moms get it."

"That's usually true."

"Not men. Or young men."

"Like I said, it should be nothing. Let's just rule it out."

That appointment would turn out to be a joke, I assured myself. I would go, a doctor would run some tests, maybe take a few x-rays. A few days later, or maybe even that very same day, I'd receive a call. The doctor on the other line would tell me it was all a big mistake. She'd go back to treating her diseased patients and I'd go back to my pro career. I didn't have a disease.

22
NEW, OLD DOCTORS

I shook her hand and thought it might snap like a wishbone. She was trembling—thin with weak hair in a bowl cut, à la Prince Valiant. I thought maybe she had her own disease. Maybe *she* had Rheumatoid Arthritis herself? Who better an expert?

"Hiiii," she said, her voice trailing at the end, seeming to already lay on the pity. "I'm Dr. Sherry."

"Hi."

"As Dr. Young informed you I'm sure, I'm a rheumatologist. He said you had some swelling that might need to be looked at."

She spoke slowly, as if to an English language learner. And why not? To all of this, I was a complete foreigner.

"This inflammation you're experiencing, Emil. Is it symmetrical? That is, in your left, and right elbow?"

"Nope." I said it like a sober kid at a DUI checkpoint.

"And do you know if Rheumatoid Arthritis, or anything like that, runs in the family?"

"Nope," I said.

But I couldn't help but think of my mom, her undiagnosed pain, her ended clarinet career, the stacks of books I'd always seen as a kid with titles about Fibromyalgia and Chronic Pain and reconciling the mystery of it all. Rheumatoid Arthritis, more or less, sounded to be in this same family of cryptic agony. But I didn't tell my doctor any of that.

Dr. Sherry took my swollen hand in hers, traced around the widened knuckles, gently squeezed, asking if it hurt. She asked me to make a fist and squeeze. She clasped my mushy elbow, asked me to touch my shoulders, which I couldn't do.

"Well," said Dr. Sherry. "I'm not going to tell you that you have Rheumatoid Arthritis today, okay?"

"Okay."

"But I'm also not going to tell you you *don't* have it, okaaaaaaaaaaaaaaaay?"

"Thanks."

"So I'm going to have my secretary schedule a follow-up appointment for about a month from now."

"Alright."

"M'kay?"

Her okay's really dripped with pity, as if the word itself bundled a *sorry*, and a *thank you* into one.

Dr. Sherry went to her office to print some things out about Rheumatoid Arthritis and possible medications. Stuff to consider, which she called "literature."

"I'm going to give you a bunch of literature to look over."

She asked me to get some blood work done before our follow up, to see if I possessed things in my blood common in Rheumatoid Arthritis patients.

"Oh, and Dr. Young mentioned something of a baseball career?"

"Yeah. I ship out to Belgium in a few months."

"Isn't that super?" she said. "That really is special."

"Thanks. Just need this elbow back in shape."

"Mhmmm."

She produced a look like she was eating an exotic dish, trying to pinpoint the ingredient in it she didn't like.

"I think I would have to advise against leaving the country. With these changes in your body? It just doesn't seem like the best course of action to leave for a long period. If this is what I think it might be, I would want to get you on meds right away, and we can't be sure of anything if you're in another country. M'kay? Maybe we can just put this trip on hold?"

23
RHEUMATOID ARTHRITIS

Reading through my "literature," from Dr. Sherry, here are some facts about Rheumatoid Arthritis I learned at the time, which was 2008. 1.3 million Americans had it—less than one percent. Of the 1.3 million, 0.0 million knew how they had gotten it, or why. 70% of them were women.

RA was the condition of the human body working too hard. It was proof that the body and mind can exist in an eternal, vengeful misunderstanding. Like Osteo (aka regular) arthritis, Rheumatoid Arthritis was the deterioration and incapacitation of the joints. The difference was, RA needed no prior injury, no repeated wear and tear. You didn't need to have played tennis all your life to get RA in the elbow. You didn't need to work construction all your life to get it in your back. You didn't need to be a stenographer or work in a textile factory to get it in the nooks of your finger. Anyone could get it. Like the tooth fairy, or Santa Claus, RA could visit you in the middle of the night, without even waking you up.

The mystery of RA had to do with the fact that it was autoimmune, i.e. self-made. It wasn't a sickness contracted from third world tap water or sneezes. The body waged war on itself. Specifically, the immune system got confused and perceived its own tissues, its own bones, its own *blood*, as a threat, and attacked it, chewed through it, left nothing unscarred, thinking it was fixing problems. RA was a glitch in the system, a finely tuned army misinterpreting a dangerous assignment, and racking up serious friendly fire as a result. The body with RA was like Boxer, the horse in George Orwell's *Animal Farm*, saying "I'll work harder. I'll work harder," not knowing he was digging his own grave.

RA made it hard to do simple human tasks without feeling like a gambler who'd been greeted by his bookie's lead pipe. Simple human tasks being: pushing the brake pedal hard enough to stop; bringing a fork to your mouth; doing dishes; putting keys in a door and twisting; wiping your ass; holding a cup as the faucet fills it with water; shaking someone's hand; flicking a lighter; moving with any sort of efficiency or haste; picking berries.

This was all due to the body and the mind having a miscommunication. If only there was a way to give your body—your own flesh and blood—a message, RA would not exist. At the time, had I known what was happening, I would have wished for the power to tell my immune system: "Take a day off, take a *month* off—you're working too hard."

Or

"That thing you're attacking right now: stop. IT'S US!"

Also learned from Dr. Sherry's literature: RA was treated by pounding the immune system with drugs that blocked it from working. The great paradox being: the immune system, in this case, was the enemy—when it was *supposed* to be the body's greatest ally in fighting enemies!

The immune system of an RA patient was like the trusted sidekick in the movies, the childhood friend who in the end double crosses and backstabs the protagonist. Another way of characterizing RA: the immune system of an RA patient was the entire Black Socks team of 1919, savvy and talented but spineless, getting paid to do something as low as throw the World Series and ruin the purity of an entire nation's spirit and pastime.

The meds for RA weren't much better. A body on RA meds was less able to fight sickness. Germs and bacteria that a normal body burned like crumb-sized asteroids in the ozone—they posed more of a threat. Because the drugs were heavy and foreign to the body, vomiting was common at first, but not to worry: this was normal. In fact, it was *encouraged* to continue with the drugs as prescribed until the body could "adapt." "Adapting" to the drugs sometimes caused hair to fall out. Sometimes the heart "adapted" to meds with cardiac arrest. The eyes "adapted" by going blind. Sometimes the liver "adapted" by failing. So alcohol while on the meds was not advised. (How would I be able to get through like this *without* alcohol?) All I'd enjoyed in excess in recent years seemed on the verge of disappearing.

There was more. The meds depleted the body's ability to filter out the cancerous agents of the sun, so going outside for extended periods, ever, was a bad idea. Cancer in general—they made sure to say—had been known to happen on the meds as well, which was why it was important to have blood tests done to make sure cancer cells hadn't crept into the picture. To catch cancer *early*—that was the aim. How reassuring!

In my next visit, Dr. Sherry dove right into treatment strategies. No chit chat.

"Again, it's too early to say that you have it, but the way things seem…"

I waited for her to mention something about baseball, to at least acknowledge the complexity of having a career, of not being able to just stop my life to futz with sinister meds and have checkup appointments every goddamned week.

"There are a number of tried and true medicines, been around for years, that have proven very reliable and effective for RA patients."

Did she even remember I *had* a career?

"If I took the meds, do you think I'd be ready to pitch in Belgium within six months?" I asked, like a businessman concerned only with the bottom line. "Remember? I'm supposed to play?"

"Oh, nooo," she cooed, "I really must advise against that.

We should be putting together a plan of action in regards to this disease."

She'd said it: disease. And worse: she'd discounted the possibility that I didn't have it.

"I still want to believe that my plan of action is not to take a cocktail of meds, but to fly to Belgium and pitch," I said.

"I'm sensitive to that? But I want you to know, in my career—and I've been around Rheumatoid Arthritis for thirty years—these symptoms are most effectively fought early on."

Sorry, but I don't have RA, I wanted to say.

She said it was unlikely for a man my age to experience any side effects from the meds, and that I should consider taking a heavier than average dose to start.

"The heavier the dose, the better the chances of getting the disease under control. Okay? As a twenty-three-year-old male, you're a great candidate to be able to really muscle through!"

Muscle through? *Medicine?* What a crock of shit! That she had the gall to speak in an optimistic tone, as if this were an exciting time in my life.

"Okkkaaaaaay?"

Stop, I wanted to shriek at her and scare her into a corner, as if she were a toy dog. I wanted to rise and show her my fists and tell her the only thing I was going to be *muscling through* was a baseball game, or some physical challenge that proved my manhood. I needed her to know that I was a man—that I was *not* in the early stages of a disease, a career ending disease.

I sat on the wax paper of the hospital bed as Dr. Sherry pointed at areas on my x-ray of significant swelling. It was getting worse in the index, middle and ring fingers on my throwing hand, she said.

"The elbow too is showing great advancement of the disease," she said in a tone that sounded sorry, but also fascinated. I had a morbid vision of being 25, unable to unbutton my pants or wave hello. What if at 25, I was like my friend's mom, driving with the little blue handicapped placard on my rear view, hobbling from point A to point B, unable to carry groceries or bend a leg. I didn't want to take meds, but what if I had no choice?

"We don't want you to live in pain, okay?" Dr. Sherry asked. "I want you to be able to play baseball again."

She said the word baseball like it was the latest teen fad, cute, yet sure to be forgotten in time.

24
DENIAL

I didn't start taking the meds.

This lady didn't understand: taking the meds meant swallowing more than a pill. It meant swallowing a new life, an early retirement, an embarrassing disease. I clung to a hope that whatever this was, it wasn't RA. I told myself, *Dude, you don't have symmetrical swelling. You did a blood test, and whatever they look for in RA patients, you don't have. Rheumatoid Arthritis doesn't run in our family. And finally, dude, it is inconceivable for you, a 23-year-old pro athlete to have a disease meant for old women.*

You don't have it, I told myself. *You don't.*

While I told myself this, my elbow remained mutilated. I woke up and couldn't bend it to brush my teeth, couldn't straighten out the collar on my shirt. From telling myself, *you definitely don't have the disease,* I started to tell myself, *it would be ridiculous if it turned out you had it.* Soon, I couldn't wrap my fingers around a soda can, couldn't push buttons on a cell phone, and I began to tell myself, *Whatever this is, it's scary,* and I wished there had just been a pregnancy stick for me to piss on to know already—two lines, you've got the disease, one line, you're in the clear—instead of playing these mind games with myself that I was beginning to lose.

My left knee was the next victim. It swelled to the size of a grapefruit. When I got out of bed, I stood as slow as a patient in post-op. Suddenly walking up a flight of stairs was harder than squatting 350 lbs., which I'd done just two months prior. I now couldn't fathom pitching off a mound. Even picking up a ball brought about a pain in my fat knuckles that I couldn't imagine playing through. My limbs were starting to feel heavy and useless, and my joints were too weak to lift or bend them.

In weeks, my knee looked like it would burst. Even when I was lying down, resting, it throbbed with a dull and incredible pain. My fingers ceased to look like fingers but more like the Hamburger Helper mascot, the jovial oven mitt. I awoke each day feeling like I'd played four quarters of football against San Quentin, sans pads.

I looked at pictures of myself in my baseball uniform, the action poses taken in those final games in April. It was now just September. I envied the person in those pictures. He was strong, determined, capable. He had the face of someone who had no idea a disease could be lurking around the corner.

I didn't know how to tell anyone. Or what to tell them. Charlie was in the minors, playing every day, real professional baseball. He was catching 90 mph fastballs, hitting doubles, and getting trucked at home plate. What was I going to tell him? That I had an injury that came out of nowhere that kept getting worse? I remembered how in high school I'd had similar pains and he'd found the whole situation to reflect an appalling lack of manhood. I couldn't deal with that now. I didn't tell Kendall because I didn't want to tell the girl that her possibly-future husband had become frail, that maybe I wouldn't be able to carry our child or play catch with him or change his diaper, that she would have to do all of the heavy lifting, literally. I didn't tell my mom because she worried when our toilet made noise after flushing; she worried when six neighborhoods away someone's car was broken into; she worried when there was a 25% chance of rain. I had no one I could tell, and nothing I was prepared to tell them.

"Contract came," my dad said later that September. He handed me a small manila envelope. The return address was The Merchtem Cats, Belgium. On it my name was spelled incorrectly (Emille). I winced as I shoved my chubby index finger across the top. I looked at the papers; everything was in Dutch. But I read dates, addresses of residences. Everything I would need to take to the consulate for my work visa.

I put the papers down and didn't sign them.

For a couple of weeks my phone rang and I looked at the 50-digit incoming call and pressed ignore. I couldn't bring myself to tell the coach the truth. I didn't even know what the truth was, but it was bad, and even if I tried to explain it to him—that in the three months since my last college pitch, I'd gotten a disease that had chewed my arm to mush—he wasn't going to understand. Why would he? To him, Rheumatoid Arthritis was probably just another fabricated American disease, a name for something that required *medication*, whereas in Belgium it was likely one of many ailments that were fixed with proper amounts of beer.

I imagined the difficult exchange:

"It's called Rheumatoid Arthritis."

"Roommate apartments? What do you say? Your living here is already arranged."

"Rheu-ma-toid…Ar-thri-tis."

"Who? *Rugby* Arthritis?"

"It affects my BASEBALL ABILITY."

"Yes, your pitching is where we are lusting. Drink ale and see you in ninety days."

Meanwhile, the burning and ringing pains had spread to my wrist. Within a week my hand hung limply from my arm like the head of a dead snake. I couldn't even wave it. Shaking hands felt like slamming a car hood on my wrist. One by one, my joints were going down.

By winter of 2009, I was bordering on handicapped. I couldn't wrap my fingers around a pen. At banks, or restaurants, when signing bills, my stiff middle finger gave the impression that I was displeased with the service. At bars, I couldn't bend my ring finger around a bottle, so I walked around as though advertising my status of eligible bachelor.

Drinking helped me convince myself this wasn't a disease. It blurred worry, numbed the bite of pain. One Friday, my friends and I went downtown. We'd done what was typical of jobless college grads *heavily* pregame with cheap liquor in the alley, arrive at the bar drunk, have one drink, then wander around picking up half-empty cocktails.

At two, the lights came on and we spilled into the streets delirious.

A bartender came out and dumped ice into the street. A friend picked up a handful and without thinking, chucked it. The ice sailed onto a passing Escalade. The Escalade stopped. Out of it came previously non-angered thugs, who were now angered, and larger than us.

"Hey man, sorry," my friend started saying.

I held my hand up signaling: *I'll handle this.*

"You guys really don't want this right now," I slurred at the thugs. I stepped closer to them so we were face to face. "What're you gonna *do?"*

They didn't use words to tell me what they were going to do, per se. Rather, they skipped to just doing it. Which was level me with a direct punch to the mouth. Then they raced away.

"What happened?" I asked, lying on my back, my mouth split open. My friends were laughing. I laughed.

"Seriously. What?"

My bold showdown was reenacted several times on our walk home, sometimes interrupted for minutes due to our keeling over in the street from laughter.

Kendall saw my scab on Skype and said it looked like Paraguay. It healed into a Joaquin Phoenix lip scar. As much as I should have been embarrassed about this, I wasn't. I looked in the mirror and was fine with how everything had played out. Mainly because someday, perhaps only months later when I was a hunched-over shell of a human with disfigured hands and a cane and smelly clothes due to being unable to change myself, people might ask how I got that scar, and I could tell them a story, and they'd know I hadn't always been like this.

That November, my dad was limbing a tree in our back yard and asked for my help. He didn't get how serious the pain was, how little I could physically do. He also sometimes just plain forgot I had a disease. And it wasn't his fault. I spoke about it so little, and put myself in few positions where my weakness would be seen. My parents rarely asked questions about my developing condition because I was prone to get defensive, and short with them.

I agreed to help him because I found it ridiculous to be unable to help with menial yardwork. It made me want to scream. He needed me to hold a rope that was wrapped around the limb he was cutting. My job was to lower the limb to the ground—like a crane with cargo—as opposed to letting it crash down.

My hands were too swollen to get a firm grip on the rope. My elbow couldn't bend to navigate the rope either. So I wrapped it around my right hand. My dad didn't notice that I had attached myself to the rope, which was attached to the massive tree branch that was about to fall. This was a big no-no in tree limbing, apparently: marrying yourself to a falling object that weighed more than you.

"Ready?" he asked.

"Yeah," I said, absently. I was only doing this to give the illusion that I could still be a man, or at least a helpful son.

The chainsaw groaned alive. Mom watched from her window upstairs.

"Careful," she said.

My dad was in the tree, his legs clinging to it like a jumbo squirrel hiding from a hawk. He worked the chainsaw into the limb and it began to crack and lower. Tree dandruff began to cloud around him. The slack of rope tightened like a tuning guitar string and started to pull me up. The limb snapped and fell in a cracking whoosh. It jerked me up by my wrist.

If I had to describe that pain, I would say it felt like there was someone in the world who *hated* me, with every fiber in his body, who had spent *years* designing a physical sensation that adequately made me feel all his bottled up hate, and had chosen to zap me with the strongest dose of that sensation, at that moment.

"Ermph!" I let out. It was one of the noises you make when you're trying not to make any noise at all.

"What happened?" Dad asked from the tree.

I unwrapped the rope from my wrist then crumpled to the ground.

"You ok?" he asked. "What happened?"

"I wrapped my fucking hand in the rope."

"Why'd you do *that!*" he cried. "You never do that!"

"You didn't tell him, Joe? How could you not tell him?" Mom snapped, insinuating that she had gone over the protocol with him time and time again. Dad's mouth opened to say something, then it closed. He didn't want to say sorry, I could tell, because that would make me a victim, and acknowledge that I was weak. The cat would be out of the bag. He respected this world of denial I lived in. He acknowledged my transparent desperation be seen as a man. So he clammed up. He kind of just sat there in the tree, with this morose, droopy face, like he'd just sat on a puppy. If I could have punched something and not been caused more immeasurable pain, I would have.

My dad went inside and he and my mom accused him of not paying attention. They argued over how they needed to be more conscious of my condition. It sounded like they were talking about someone they didn't know, like a foreign exchange student they were hosting for a semester who couldn't make friends. Though these discussions only made things worse, made me feel like some charity case, I couldn't blame them. With all my changes, and the quickness with which they had happened, they *didn't* know me anymore.

"Weird stuff is happening," I finally told Kendall. She was coming to visit for Christmas, and when she arrived I knew it would be impossible to hide my thin forearms, my wincing from some small, seemingly insignificant movement.

"What kinda weird stuff?"

"Just, my body. I'll show you when you get here. Just don't want it to alarm you. It started on our trip to Manteca. Just seems to be getting worse. Making it pretty hard to play baseball, or do much of anything."

That winter she and I went to Yosemite and stayed in a cabin with my parents. On the drive, I had to constantly lay my leg across her lap as the knee was too swollen to bend. She eyed my leg with sorrow while clearly trying not to stare. One morning she tickled me, which was something we used to do in Hawaii. It had always led to breathless kissing and laughter. This time, I tried to wrestle back but just flinched and cowered, so we sat there in awkward silence. I could scarcely make love to her in more than one position. (The position was boring). Our hands, due to my fingers, no longer fit together. On the hikes through Yosemite, I anchored the group. I was the unflattering combination of swollen and bulbous, while thin and frail. My idea of exercise now was treading water in the lodge pool.

I feared losing Kendall, that she would go back to South Carolina after this and think: *I didn't sign up for this. I don't deserve, at age 20, to be a hospice worker. There are plenty of men right in my backyard, who aren't crippled, who will be able to protect me. I should not be the guardian and last line of defense in our relationship. I am not drawn to a limping, disappearing sob story.*

"I love you so much," she told me often, with the calm certainty of a wife who'd survived war with her husband.

"Whatever you want me to do, I'll do. If you want to talk about it, we can. If you want to ignore it, pretend it's not there, we can."

"I don't want anyone to know. I want people to think I'm on a diet, and that baseball ended from a fishing accident."

"I'ma tell my family you lost your elbow *fishin'*? You gotta give me something better than that."

Telling the Belgian coach that spring was not easy. It did not have the comedic tones I thought it would. That is, there was no language barrier, no who's-on-first moments.

"Oh," he said.

"I'm sorry."

"You are not coming?"

"I can't. I have a disease."

A silence took over that was thick with the sting of betrayal.

"Ay-meel, this is not good. We are counting on this, yes?"

It was as if he suspected I was changing my mind about this, making up a lie to get out of it. Or worse: he thought I was bitching out, that I was passing up a lifetime opportunity over a little arm fatigue.

When I hung up, my career was gone, my disease was here.

"How's it going out there?" I asked Charlie in a conversation that spring. It was about nine in the morning in San Francisco. I assumed he had a couple of hours to kill before he had to get to the park for a standard seven o'clock game. Rookie ball had gone well for him. He hit over .300 for the Batavia Muckdogs, a team that won the division championship. He got a championship ring for it, showed it off during the offseason, while I was busy avoiding his questions of *wanna play catch? Wanna throw a bullpen?* Now he was in his second year of the pros.

"It's good man. Just grinding through the season. I'm the starting catcher in Quad Cities."

"That's great, man."

"Living the life. You'll know soon enough."

I could tell he had a chew in from the spitting. I badly wanted to be in his position, sitting out on the field, listening to country music, and shagging balls. I could still feel the humidity of purple Hilo dusks as the stadium lights hummed alive, the chatter and burps of my teammates, the batting practice, the smell of the forever wet grass.

I put the phone in my right hand and painfully brought it to my ear. Mornings with RA were the worst. The tips of my fingers were icy, everything was heavy. I moved slow and cautiously, like walking across a war-torn field where dormant mines still existed. The slightest poke at a swollen area was electrocution.

"What's up with you?" Charlie asked.

"Not much."

"Yeah."

"Well, actually. You know how I was going to play over in Belgium?"

"Oh yeah, that league."

In his tone, *that league* sounded like continuation school—a great resource for people who can't hack it in real life.

"The contract came in the mail," I said, an attempt to prove that my league was legit enough to pay its players, momentarily letting me feel like we were on level playing fields as pros, if only for a moment.

"It did?"

"Yeah."

"Sweet. So when do you leave?"

Was I going to cross the threshold, though? Was I going to break the seal and tell him? Once I told one friend, it was out. Everyone would know. Friends, their parents. Anytime I saw people, they'd ask, "how're you holding up?" as if I'd been left by my fiancé and had spent the last month watching "Friends" reruns and eating Chinese takeout in bed.

"Thing is, I don't think I can go."

"Why?"

The tone was presumptuous, as if there was no reason on earth that wasn't invalid or fickle. I knew whatever I told him, short of the truth, would sound lame. Shit, even the truth would be lame.

How do I tell him without telling him? I wondered.

"My elbow's shot," I said vaguely.

"Shot? How?"

"I'm not sure, I can't straighten it, hurts to throw. Couldn't pitch a full season right now."

"What about rehab? Surgery?"

"Seems beyond that."

No human injury, as far as Charlie knew, was beyond rehab and surgery.

"Damn. Oh well," he said. "Shit happens."

I knew he was thinking, *if he really wanted to play he would find a way. There's always a way.* By his quick and casual dismissal of the topic, "Oh well," I knew he thought that Belgium never was a serious thing to begin with. Or perhaps I was never as serious about baseball as he'd thought. I wanted to tell him, *Dude, listen. I'd give anything to play. But this thing going on in my body? It doesn't give a shit about what I want. It's real. There's no Manning Up this time. I've Manned Up through plenty in baseball, and I'll tell you, that doesn't work with this. This thing—you've got no fucking clue.*

I fell out of touch with Charlie, lost interest in his pro career. I didn't care if he was promoted to single A or high A or however many goddamned leagues there were with people actually getting to play baseball.

I fell out of touch with Saff and my other roommates, as well as Coach Clark and the Hawaiians who I'd considered brothers one year before. I stopped dressing like a jock. No more half-crooked ball cap and, "Property of UH Hilo

Baseball" shirts. I cut ties with all of that. I started wearing a beret, and jumpsuits, like in "The Sopranos." I'd go to Ross and sort through the active wear with the old Filipino men, find a track jacket to my liking, then head over to the pants and look for something that matched. I told people I was going for the mobster look. I tried to convince myself I looked tough, like an enforcer, or a made guy. But really, I wore old man clothes because it hurt to button and unbutton pants. If people were going to think I was lazy, or devoid of fashion, or a delusional Italian? That was fine. I was OK with all of those labels, as long as they didn't think I had a disease.

25
THE REAL WORLD

"Wake the hell up and get a job."

Mom was starting to greet me this way each morning. She liked to follow-up with a gavel-like knock on my door. In her defense, I *was* jobless and sleeping in till 10:30, at which point I usually oozed out of bed and sat at my computer until the afternoon, ace bandage around my right wrist, ice pack strapped to my left knee, gloves with the finger tips cut off like the underground renegades of *The Matrix*. I spent this time conceiving un-publishable literary works. Mom was starting to worry.

My pain made it hard to do anything—open the fridge, shower, brush teeth, get out of bed. And so I'd been hermitting myself in my room, praying to put together some award-winning fiction (writing was one of the remaining things that brought me joy, or at least distraction, and spared me pain). And while I did this, I'd hoped my mom would forget about me; she didn't. Au contraire, she took issue with my being a 23 year-old with two college degrees sitting around in my pajamas until the afternoon. While I hid in my room to write, and prevent her from seeing the worsening state of my disease, she started to suspect that I was indulging in marathons of porn. She developed this unfortunate penchant for reminding me that life goes on. Baseball fantasyland was over. This was the real world.

"In the real world, Emil, people get sick and they still have to work."

She was of course referring to her own hodgepodge of woe.

One morning, I walked to the kitchen table and asked, "Mom, what can I even *do?*"

"Don't know, but you sure can button up a shirt, hit the trail, and knock on some doors."

I knew this was her way of coping with my disease; she felt if she let herself sit around and think about how her son was debilitated, and the possibility that her genes might have been the cause, she might get depressed. So she dished out some tough love, when really I could tell she was feeling like a spooked horse, and dragging me by the boot spurs.

"Mom, you're telling me to put on a tuxedo and walk in unannounced to Radio Shack."

"You know what? You have to start somewhere."

"This isn't the Great Depression. Nobody gets jobs like that anymore. You can get *bullied* doing that, but not hired."

"You can be sarcastic all you want. But the reality is, we're going to start to charge you rent."

"What?"

"Three hundred dollars a month. Starting next month."

"To live in this house? With my parents?"

"And eat our food, and drive our car, yes."

"Or you're going to put me on the street?"

She shrugged and raised her eyebrow, implying, *do you really want to find out?* I limp-stormed from the kitchen to my room. My rage was the kind I felt after pitching badly in college. Teeth clenched, needly sweat under the armpits, tight chest, the kind of feeling that, later in life, would probably result in a heart attack. In college, when I'd felt like this, I'd gone and done sprints until I was heaving for air. I'd thrown chairs in the clubhouse. I'd exorcised the fury until I was too tired to be upset. It had been a healthy method to deal with anger, I thought. But now, I physically couldn't do any of that, couldn't even make a fist. So the rage built and compounded and calcified into this acidic lump inside me.

My big tantrum culminated in picking up a pencil and flicking it. It spiraled into my laptop and broke the screen. My mom came in and put her hands on her hips, like a sensei disappointed in her pupil's poor discipline.

"You'll pay for that too."

26
POOR, UNFORTUNATE SOUL

"It's not a career," Mom said.

"I know that. Do you *think* I think working at Jamba Juice is a career? What else am I supposed to do if you're making me pay rent?"

"Maybe you ought to go out and get an actual job."

I'd had just about enough of her employment sermons when we both knew she had no experience doing anything she was telling me to do.

"Mom, you are a music teacher. You get students from a brochure you pin on bulletin boards in schools. You haven't even interviewed for a job since Denny's in '74."

"You know what I'm doing when I go from school to school, pinning my brochure up? It's something you're *not* doing, and it's called networking."

Oh Jesus. She'd said it. *Networking*. The buzzword of the 2009 recession. She'd heard it on "Oprah," or read it in some bogusly vague article on Yahoo titled "Simple Tips in These Tough Times."

She was worried about me again, and she showed it by relentlessly picking at my soul. We butted heads in our small house because, how was she supposed to know the *right* way to deal with my spontaneous disease? *Was* there a right way?

Jamba Juice had been different when I was a college kid home for summer. I'd actually found the job to be fun, at least compared to other shitty summer jobs. For instance, Jamba's inventory system was the shits. Meaning, I drank smoothies and ate baked goods at staggering rates, then explained on the "waste chart" how muffins had "accidentally dropped in the garbage." When I was hungover there was nothing like a smoothie. The worse my hangover, the more I looked forward to work. (How many people were lucky enough to say that?)

All of my other coworkers were in college or high school, just getting extra bucks. We were a union of adolescents, ignoring the corporate mottos, ignoring the customers, daring management to fire us, experimenting with fruits and juices and yogurts for the ultimate hangover remedies and stoner medleys. Because who cared? We were kids in college, and this was a summer job.

"Dude, you gotta try the orange juice, the uh...*soymilk*, with the peach and banana. And the *blueberries*, uh, and...no wait, that's it. Wait what did I say?"

Entire shifts were spent like this. Not to mention, the endless amounts of protein powder at my disposal. A college athlete with an unlimited supply of protein was like Homer Simpson at an unmonitored spigot of Duff.

But now, I was no longer in college. I was a college *grad* in need of a *profession*. If I returned to Jamba Juice, I would be doing it because suddenly I *needed* money, to pay rent, so that I could continue to live in the *same room* I'd lived in for free since I was three years old, to sleep in the same bed with broken bedsprings that my feet practically hung over. If I returned to Jamba, I would no longer be able to blow off all the things about the whole corporate scene that I had once laughed at. Things like, Jamba Juice practically put a quota on how many smiles to give per shift. There was propaganda everywhere in the store that begged/threatened employees to uplift customers. Signs like:

Have you wowed someone yet today? Show them some pizzazz! Show them some umph! Show them that AWESOME smile of yours! Try showing it MORE than once!

When the doors of the store opened, employees were

supposed to go ballistic with hospitality. Posted in back were profiles and bios of exemplary Jamba Juice workers from all over the country. I always suspected that the people in the bios did not exist, but were low-grade models hired by Jamba Juice headquarters to brainwash workers into truly believing there was no more euphoric an experience than making a stranger a smoothie. The profiles usually had pictures of someone in an apron and visor (no two things on earth looked dumber when worn together), smiling genuinely, with a cartoon bubble coming from his face that said:

"I try to make every customer's day a little bit better. Making other people happy makes me happy. That's what it's all about."
–Todd, 19, Arizona
(Following these dim teenage proverbs, there was always a written response from Jamba)
Keep it up, Todd! –Jamba Juice

"I think life's all about being crazy and having fun. And I just want everyone else to feel that way. Because, it's good!"
–Amanda, 21, Colorado.
You *go!* Amanda. You go...*bananas!* –Jamba

My manager was a wiry, coffee-overdosing Jamba lifer in his early forties. He greeted customers with "Hi!" excessively, sometimes without any customers in the store. He was a nice guy, and he meant well—he was just caught in this pickle of having to please corporate with sales and good reviews while keeping his employees happy, who were a bunch of potheads who stole.

"Say thank youuuuuu," he would remind-hiss when we completed a transaction with a customer. On slow days, he would have us scrub already clean windows, sweep swept floors, restock overflowing napkins, take out empty trash.

"What's wrong?" he'd ask after I'd undergone such labor. "Just not in a good mood today?"

On sunny days, or 4th of July, or during BOGO promotions, he marched around the store in frenzied circles screaming "hiiii!" like a malfunctioning toy.

"You guys need to get these orders out *faster!*" he'd whine. Female employees rolled their eyes. The soundtrack of Jamba nearly drove me to consider dialing a suicide hotline. Song after song was either about being irrationally happy, or being a clumsy hipster in love. Jamba's line would be out the door with teenage girls, and double strollers of wailing babies flinging bags of Pirate's Booty. Customers complained about smoothies, asked for them to be remade and then gave us looks like they wanted us to thank them for their honesty. Then our manager would come out into the hell zone with the fucking blenders going nonstop and the trash everywhere and the employees wiping sweat from their brows and the vegans and lactose intolerant subbing fruit for fro-yo and the pimply teenagers on dates subbing fro-yo for fruit.

"Act *happyyyyyyyyyy!*" he would scold.

All of this we had to do while wearing an orange visor.

Believe me, I didn't want to go back. I'd spent a couple of months searching for other jobs. If I wasn't going to be able to play baseball, I figured I should at least look for a job I wanted to do first. I'd perused the "Writing" section of Craigslist daily, where the bulk of the listings seemed to be non-paying sports blogs. These were opportunities to "build a readership," allegedly.

Also in the Writing listings were things like "Senior Technical Editor" or "Administrative Content Consultant." The job description typically took four cryptic paragraphs to say that you would be doing Excel spreadsheets. A minimum of five years of job experience was usually needed. These postings reappeared daily because, ostensibly, no one was qualified enough, or interested.

Another recurring post:

$5,000 A WEEK!!!!! WORK FROM YOUR COUCH!!!!!! NO JOB EXPERIENCE NECESSARY!!!!

I worried, *if I click this, might my computer explode?*

Hours trolling Craigslist led to a whopping two interviews. One was for a dog-walking company, who in the end said they were looking for someone with "a little more experience." I'd had a dog growing up, and I'd walked this dog. What the hell more did they want? My second interview was with a company that acted as the agent between engaged couples and wedding photographers. It was the kind of job you heard about and thought, that's a *job?* I passed the initial phone interview, which a banana slug could've passed if the phone was held to its antennae long enough. The second interview was at their office, where they cranked it up a notch. I was asked to have a mock conversation with an unhappy customer. This "customer," was the CEO of the company. He simulated a bride who just did not find it necessary to have his (her) wedding photographed. I was supposed to convince him (her) otherwise.

"I think I'll just have my cousin photograph it," the CEO said in his best Skeptic Voice.

"But sir, or ma'am, I assure you our photographers are top notch professionals and when you look at your pictures in years to come you want the memories to be pristine."

"What's to stop me from going direct to a photographer myself?"

"Well, ma'am, with so much else to worry about for your wedding—the invitations, and uh, silverware—the last thing you want is to have to put in the time to arrange the trustworthy and fantastic photographer you deserve on your big day!"

"I really don't see the logic in paying a *middle man* when I can find a photographer myself."

And my thoughts were, *you and me both. This job is a fucking joke!*

Eventually I said, "I give up, you're right! You *shouldn't* use this company!"

The CEO blinked. I got up and walked out. In the lobby of the company: quiet, drab carpet colors with square shapes like old Microsoft screen savers. There were water coolers, humming electronics, fresh-out-of-college kids speaking with strained politeness. The workers looked like the shriveled aquatic nubs in *The Little Mermaid* who sulk as Ursula sings "Poor Unfortunate Soul."

They probably wondered each morning, taking the bus or paying for an overpriced downtown parking spot, walking into their beige lobby: *What have I gotten myself into? I'm cold calling people about wedding photographers? What happened to college and high school and traveling and youth? When will I have my life back? Will I get it back?*

As I limped out of there I wanted to salute them, or hold up a fist, like the Black Panthers or Che Guevara, except with no political or racial affiliation and only the unifying admittance that I was struggling, I too wondered when/if I'd get my life back.

"Hiiiii!" my manager at Jamba Juice shrieked.

Walking back into the store for the first time, it occurred to me that over periods of time, some things can change greatly, and others can remain so stubbornly the same. For instance, Jamba Juice itself was the same: the manager still sounded nervous and unhappy and tried to mask these traits with borderline-violent cheerfulness. I could tell the workers still didn't take the place seriously and stole everything. No one cared if customers smiled or if their smoothie tasted remotely good.

I, on the other (swollen) hand, had changed a lot. I'd lost

fifteen pounds. My muscles were gone. I could not crouch, could hardly walk up a curb. I could not grip anything, couldn't turn the employee key in the bathroom. I could not make a fist or shake a hand. I could not dry myself with a towel, couldn't take off a sweatshirt or bump into something without cowering. I was a walking bruise. And now I was back at Jamba Juice, stuck in a weird limbo of needing hours to make money, and dreading the hours because of the pain of the menial labor.

In college, I had always been the guy people asked to do the heavy lifting in the store: carry a ladder, bring out boxes of fruit from the stand-in freezer, then throw the boxes around to break up the stuck-together fruit. It was fun. Sometimes I turned the task into a workout. I would curl the boxes, or thrust them over my head like Olympic lifting. I would be sweating afterwards. Then I'd make a protein shake, and not pay for it. I'd relished my role around the workplace as the grunt, the jock. A couple of times, sketchy homeless guys came in and seemed to be casing the joint, maybe to steal some breaded goods, or our tips. The girls would come back and say "Emil, there's a scary man up front," and I would stalk out into the lobby with my shoulders broadened and a Clint Eastwood scowl, and save the day.

This time around, on my first shift back, my manager asked:

"Tough guy, can you bring out the ladder pretty please? A light in the lobby's out."

I went to the back, and tried to pick it up, but couldn't squeeze, couldn't even lift it. With Rheumatoid Arthritis, technically you had hands, but they were just for show. I came out with no ladder.

"Uh, hellooooo, earth to Emil?"

"Got stuck," I said.

Moments later, he came bounding from the back with the ladder slung under his armpit as if it was as light as cardboard.

"Oops," I said and walked away.

"What happened to Mr. Tough Guy? Sheesh!"

I couldn't pick up and throw the boxes of fruit anymore. I began to delegate those duties to other employees, like skinny girls, who trembled trying to lift the boxes, and then looked at me annoyed. Stuff a normal person could never imagine hurting, now killed me. Scooping ice cream, changing toilet paper, taking wrappers off straws, holding blenders to fill with fruit. Some days I would be so ashamed of myself, my declining body, that I'd volunteer to bring out the heavy fruit boxes even though I knew I couldn't. I would close my eyes and clench my teeth and my fingernails would bend backward as I squeezed as hard as I could to pick up a cardboard box. I hated myself. I hated my body and wanted to cause it pain.

"So what happened with baseball?" my manager asked once.

I looked at my hand and my wrist. My fingers looked like pregnant geckos. I knew he'd seen me limp from station to station. *Isn't it clear,* I thought?

"Just wasn't for you, huh?" he asked.

This made me smile. What a funny concept: that there could be people for whom pro ball just didn't seem right, who chose to hang it all up to work at Jamba and live with mom and dad.

"I don't blame you, buddy," he said. "I can't stand the sport."

And in some roundabout way, I agreed.

27
MY (SHORT-LIVED)
TREK TO THE EAST

The meds were sitting in my cabinet. Sealed, the cotton ball still inside. I was going back and forth with Dr. Sherry in emails, butting heads with her about starting them.

Dear Emil,

I don't want to see you in pain. The meds are powerful and effective. I truly feel the earlier you start taking them, the quicker you'll feel better. Please get in touch with my secretary in order to schedule our next appointment. I'd like to talk about this with you in person.

Best,

Dr. Sherry.

Dear Dr. Sherry,

I think I'm going to pursue alternate approaches. Holistic approaches. I've heard of a few. I'd rather put natural things into my body if I can help it.

Thanks,

Emil

Dear Emil,

Many alternate approaches have no scientific data to back up their results. The research and testimonies are unreliable. I urge you to stick with the plan here.

Dr. Sherry.

My mom had been instrumental in spring-boarding this

holistic quest. She believed it was better to try alternative medicines that weren't potential health risks before resorting to pharmaceutical drugs.

She wanted to believe that ailments of all kinds could be treated naturally, from the earth. She worried that one of the medications I'd been prescribed, Humira, had only been on the market since 2002, and therefore did not have a long enough track record to be deemed safe. She felt the FDA regularly approved drugs prematurely. She'd gone to the deepest depths of the internet and read that Humira had caused cancer in adolescents. She thought I was being used as a guinea pig. She would relay these concerns via email, and I would email Dr. Sherry with these concerns, and she would reply to assure me all was well.

"I want you to give my Chinese herbalist a try," Mom said. This was the beginning of spring, 2009, and my symptoms were getting worse by the day.

"What did you see him for?" I asked.

"My back. Also my chronic thirst."

"Chronic thirst? That's a thing?"

"It was a dangerous thing, Emil."

"Did the herbs work?"

"I *think* they did?"

The herbalist was in Oakland, in a house in a quiet neighborhood. My mom took the day off work and we coasted over the Bay Bridge at noon when the morning traffic had dissipated.

"The man is very nice," Mom said, crossing the bridge. "Make sure you're polite. No farting."

"Really compromises the *chi?*" I asked.

"Just don't."

In the hallway of the house, which doubled as the waiting room, was a creaky cabinet and matching grandfather clock, both looking like they might splinter away at any minute. The house smelled of incense, and a bonfire of dog hair. Mom and I sat quietly; only the noise of our breathing could be heard.

"Hello," I heard softly from upstairs. "Come."

Upstairs, the old man motioned for me to sit down. I realized I was essentially in a bedroom. There was a dresser with framed pictures on top. The doctor's bed, which typically had wax paper stretched across hard cushion, had a powder blue quilt on it. This doctor's room had a window, which gave the view of nice neighborhood front yards.

The old man closed his eyes and took my hand in his. I looked at my mom, who nodded. Never had I been held by softer hands. He didn't do much with my hands, just held them. The hands were not cold, not hot, only soft. Little time passed before I was nearly asleep. The doctor then prodded lightly and slid his ancient fingers to the part of my wrist where my pulse was, then pressed, studying me. He trickled his fingers around my puffy wrist, tapping and pushing and holding still. It was the quietest doctor visit humanly possible. His son, in a white smock, studied his father, his hands folded in his lap. After some moments—perhaps seconds, perhaps minutes—he opened his eyes, turned to his son, and said something.

"My father, he says weak pulse. Which is bad circulation. That makes the joint pain."

Weak pulse. The diagnosis sounded scary, like the diagnosis of someone facing imminent death. Literally, a fading heart. But then, I thought: this man *did* just identify the cause of all my swelling, all my pain. Bad circulation. Surely, in the history of China, bad circulation had been suffered, and surely, the doctors and healers had discovered the remedy.

In a way, I felt this man had just cured me.

All I would need was whatever herbs the Chinese took for bad circulation, and that would be it. These few months of pain, and loss of baseball would all turn out to be a misunderstanding, a *misdiagnosis*. Maybe Mom was right in distrusting Western medicine, and preferring the earth-given, centuries-proven antidotes of the East. I'd be back to my normal self in no time.

"Ok," the old man said, bowed, and disappeared down the staircase.

"My father. He go to get you the herbs," said the son, then he bowed, and exited as well. Mom and I sat there. We said nothing. Outside, the streets had no traffic. I had never been in a place so devoid of noise. It felt like I was floating in the solar system.

"How do you feel?" my mom whispered.

"Deaf."

The old man returned with a grocery bag of smaller paper bags. There were instructions for how to prepare the herbs, along with a list of foods I was not to eat, foods which were thought to aggravate my condition: milk, cheese, poultry, pork, beef, potatoes, tomatoes, shellfish, lettuce, avocados, citrus, bananas, salt, pepper, alcohol, and ice. No cold or hot beverages. No condiments or spices. I was permitted to eat… broccoli, and radishes maybe? Some tortillas? Also, it's worth reiterating: no alcohol. None. I was going to be going about this journey of pain and hope and worse pain without a drink, when booze was often the one thing that helped me escape, helped me think that this wasn't happening. My 15-minute appointment was over. For this, I handed over 100 of my own dollars. To ease the financial burden, Mom allowed the money I paid at holistic appointments like these to count toward rent.

The herbs took some getting used to—both their taste, and their appearance. Nothing looked like a plant or an herb, but more like wooden toys of ancient sorcery. One herb resembled furry, prehistoric clams. I was to boil these relics down to an eight-ounce dose of pulpy tar. When preparing my brews, the windows of my kitchen fogged. The house smelled like garbage that needed to be taken out. I drank the concoctions twice a week and mixed in a weekly $100 appointment, for the next two months. For those two months, I spent great portions of the day concentrating, trying to determine whether my symptoms were changing. And if they were, I worried the changes were so slight that it was a placebo.

"What you here for?" a woman asked me once in the waiting room.

"Allegedly Rheumatoid Arthritis," I replied.

"Are the herbs working?" she asked in a way that implied she knew the answer was yes.

"I'm just getting started, so, still waiting."

"Well, I'll tell you this. Without Dr. Chang, I would have already taken my own life. My sciatica was a medical mystery. No western medicine helped. All it did was give me side-effects that were worse than my sciatica. I couldn't get out of bed? Couldn't use the toilet? But then, a couple of years with Dr. Chang? The herbs, they saved me. They can cure everything."

This lady looked to me like someone who might read Tarot cards. She wore a couple of shawls, a tube of clanking bracelets up her arm.

"I've got my fingers crossed," I said.

"No," she said. "They cure everything."

I felt myself getting defensive. I wanted to say: "No. I don't know you and don't enjoy the certainty in your tone, because guess what? You *don't* know. You *don't* know me. I've been coming here for two months now, and I feel zilch in terms of improvement. The only thing that is currently less swollen in my life is my wallet."

Each appointment, the old man massaged my hand and held it still, relaying news that the "my circulation was improved." But I didn't *feel* any different. The testimonies for the herbs said they took time, and called for patience, because traditional Chinese medicine, unlike Western medicine, did not address the symptoms, but whatever was *causing* the symptoms, and this was no quick fix.

$400 bucks a month, living on a prayer.

I wondered about the lady with the sciatica who was healed after two years: were finances simply not a concern for her? Because, $100 a week, for two years, was over $10,000, and if $10,000 over two years was chump change, then a salud, lady!

I was looking at the meds in my cabinet more and more. Methotrexate, Humira—the stupid fucking *drugs,* with their stupid fucking *names,* and their stupid fucking possible *side-effects* that always sounded worse than the disease. But, nothing could be worse than this disease. I needed results and the herbs weren't working. After two months of the herbalist, I had to make a decision.

"I don't think I can come back anymore," I said to the doctor's son on the phone.

"But my father, he said improvement is soon. To feel better."

"So sorry, not soon enough."

28
FORUMS, FACELESS SUPPORT

UH Hilo baseball came to town on a road trip to play Academy of Art that April. My parents wanted to cater a postgame spread from a local taqueria to express how grateful they were to the program, and Coach E, for funding my college education, and watching after me during those unstable years. Coach E reacted to my parents' gesture as if we were providing food and shelter for thousands of displaced Hawaiians after a tidal wave. I missed him, his big heart, his genuine compassion, his concern for the *wellbeing* of his players over anything else (even winning).

It was an afternoon game at USF's home field (Academy of Art didn't have a home field, so they played where they could). The sun dipped past the dorm towers and the temperature plummeted. I was learning that cold weather brought Rheumatoid Arthritis to a new dimension of nightmare. You couldn't snap your finger. You moved like you were in quicksand. You couldn't carry anything your parents asked you to carry, not the full trays of carne asada or beans or rice— just the paper towels. You hardly could open the program that had the roster listings for both teams, the program you'd appeared in just one year earlier. You sat down like a 90-year-old, groaning and hoping gravity did the work without causing you to fart loudly.

Shivering in the bleachers, I watched Coach E hit infield, watched the players take their 90-foot warm-up sprints, watched all the poles jogged by the pitchers, all the casual grounders and flies, all the practice hacks, the meaningless conversations. I heard all the generic pregame songs, the "Sweet Home Alabamas."

College ball was so beautiful I bit back tears.

I looked at my hands, like disfigured dead branches out of a Tim Burton film.

After the game (which Hilo managed to lose), the boys came up one at a time. The freshmen had all grown taller and wider in the shoulders. They were all so big, well-fed, and oblivious. The love-felt hugs and hand-slaps as they pulled me in and thanked me for the food: each one shattered my hand, broke my elbow, ripped me in half.

It wasn't easy for me to admit, but I needed support. At the same time, I couldn't bring myself to tell anyone. My parents were always available, but I couldn't stand to be babied by them, so I gave my best shot at limping stoically in their presence and telling them vaguely "It is what it is." Same with Kendall. She was still in South Carolina, finishing up school. Rheumatoid Arthritis was easy to hide on Skype, and I didn't open up to her about how hard this was, because our relationship was still new, and I was desperate to preserve her image of me as healthy and strong. I couldn't tell friends. I couldn't bear *anyone* my age who knew me to have a new image of me as sick, weak. I started to seek support online. There, I could be faceless, thus I could be honest.

There were many online forums where people with Rheumatoid Arthritis talked of their ailments and offered cyber support. People shared their most intimate bouts with the disease, shared their unusual habits that seemed to alleviate pain. They shared their hatred of the disease. They shared their hope. Sometimes people became passionate about topics I didn't know people *could* get passionate about. On one forum a woman decried the name "Rheumatoid Arthritis." Evidently, because of its name, it was often confused with the more common osteoarthritis, which to her, was like confusing army boot camp with freshman PE. The woman proposed alternate names which she hoped would be considered for an official name change. Names like:

- Chronic Swelling Syndrome
- Autoimmune Joint Deterioration
- Inexplicable Compounding Pain Affliction
- Random Reckless Disorder

Which, to me, all sounded like heavy metal bands.

Ultimately, these forums were not what I'd hoped to find. They did not enlighten me much to the natural, diamond-in-the-rough remedies (the proverbial Tibetan on the mountain with all the answers), or the inspiring anecdotes I had hoped to find. Mostly, they enlightened me to just how bad RA could get. People's experiences made mine seem as inconvenient as a hangnail. Here are just some of the hundreds of forum topics I came across:

- Muscle But Not Joint Pain. Help??
- Fleas
- Muscle Spasms
- WE SHOULD HAVE A JOKE SECTION HERE!
- Can't Use My Fingers
- All In My Head
- Does Anyone Else Have Mood Swings With Rituximab Infusions?
- Can't Sleep
- Flatulence
- Ouch And I Feel Stupid
- Feet Again
- I Feel Like I'm Falling Apart and No One Believes Me
- Rheumatoid Arthritis AND Leg Ulcer (the message of

which begins cordially "Hello, I hope everyone is well…")

- Please Help Me, My Son Is 12 with RA
- Bruises
- Hip Replacement
- Anemia and Swine Flu
- Feeling Sad
- Methotrexate And Hurting Hair
- Methotrexate And Loss Of Hair
- Sex Probs (where, in addition to talk of spasms and joint agony, there were messages like: *I would much rather go to sleep nowadays than have sex, it feels like too much effort LOL)*
- Do I have a future? (clicking on that forum led me to an 18-year-old male who had considered suicide)
- Feeling Strange
- Booze and Meds (the entry that followed this title was:)

True. Blood test every four weeks, so far so good, however, must state that I don't drink too much, few glasses a week at home…social life is zero, so I guess I deserve a little tipple now and again…sadly I can't have any tonight or for a week as I'm on Antibiotics as I just had four teeth removed due to my crap immune system and toxic Meds! Now that is annoying, losing what were perfectly good teeth until a recent flare up a few months back! oh well, I guess false choppers aren't so bad in this day and age LOL!

- About eight messages in a row with the subject "Hi."
- Telling People And Work
- You've Got To Laugh About It (directly followed by:)
- Tonight I've Hit Rock Bottom
- You Will End Up In A Wheelchair

Contributors came from all over the world—I could tell from phrases like "me mum," and "the loo" and "heaps of pain." People tried to stay positive, concluded messages with smily faces or biblical reassurances. They apologized for the burden of their long posts. People supported one another, saying there was hope and that they had been there. And there was no cure, and there was no telling how people with this thing would end up.

Going through these forums reminded me of this one day in high school when the team had to sit through a cautionary video on chewing tobacco. It was essentially a long interview with an ex-pro who'd had half his jaw removed. When he spoke, it looked like his jaw was trying to gnaw itself.

"I'm telling you," he mumbled in his half-face language, "don't start it. Take it from me."

A few of us laughed. Partially at the morbid spectacle, but mostly because we felt safe. We were young and invincible, staring at a mutant that we would surely never become.

Now, as I read through these horrifying accounts of RA, I couldn't resist scrolling down, reading one at a time, cringing, like slowing at a car crash. Only this time, I couldn't laugh. I just feared—between the people who lost their hair, or were in a wheelchair, or had hip replacements, or got swine flu—which one might I become.

29
WORTH A SHOT

Mom often sent me emails while sitting in the same room as me. An email would pop up. I'd laugh and look at her. "What?" she'd ask.

One morning, while I was working on another doomed short story, Mom forwarded me an email with the subject "Worth a Shot." Her friends, who seemed to have incalculable amounts of time to surf the web for obscure articles, liked to forward her links and say, "reminded me of Emil," or "worth looking into for Emil ☺," and she forwarded them to me. Many were articles about underground RA cures, cures that the FDA and pharmaceutical companies "didn't want anyone to know about," because they would disrupt their agenda of being filthy rich.

Food Allergy May Simulate Rheumatoid Arthritis was the latest link to make it to my inbox.

I read that article, then read the suggested next article. One led to another. In the comment sections, I began to read people's accounts of being diagnosed with RA, then discovering their symptoms were from food allergies.

I read such comments as:

"I tried *everything*, all the hardcore meds, and none worked! I had resigned to living the rest of my life in agony. Then I heard about food allergies. So I figured, worth a shot! After a few trials, I learned my swelling wasn't RA after all. But cinnamon allergies!"

Cinnamon. I *wished* I was allergic to cinnamon.

I wanted all of this to be true. I went back and forth in my head. I told myself: *if this was real, then it would be widely known. This information wouldn't be so hidden from the public.* Not to mention, with the severity of my pain—my inability to wash my own hands or bend my elbow enough to comb my hair—I had a hard time believing it could all be from something like cinnamon. But at the same time, I figured there was no way that people were just *making* all of this up. What would be in it for them? I figured, as my parents' friends wrote in their emails: it was worth a shot.

The next day, I made an appointment with a food allergist. I fell asleep thinking that I could be just like all of those women on the websites. I romanticized the moment when I discovered *my* allergy. *It's out there,* I told myself, *somewhere, waiting for me.*

"My father-in-law actually had Rheumatoid Arthritis," the nurse said, sliding the blood pressure pump up my arm. She said this like it was something cool we had in common. "He was completely crippled by it."

"Really."

"They had to take out part of his intestines because years of taking the drugs had messed up his whole stomach lining."

"Ah."

What the hell was I supposed to say? Was this supposed to be small talk?

"He was in the ICU in a wheelchair, could barely whisper. And he asked, *whispered,* for more drugs for the pain? But he couldn't take no more."

"Alright, thanks."

"Do you have high blood pressure?" she wondered aloud as she left. "The food allergist will be in here shortly."

Minutes later, another woman entered and introduced herself in a thick eastern European accent. She had the round cheeks and puffed, white eyebrows of a Keebler elf.

"What eez it you think you are allergic to?" she asked after typing on her computer, squinting through her glasses at my file.

"Nothing that I know of, yet."

She gave a puzzled look. It was 5 p.m. I was clearly her last appointment of the day, and she was not interested in a whimsical patient.

"Have you heard of food allergies being confused as Rheumatoid Arthritis?" I asked.

She looked away from her computer, eyed me.

"Tsk tsk."

Then she looked up, as if thinking of how to put it in English.

"It is a…lost cause."

"Lost cause?"

"Quack literature. Yes."

Delightful, I thought.

"People are looking for ways to make money, with new diets and products. People say gluten free diets zis and vegan dat, but it is all money maker. If it worked, then it would work, yes? There would be real articles in real publications, Arthritis Today, Web MD. Everyone would know. Yes?"

I slumped in my chair. I considered saying mysteriously *But what if they don't want you to know?* but I had a feeling she'd laugh as if I'd suggested there was no moon landing, or no moon.

"Ve must hurry, the lab is closing. What foods would you like to test for today?"

I was now embarrassed to say any.

"I've read about gluten, dairy. Also, 'nightshade plants?' Whatever those are."

"We will do all inclusive test. And we hope for ze best. But I must warn you, often people come expecting answers, and it turns out they are not allergic to…tiddly winks."

In the lab, she pricked my skin with a panel of the active ingredients in known food allergens—dairy, shellfish, citrus, wheat, nuts, nightshades. This made twelve tiny scabs which dotted a grid up my arm. I looked like the world's most organized heroin addict. On my other arm, the same was done with atmospheric allergens, pollen, hay, cat dander. Both arms were lined with scabs. Now I looked like the world's most organized, and *fiendish*, heroin addict.

I waited for one of the scabs to puff up, or sizzle and boil. I hoped to get faint and sweaty and perhaps vomit in my lap. Breaking out in hives would have been nice, even spending a night in the ER. Anything to show I was allergic. At one point, I thought I saw one of my arms start to bubble. I thought I saw the needle point enlarge into a mini-red mound.

"Is this something?" I asked.

"No."

The dots on my arm healed over and eventually disappeared.

"So. Do you have any knowledge of alternate methods of treatment for Rheumatoid Arthritis?" I asked, hoping to get something out of this appointment. I knew she wanted to leave, and I could tell she was already annoyed for having to go through with this when she knew the answer all along.

"Well."

She looked at her door cautiously, or perhaps longingly.

"Please, do not quote me, I am not rheumatologist, yes? I can get in trouble."

"Right."

"It is known that protein-rich diets have caused Rheumatoid Arthritis to be more, eh, intense."

"Really? Protein?"

"Mm. Yes."

"I haven't heard of this."

"Ze, what do they call it, *flare* ups, are worse, yes?"

"I see."

Leaving the hospital, I thought this whole day was a wash, another wasteland destination on my path to a cure. An allergist had given me some haphazard tidbits, some seemingly imagined insight. Perhaps, she'd just made it up because she'd seen my long face when I'd learned I was free of allergies.

Protein, I thought as I walked through the parking lot. *What a joke. What am I doing asking an allergist Rheumatoid Arthritis questions anyway?* But as I got in my car, everything she'd said started to make sense. Or at least, I made myself *think* it made sense. Since childhood, and especially in college, I'd always maintained a protein-rich diet. *Heavily* protein-rich.

My teammates' bathrooms in Hilo had looked like meth labs from the round containers of powder stacked on each other—whey protein and soy protein and creatine, plus a whole bunch of other stuff that I could never afford or pronounce. And as an athlete I'd felt pressure to keep up with them. Trainers had advised me to take in over forty grams of protein a day. I went through cartons of eggs for breakfast, ate chicken and beef for dinner and washed everything down with protein shakes. At Jamba Juice, where I'd worked five days a week for four summers, I'd overdosed on free protein shakes. Basically, I'd spent all of college overloading my body with protein. So after that appointment, I considered the possibility that perhaps these RA symptoms were my body telling me: enough was enough. Perhaps these symptoms were my own doing, the results of trying to be the best athlete possible.

This was pretty much my last chance; I was certain I could not go on much longer with the pain. I would give this diet a shot, and if the diet didn't work, I'd have to start taking the meds. So no meat, no cheese, no protein. I also decided to cut gluten out of the picture for good measure, because in 2009 everyone everywhere was starting to blame Mother Earth's problems on gluten. Much like the diet mandated by the Chinese herbalist, I was left with very few conventional foods to eat.

Thankfully, San Francisco was a great place to be on a berserk diet. Everyone was on one. And I'm not talking Jenny Craig or Atkins. That shit was child's play in San Francisco. The diets here were inconceivable, as though inspired by a POW camp. Diets like: *just* broccoli, or *just* juice. Or *just* broccoli juice. Stores tried to accommodate everybody's weird food habits by having signs stating which foods were gluten free, organic, vegan. Big food companies were beginning to join in on this sudden trend of humans wanting to be healthy too, so their packages bragged with buzz phrases like "with real sugar" and "sea salt." Suddenly, everything was made of "superfoods," even fruit candy. No shit: I saw a 7UP bottle with the word "antioxidant" on it.

After a few days, I was famished. I felt like I was floating—weightless in body and in mind. I had willingly whittled my menu to that of a deer—all berries and stems, no meat and no carbs. I was in a Zen-like state of dazed inattentiveness. I told myself that from my suffering, good things would come. I romanticized my circumstance, imagined myself on a Himalayan mountain, sitting in a Sherpa blanket with a shaved head with nothing but a cup of grains to last a week. All because I'd forfeited burgers. In this image of myself, I was disease free. Hungry, but painless.

After a few weeks, there was no noticeable change, which I actually found encouraging: for the first time in months, my body hadn't gotten *worse*. Maybe this was the slow path of RA disappearing. Maybe the disease needed to plateau before it went away. Then for a glimmering few days, symptoms *did* improve. The change was slight. So slight I might have been imagining it as a result of my Buddhist fantasies and delirious hunt for a cure. But my elbow was almost moveable. My knee too. I could make a fist, and even squeeze. I was *not* making this up. For a couple of days—truly glorious days—I felt like this. I thought, *maybe all I have to do now is reintroduce the foods slowly, one at a time, and the one that causes me to swell up in pain is the winner!*

I'd always thought the body and mind were one entity, functioning in tandem. But if I'd learned anything from this disease, it was that the body and mind were separate. They were, in my case, a toxic marriage. At night, I found myself speaking to my body:

Ok, listen, body, I'm sorry. I've spent years abusing you in vast and creative ways. You want me to get into specifics? OK, fine. You deserve that. For starters, pitching. Throwing a baseball is one of the more unnatural human motions. Of course, doing it once or twice, or even a couple thousand times—big deal. The body is a healing machine. But I did it for twenty years, often times not just throwing, but throwing as hard as I could for hours. I know I didn't throw that hard, but that's beside the point. All that throwing was serious trauma, I'm sure. And even when you were in pain, and needed a break, I just kept throwing and throwing, breaking you down. And you held together for me. I'm really sorry for not taking care of you, and for pushing you to the limit. OK.

Exhibit Two, my drinking. It's probably taken a few years off of my life, I know. There were some good times there, some funny nights indeed, even you have to admit. But mostly, deluging your brain and liver to the point where I couldn't function, and then even in that state drinking more: that has to have taken its toll in the past five or so years. I'm assuming there is a strange blot in my liver, like an aerial view of an oil spill. The booze has made me depressed; I've puked blood; I've been twisted into pretzels by bouncers. I'm really sorry for that.

This leads me to exhibit C. Because for me, alcohol and anger go hand in hand. I have abused you, body, with my anger. Which, who knows where it comes from, but it comes out at night. Fighting has concussed your skull. It has purpled your eye. It has cracked your tooth. And so, for the past 20 years, I have abused you and when you heal, which you've always done, I have never said thank you. I've barely even noticed; I've just expected it. It's been childish and spoiled. But now, I've got something that you seem unable to heal from. It came at a time when I needed you most to be healthy. And I really need you to fight through this thing now. Do I deserve to have a full bill of health? Of course not. And I'm not necessarily asking for one. I'm not asking to be able to play baseball again; steadily, I'm letting go of that, albeit reluctantly. Really, there's nothing like pitching, and sitting in the sun all day with people you call brothers. But I'm willing to sacrifice that, ok? I don't have to be in top physical shape with definition and bulk and a profound Adam's apple anymore. But I really don't want this disease in my body. I'm asking. I'm begging you, fight this one last fight for me, please? Show that I'm allergic to some food, pick a food, any food. I'll give it up for life. And I promise, I will mind my drinking, I will live with Ghandi-like passivism, I will abuse you no more.

Pretty soon the wheels started falling off my diet. Whereas for a couple of weeks, the morning stiffness had been milder, I'd been able to make fists without cringing, I'd been fearless of simple tasks like filling up a cart with groceries—the swelling had returned. It started in my elbow, like the beginning of the disease all over. I felt cold when I woke up. The swelling went to my fingers. My knee felt like a stuffed nose during sickness. How could I have a food allergy if I hadn't been eating any food? I could not spend any more time on the holistic options and folkloric remedies my mom's friends discovered. I'd reached the end of the line.

It was wet and cold in San Francisco, the kind of weather where a room without carpeting and heat was no different than a meat locker. My joints ached and felt unmovably heavy. I decided I had no choice, that the time had come for the drugs. I went into my bathroom cupboard, opened the cabinet that held the hair gel, the cologne samples and the Band Aids—all the stuff I barely ever used and often forgot I had.

I stared at the bottle. Methotrexate. Its hideous, compassionless name. Not even trying to cushion the blow with that name. It was a "tried and true" medication, according to Dr. Sherry. I opened the top, pulled out the cobwebby cotton, poured out eight pills, flung them into my mouth and swallowed. They tasted dry like cotton swabs, with a toxic sweet aftertaste. I stood still, waiting to projectile vomit. I wondered if my innards would melt like hot wax.

Then I went to the fridge, took out the Humira that had been sitting there for months. I went to the bathroom, pulled my pants down half way, rubbed alcohol on my leg—that skinny, saggy, white leg—and stared at the needle. It was a pathetic feeling. Literally, and symbolically, I was naked. I felt like if a pack of wolves were hungry, I'd be the easiest prey they'd ever come across. I didn't even care that the drugs could render me blind, hairless, and dead. The pain dominated any other concern. I felt like a druggie, focused on the needle and the feeling it promised. Or in my case, the *disappearance* of feeling it promised. The disappearance of pain. I stuck it in my leg, felt the subtle prick, pushed the syringe slowly and watched the drugs empty into me. I waited, waited to go blind, waited for my heart to stop. I felt cold sweats, sitting on the toilet naked. And I waited.

30
FOCUS GROUPS

Mom was on a mailing list that sent ceaseless alerts for "Upcoming Focus Groups in Your Area." And in a metropolis like San Francisco, there were always focus groups. This may very well have been her idea of "networking."

Focus groups were glorified surveys on consumer products, like sodas, toothbrushes, remote controls. You went into a room for a couple of hours and shared your insight and then got paid heftily. Qualifying for focus groups was easy, too; often the requirements were just *slightly* narrower than: applicants must be humans, breathing. They would be something like: "Men, ages 21-75, who use money" or "People between 25-50 who eat." The sessions tackled crucial issues like breakfast drink preference (pulp or no pulp, or *some* pulp), or cell phone case color preference.

Mom forwarded me ones that I qualified for because, again, they paid you to do nothing, which was perfect for someone with RA. I was still at Jamba Juice, getting paid minimum wage, wincing as I scooped frozen yogurt into blenders I couldn't grip.

One day—while sitting next to me on the couch as usual—Mom sent me an email about a focus group for Rheumatoid Arthritis patients.

"You're a shoe-in!" was the subject.

"Mom..." I said.

For a couple of reasons, I didn't share her gusto about this focus group.

1) I didn't like the idea of talking about my disease, i.e. pain, weakness, and failure. It was one thing to have this

disease and come to terms with it privately, personally. But to talk about it with others? That sounded terrible.

2) I didn't like the thought of being in a room with other RA patients, where I would probably be the only male, and young person, sticking out like a sore thumb (which everyone present was bound to have).

Mom's rationale was different. She thought it would be an opportunity to get help, to receive comfort. And if it paid? Even better.

"Think of it this way. The disease owes you. Here's your chance to collect," she said. "All the money you'll pay for meds and appointments over the years. Any chance you get to be compensated, you need to take."

I didn't like that: "All the money you'll *pay over the years.*"

I hated thinking about my future with this disease. It wasn't enough to come to terms with having a disease *in the moment,* as a 23-year-old; I also had to come to terms with this thing being here *forever.* Emotionally, as well as financially.

The day of the focus group, I entered a windowless room downtown. There were three other women, one middle-aged, and two seniors. They gave me scornful looks. I could tell they didn't believe I had RA; what 23-year-old male had it, after all? They thought I was one of those people who lied in order to qualify for 200 bucks. My mom's friends had lied to get into focus groups. One of her friends, a woman, once tried to get into a group about shaving razors by saying she had an occasional beard.

"What I'm going to do is show you a series of RA drug advertisements," the facilitator said. She was a part of a marketing firm.

"As a patient who could potentially use these drugs, what

does the picture make you think? Feel?"

For an hour we sat in a circle, analyzing poster board and magazine ads, sharing our opinions on the effectiveness of one ad versus another. *This* picture versus *that* one. With no windows, the air became stale, and I felt like I was in a scene in a dystopian novel in which the villains try to break the hero's will to live.

"And what is happening in this picture? Are you more prone to trying the drug as a result?"

It made me wonder if people actually based their medicine choices on what pictures were more influential between gray-haired women cooking spaghetti versus Hispanic ladies pushing grandchildren in a double stroller.

"Neither," I said.

I was asked again about the old lady spreading mayo on a sandwich, and the black lady zipping her suitcase.

"Neither."

The grandpa shooting hoops with his grandchild, or the lady with the silver bun pointing to the chalkboard with her yardstick?

"Neither."

The other women in the group looked at me pitifully, as if I were standing in front of a class being asked "what's two plus two?" and insisting it was five.

"Maybe if there was an ad with a 20-year-old pitching in a ball game, or a guy putting away a pitcher of beer and laughing with his bros like a 90s cigarette ad. Then I might pay attention. As it is, I'm not sold by seeing Nana joyously push buttons on a TV remote."

The facilitators took notes.

"Really, I only want what will work," I said. "I guess I'd rather trust my rheumatologist about that, not an advertisement wedged between recipes in *Southern Living*. Honestly, I've never read an ad for Humira because I don't read any of the magazines that have RA ads. I don't garden, I don't decorate, I don't bake pies. I'm a baseball player. I'm supposed to be in Belgium pitching right now, and now suddenly, I'm walking with a limp. So it's all very new to me."

I didn't belong in this focus group. Young men were not in RA advertisements. Young men didn't have RA. The women saw me grappling with this. They saw in my face that I felt I should have never come here, that 200 dollars was not worth having my face rubbed in this disease. And I hated their pity.

* * *

I opened the door to find three business-women, of the intimidating variety—high heels, tight fitting gray suits, hair fatigued from product. They looked like they weren't looking for romance, but a lucrative divorce. Without question, they could beat me up. They had briefcases. I was terrified to talk to them for two hours about Rheumatoid Arthritis. But I had agreed to.

A week before, my healthcare provider called asking if I was interested in doing a study on RA.

"Not really," I said, remembering my first experience.

"It pays two hundred and fifty dollars, and you don't have to leave your couch."

"Dammit."

The mom in me said, you can't turn down free money! I heard Charlie, somewhere, agree. *Man up, it's just sitting and talking. You won't ever see these broads again, so who cares? Get paid, dude.*

"If it's alright with you, we're going to videotape this session," one of the women said, situating herself on my couch. "In case we miss something in our notes."

She smiled, as if to say "I just lied. I'm not telling you the real reason."

"I guess."

Out of a briefcase came a light. They bent its long neck and aimed it at me, giving me the feeling of lying in a dentist chair. It wasn't long into the interview before the light had me sweating. I could hardly see the women, just the silhouettes of three perfectly manicured heads of hair. The ambiguity of this was unsettling. Surely, a medical organization wanted to learn how to improve their product marketing, but the conspiracy theorist in me couldn't help but wonder: what if there's more? What if these medications are cancerous, and these women have been sent by the company to gauge whether patients are onto them, or to be sure they remain in the dark?

"Do you have an open dialogue with others about your medication?" they asked.

"Generally, I don't talk about the disease."

"Why is that?"

"A lot of people in my life, even people who have known me for years, don't know that I have it."

The women whispered. I squinted.

"Can you expand a little, if you don't mind, why you don't like talking about it?"

"People treat me differently when they know I have a disease."

"How so?"

"I sort of see the disease as a weakness. I mean, it is. Literally, I am a very weak person. So when people think I'm weak, they treat me like it. They observe me doing menial tasks, watching for me to cringe, or wince. But when I *don't* talk about it, people forget I have it, and then I'm able to act as though I don't have it."

"Can you explain what is toughest about the disease?"

"Not being able to do anything I used to do."

"Can you be specific?"

"Baseball."

"Anything else?" they asked.

"I guess, up until now, I always felt…masculine? I was a little Neanderthal-ish, I'm first to admit, but it was my comfort zone. Then disease came and bam, I felt like I was in Mario Kart when the lightning strikes and shrinks you to a mini-you that just gets run over. Or, another way I look at it is like, being in the wilderness. A couple months ago I was at the top of the food chain, fast, strong, confident. I had no natural predators, right? Now, I'm shrinking, I'm slow, I'm weak. I'm like a slug or something. If this were the wild, and I got this disease, I wouldn't make it one day before I got shredded."

My breathing quickened as I spoke. I heard my volume rise. I sounded like I was yelling at them.

"I also hate that I'm on drugs."

"Why do you say that? Don't they help?"

"I fear the drugs are slowly killing me, for one. I don't trust the pharmaceutical industry to prioritize health over profit."

They asked what meds I was on. I told them Humira, an injection. They asked where I injected it. I said my leg, and they asked if I currently had a dose that they might be able to record me injecting. I told them I only did it once a month, and it wasn't time yet. They asked if I might be able to "cheat" and inject it a little earlier for the sake of research.

"No," I said. They frowned

"Would you be able to take us to your bathroom, and go through the process of an injection, without injecting?" they asked.

"Huh?"

They made thin-lipped adult smiles.

"The people at your headquarters can't envision an injection?" I asked.

"Just in case."

They followed me to my bathroom, watched me as I undid my belt, unbuttoned, and pulled my pants past my knee. The video lady craned to get a better angle. Then, to the women in business suits with their healthy hips and authoritative busts, I unveiled a weak, pasty leg. Looking at it, I panicked, like a realtor showing a particularly unsightful room. Skin sagged from lost muscle like a turkey throat.

"Then," I said, looking at the camera, loud with meant sarcasm, "I execute the very complex and bewildering task of sticking a needle in my leg."

I buckled my pants.

"How do you feel right now?" they asked afterward, back on the couch. They meant my symptoms and their improvement since I'd started the drugs. But I didn't answer it that way.

"Honestly?" I said into the blinding light. "Right now I feel like a zoo animal on display with a huge lump, or a neon ass, or something else that haunts me and fascinates the science world."

"Can you elaborate?"

"People nod and take notes and leave, and I go to sleep and wake up in the same cage."

PART IV:
THE MECCA

31
A CHANCE TO ESCAPE

On a dismal day in late May, 2009, while wearing an orange visor and shouting "Hi!" to thirsty strangers, I got a phone call.

"Sup?"

"Sup."

"You graduate?"

"Yeah."

"Sick."

"Congrats. You comin' home soon?"

"Sort of. Hear me out on this."

I'd known Dave since middle school. We'd played ball at Lowell. He, Charlie and I had been the ambassadors of shenanigans at the school, the beyond-class clowns, the kinds who bordered on expulsion. At school, we'd spent close to every waking moment together. We were both in symphonic band and jazz band. He and I were the only two jocks perhaps in the nation who drove to baseball practice listening to Charlie Parker and Dizzy Gillespie. We drank beer together in the school parking lot before our concerts, spent afternoons hitting in the batting cage. He was a year younger than me, now graduating from UC Davis with a degree in International Affairs. We gave him grief for that because, what was that? I figured he'd be moving back home shortly. Surely, he'd be joining the dismal rat race of college grads moving home with Mom and Dad, needing a job desperately to move out of Mom and Dad's, just like me. Possibly, he was calling about job leads in the city.

"I just got a job in Miami, dude," he said.

Fuck me, I thought.

"Seriously?"

"Yeah."

"Congrats, dude. What is it?"

"It's not like a real job. I mean, it is, but. It's called AmeriCorps. You basically just try to give inner-city kids a chance at a good life."

"Nice."

"It pays dogshit."

"Holla."

"Anyways, check it out. My parents are bequeathing upon me The Rapist Van."

Their Dodge Caravan had over 200k miles on it. A good chunk of those miles were driven in high school, taking us to all of our games, or taking us home after parties. The steering wheel rattled if you went over 30. It looked like something only owned by skinny, pony-tailed creepsters who like to coast slowly by elementary schools.

"I'm driving that thing to Miami."

"Slow lane pimpin'."

"You want in?"

"Cross country in the Caravan?"

"You're just killing time before Belgium anyway, right?"

"Pretty much."

I was pathetic. Hadn't told him, or anyone. Just Kendall, and my parents. I'd mentioned a blown-out elbow to Charlie, but that wasn't the same. It had been nearly a year now with the disease.

"So, you're in?" he asked.

Jamba Juice was going nowhere. I wasn't receiving the national literary acclaim I'd hoped for. My disease was somewhat contained from the meds and I guess from that standpoint things could have been worse. But I was feeling antsy and stagnant in my house. In less than a year, my transition had been: Hawaii, partying, baseball, professional baseball contract, disease, baseball never again, move back into a small room with parents, *pay* money for this room, work at Jamba, feel intense pain in all waking moments.

I'd been telling myself things like, *hey man, it could be worse: you could be homeless. You could be a drug addict. You could have had parents that didn't love you. Your parents could be dead. Or you could have been killed when you were four years old in a civil war in some African country.*

Then I'd think, *no wait, things really do suck, dude. No one else you know has a disease that swooped down just in time to cancel your dreams. No one else has trouble tying his shoes or picking berries at age 24. No one else gets so mad they wish they could punch something, but can't due to having brittle, senior-citizen bones.*

A few days earlier, my high school coach had called, asking if I wanted to come back and help out during the next season. To me, the prospect of being on a baseball field, unable to play, while pimply twerps took the game, and their able-bodied selves for granted, was untenable.

"Let me get back to you, Coach," I'd said. Other phone calls I was receiving in bulk were from Dr. Sherry. I'd see the phone number, click ignore, then feel my phone vibrate with another voicemail that undoubtedly said:

"Hello, this message is for Emil DeAndreis. It's Dr. Sherry and I'm calling about scheduling a checkup, m'kay? I'd like to know how the meds are working. I'd also like you to come in and do blood tests to make sure the meds are not having adverse effects on your organs. How does that sound? M'kay? Please give my assistant a call back soon. Okkkkaa—"

I would have rather been hearing from the CPS agency about a kid I didn't know I had.

"Dude, do you think the Caravan will even make it to Miami?" I asked.

"Probably not."

"I'm having this vision of all four tires simultaneously

exploding somewhere in the dead of Route 66."

"So, you're in?"

All I had in my life was stuff I wanted to get the hell away from. This trip would allow me to drive away from my disease, hospitals, worries about a new job, calls about coaching baseball, calls about the disease. Waking up in a new city each day, sharing the road and diners with strangers—no one had to know who I was.

Days before our departure, Charlie called. We hadn't spoken in months at this point. I hadn't kept up with his stats, didn't know how he'd been playing, or even if he'd been playing. With baseball season in bloom, I'd been doing my best to forget its existence. "I just got promoted," he said.

"What? No way!"

I had to strain to get my note of enthusiasm right. I didn't want him to detect bitterness. To think, in a year or two he could possibly be in the The Show.

"Where's the next stop?" I asked.

"High A ball."

"Where's that?"

"Palm Beach Cardinals, Florida."

"Wow," I said. "Seriously?"

Dave and I would be driving into Florida in ten days.

"Yep."

"When do you leave?" I asked.

"Tonight."

And so it seemed there was something in the cosmos, something spiritual taking form, because suddenly the trip that I'd hoped would take me away from baseball, was going to drive me right back into it.

32
THE NO-HITTER

Originally, it was going to be just me and Dave, taking turns driving through the sunbelt. We would stop, sleep, and eat where we pleased, check out landmarks, have drinks with strangers in unheard-of cities.

Days before our departure, another friend decided to join. Carl also played on our high school baseball team. He was a benchwarmer with muttonchops who often pondered loudly why he wasn't playing. He abandoned summer school at San Diego State for a near-failing grade and drove up to meet us. On the way, his car broke down, permanently, and he rode the rest of the way in a tow-truck, making it just hours before we were to head out.

We left on July 11th, 2009 in the late afternoon. Our first stop: Vegas. We planned to roll in sometime around midnight, check into a greasy off-the-strip motel, gamble what little money we were willing to part with and catch a few hours of sleep before getting back on the road. For the first leg of the trip, Carl was behind the wheel. The weather was mid-90s outside the city. We were past the midday Bay Area traffic of union pickup trucks switching three lanes at once to get the hell home from their jobs. The roads were quiet. Surrounding us were sawdust-gold hills topped with electrical line posts and windmills, filling the space between turnoffs of sunburnt Chevrons. We were listening to old-school Outkast, in tank tops, spitting chew and sunflower seeds into empty water bottles, and I was brought back to high school. I had the distinct feeling of driving in the blazing heat to play a glorious summer game under the lights.

Forget baseball, I told myself.

"I hope Sanchez brings his A game tonight," Carl said. He surfed the radio for KNBR. The Giants game was about to begin. Jonathan Sanchez was the starter. The idea of shutting out baseball was becoming increasingly unrealistic.

In 2009, the Giants hadn't had a winning season in a few years, and all the die-hards were getting ulcers over it. Carl was among the many die-hards I knew, and once he got himself started on the Giants, (or pretty much any topic for that matter), you could forget about peace and quiet for a while.

"The way I see it, the game can go one of two ways tonight," he said. "Sanchez'll either have it, or he won't."

Carl stated this as if it was a bold theory, and not a simple fact of life.

"Sanchez is a feast or famine guy."

Carl was one of those guys who heard ideas on talk radio, then repeated them verbatim as though they were his own.

"He should go back to the bullpen. We need someone else while Randy Johnson's on the DL. I'm not saying I don't like the excitement of Sanchez, but I don't get it. If you can dominate one night, how can you plain *lose* the strike zone another night? And, you know another thing? His attitude doesn't sit with me. It seems like he could take it or leave it, pitching that is. The guy's a pro, and he can take it or leave it? Think of all the guys that don't get a shot."

He was talking about himself. He still held a grudge on our coach about scarce playing time in high school. He believed he had been one good chance, one good coach away from being a pro prospect. Once, he told us: "I'll tell you guys one thing. If I had been 6'6" I would have made it to the NFL. That's a fact."

The thing was, Carl quit football after freshman year.

By eight o' clock the sun had disappeared behind the hills. We were on two lane freeways, tightly passing big rigs with the divider unsettlingly close. There were sudden inexplicable gusts of wind that would jar the archaic van. I was driving and we were listening to the Isley Brothers because the Giant's station was too fuzzy, though last we'd heard, Sanchez was dealing. Carl mentioned how he'd had a feeling all along that Sanchez would be on point that night. Dave let out a deep sigh.

Some more about Carl: he was a connoisseur of the one-sided conversation. He took pride in his capacity for excess, particularly talking. And food. And *definitely* booze. He had an advantageous body for this that turned whatever he ate into freakish muscle. He would often eat two-pound steaks and lick the plate clean, then lick his fingers, no matter who was present. He drank three 40s of Colt .45 to start the night, then got into liquor. And somehow he'd wake up the next morning at five and wonder why no one else was up yet.

"My skills weren't ever put to use on the baseball diamond," he mourned, while dipping Wheat Thins into peanut butter to maximize the calories. "I had at least three tools."

Dave and I both thought to ourselves: *Carl, you had one notable skill, which was hitting a ball five hundred feet foul.* My urge was to say, "Boo-hoo, Carl. If you wanted to play that bad, you should have taken a hundred hacks off the tee a day, you should have honed your swing, you should have put your abnormal muscles to use, you should have given Coach no choice but to play you. Instead, you bitched. You don't have an excuse. You don't have a disease."

I hated these toxic thoughts. I needed to switch the subject. Dave fumbled determinedly to get a clear signal of the Giants game, anything to reroute Carl from his lamentations.

Somewhere along the thin and straight stretch of freeway to Vegas, the signal came in, the unmistakable fuzz of AM radio that blended so smoothly with the ongoing hum of the crowd. It was the eighth inning and the Giants were ahead. Sanchez was throwing a shutout.

"Knew it." Carl said.

Evidently, Sanchez's curve ball was dominating. His fastball was alive, and apparently getting stronger as the innings went on. Then, through static, we gathered from Dave Flemming's careful choice of words that Sanchez had not yet allowed a baserunner. Dave and Carl looked at each other. Had they heard this correctly? It was the eighth inning, and Sanchez was throwing a perfect game? Dave burrowed into the back of the van and pulled the cooler into reach. It had beers icing for later when we were situated in our slummy Las Vegan hotel. Carl giddily rubbed his hands together.

"Dude, our moms are at this game!" Dave remembered. "You think they're aware that a perfect game is taking place?"

"My mom is liable to not know what a perfect game is," I said.

"Our moms may be so worried about our road trip that they don't know what teams are playing."

"On the ground, Uribe…off his chest" John Miller called through the radio. "It'll be a baserunner. And for the first time tonight, Sanchez will pitch from the stretch."

Just like that, in the time it took for Dave to grab beer, the perfect game was gone.

In the end, Sanchez salvaged the no-hitter. It was San Francisco's first no-no since '76, and one of the first reasons for Giants fans to celebrate in years.

And he had to do it on the first night of our road trip.

Dave and Carl put on some Bee Gees to get them in a Vegas mood. They cranked the volume and opened beers. They danced in ways that would repel women completely out of a place of business: violent punches of air, head bobs like chicken seizures. I elected not to dance, using driving as an excuse. Really, I just wasn't that thrilled about the no-no.

My pocket vibrated. It was my dad. I turned down the music and before I could even say hello, Dad was shouting:

"He did it! He did it! Can you even believe it! And, can you believe Mom's there?"

I didn't want to be happy for Jonathan Sanchez. I wanted to *be* him. I didn't want to be a fan. I wanted to be a player.

When I got off the phone I turned the music back up. I wanted to be in Vegas soon, throwing down a few drinks, in a place of lights and noises and distractions. I needed that. Even if I lost money at blackjack, even if drinking wasn't the best idea on my meds. I didn't care. Anything but baseball.

33
THE GRAND CANYON AND ITS HUMBLING WAYS

Carl's hunger began as mild interest.

"I wonder what kind of food Arizona has."

He said it as though there were some culinary allure to the state, as if the turnoffs might yield anything besides gas stations and burger joints.

The last food Carl had eaten was earlier that morning at a gas station on the way to the Hoover Dam. He'd had pink popcorn, and while eating, spent a good deal of time congratulating himself for his success at blackjack the night before. I'd lost $40, Dave had lost $60, and Carl accidentally won $60 while being hammered and not even looking at his cards. He'd almost gotten himself blacklisted for heckling the dealer, "where the fuck is my *cocktail?*" when it was his turn to hit or stay.

Now it was mid-afternoon, we'd just visited the Hoover Dam, and Carl was at a point where he'd have traded every dollar he'd won for some sirloin cuts. We continued down the skinny interstate through Arizona. To the left and right was nothing but flat hard desert and empty powder skies.

"Hmmm. Not a single restaurant," he said. "Where do these people eat?"

"What people?" I asked.

There were makeshift shops under tent overhangs selling Native American dolls. Workers fanned themselves as we passed. Usually there was one rental car parked with a couple of people perusing the goods. But no restaurants.

"Wherever we end up, I'm thinking a steak and shrimp fajita," Carl lusted, "with cheddar. Can you pass me the chew?"

Carl was entering a state of panic. We could see what seemed like hundreds of miles ahead, and there was nothing but dirt, mountains, and sky. No restaurants. Not even a gas station. Not even a vending machine. Dave passed Carl the tin of tobacco. Carl stared at it.

"What?" Dave asked.

"Can you open it for me?"

Dave opened it and handed it over.

Carl stared.

"Can you hold it for me while I pinch?" he asked. "I gotta steer."

"Jesus," Dave sighed, holding the chew.

Carl then overcomplicated the task of steering with one hand and pinching with the other. He spilled half of it on his lap, then smeared the rest into his teeth.

The scenery did not change. The mountain ranges—the enormous rust and auburn colored towers—were like a kind of geological chess game in progress. The ground was cracked and colorless with an infrequent shrub waiting to be struck even more dead by an Arizona thunderstorm.

Then, finally, a sign of civilization graced us: Rosie's Den Café, five miles ahead.

"This place better have some *burgers*," Carl snarled, as though offended the restaurant had not been built 30 miles earlier.

"For all the shit you've been talking, if this place has an eating contest, you're doing it," Dave said.

Leading up to the trip, Carl had repeatedly expressed his excitement at the prospect of our nation's great eating challenges. He'd seen "Man vs. Food" and "Diners, Drive-Ins, and Dives," and watched as overweight semi-celebrities went to small cities and ate their famous heart attack challenges. Carl, derived an exhilaration from eating challenges that bordered on sexual arousal.

We pulled into what looked like a residential house. The sign for the restaurant, Rosie's Den Café, looked sweetly like it was painted for a kindergarten art project. There were three gravel parking spots. Inside smelled like cigarettes and greasy aprons. A biker couple sat at a table, speaking tenderly over patty melts. We sat at the counter and menus were flipped to us by a frumpish-looking waitress in her early 40s. Dave smiled and pointed to the menu.

"Ladies and gentlemen, we have a winner."

"Oh yeah!" Carl said.

"Pancake challenge."

"Nice! Wait! Pancakes?!"

The small diner was silenced.

"Rosie's World Famous Flapjacks. Take the challenge. C'mon. It's only two…" Dave read from the menu. "Let the games begin."

"I HATE PANCAKES."

"Shut up," Dave said.

"I've never ordered a pancake in my life."

"So?"

"I've been waiting all day for some *burgers.*"

The waitress waited.

"Or a T-bone."

He looked at her, as if she had a say in the matter.

"It's just two pancakes," she said, and winked.

"He'll have the challenge," Dave said.

"Pancakes?" Carl cried, to the restaurant, now his audience. "I been dreamin' burgers for hours."

In case this wasn't already crystal clear to everyone.

"What'll ya'll have?" the waitress asked us.

"Burgers," we said in unison; Carl looked like a dog being put out in a storm.

Our burgers came out quick and Carl's dish followed, which

wasn't even fair. My heart clogged on sight. The pancakes did not look like food, but more like slabs of adobe tile. A tank of syrup accompanied them. Carl sank into his chair. Everyone else applauded. The waitresses waited for him to carve his first bite.

"You guys got any fruit?" he asked, annoyed.

"Pardon?"

Carl eyed her, as if to say, you heard me.

"You want *more* food?" she asked.

"Helps my digestion."

"Alright, sport." She disappeared and Carl regarded the plate dourly, like it was the ninth inning and he was up with the game on the line. A bowl of pineapple and strawberries was set next to him. Carl oozed syrup onto the doughy manholes, tore off a sizable flap, wrapped it around a pineapple wedge and commenced his charge.

Half way through the first cake, he was also through half a pineapple, attributing his impressive pace to the fruit. Come the second one, he looked weighted down, constipated. His breathing was heavier. He was being tasked with quite possibly five pounds of dough.

"Strugglin', hun?" the waitress asked.

"No," Carl shot back.

He was not using utensils. Pineapple juice streamed down his arms. He addressed this nuisance by licking his arms, which embedded pancake crumbs into his blonde arm hair. He chomped, sucked, popped and made strange animal noises, and it was clear when he surveyed the small cafe that he was happy to disgust everyone.

Thirty minutes later, Carl was wearing an XXL Pancake Champion shirt from Rosie's Den. We were back in the van, headed east on the lonely, late-afternoon Highway 93 toward the Grand Canyon.

"It was all thanks to the fruit," he said. He wiped his mouth with a napkin. "Couldn't have done it without it."

He was fielding his own postgame interview, answering questions that hadn't been asked.

"I can't wait to find a burger challenge."

As we headed for the Grand Canyon, we listened to Hendrix, Curtis Mayfield, and Wu Tang, and rolled in just as the afternoon began to age into early evening. Everyone in the parking lot seemed appalled as we entered. We didn't understand why until we realized we were blaring "Slob On My Knob" with the windows down.

Moms in summer mumus stood next to their husbands who had cargo shorts and broomsticks for legs. They leaned over and snapped photos of the dam while their kids waited in idle cars playing video games and drinking Mountain Dew.

At the Canyon, we sipped High Lifes, leaning over the edge as the sun moved behind us. I reflected on something I'd seen at the Hoover Dam earlier that morning. Driving through the monument, we'd passed a bronze sculpture of a worker in a hardhat sitting in a rope harness, smiling. I imagined men back then, hundreds of feet in the air, swinging in raggedy lifts, hammering bolts into a mountain, getting sunstroke. And yet there they were, just like the man in the sculpture.

"One day out there and I'd be dead," Dave had said of the statue.

"Oh, yeah. Me, too," said Carl. We stared silently.

"Ah," Carl rethought, "I could probably handle it."

I pictured myself as a worker on the Hoover Dam, having to carry my weight, operating wrenches and sledgehammers and 10-pound bolts, and maneuvering to carry heavy rock from dynamited quarries, pouring millions of pounds of concrete, and having to grip and pull metal cords and crank shit into place. Every day, over and over, to survive.

What if I'd had that job and got Rheumatoid Arthritis?

What if I'd had a family to look after, and gotten this goddamned disease? That would have been it for us. Sometimes I couldn't even pop open a shampoo bottle; how could a family have depended on me?

"I heard he got the Rheumatism," people would grumble about me at the tavern after work when suddenly I stopped showing up.

And that would be that.

Now we stood looking out over the Grand Canyon as the sun moved behind us. Little was said, which was partly because we'd just spent the whole day in the car talking without cease. But I also thought we were intimidated by something so big as the Grand Canyon and how small it made us feel. The cliffs grew a deeper and deeper orange with the sunset, and then looked like rare and medium and well done tri-tip once the sun was gone. The air got crisper.

"How far do you think it is across?" Dave asked.

"I'd guess but I'd be wrong," I said.

Carl closed one eye, doing the math, opened his mouth to speculate, then decided against it.

As long as we could see it, we stared.

"How is this thing even possible?" Dave asked after a while.

34
COACH CLARK

"Albuquerque Isotopes Park, next right," Dave said, noting the road sign as we passed by. I had an urge to say something, but held my tongue.

"I've heard that stadium is sick," Dave said.

We'd awoken early to a calm and blue Arizona morning. The air was crisp and dry and smelled like trees. Our Flagstaff hotel looked like it had been plucked off an interstate and dropped directly on a forest with hardly even a road leading to it. Dave and I cooked oats on a little burner he brought. We felt rustic and from a past time, like maybe Jack Kerouac, or Lewis and Clark forging across the west. Carl ordered a chicken fried steak from the hotel restaurant for $20 dollars and ate it with his hands and then spent 40 minutes in the bathroom launching pyrotechnics. Now we were on highway 40. Our next stop was Houston. Coach Clark lived there now, and we were bunking for a night at his apartment.

The Albuquerque Isotopes stadium was shrinking behind us. I craned my neck to watch it.

"I pitched there," I blurted. "2007."

"Isn't it a minor league stadium?" Carl asked.

"Yeah, but University of New Mexico also plays there."

I told them about how I came in after the starter had given up three straight homers. I told them about the check-swing triple I gave up, about the bullpen phones, our trainer Dick threatening to strangle us. We all laughed. The memory felt nice. I wasn't sure why. Of course, I'd tried to avoid thoughts of baseball because inevitably they led to thoughts about my disease and crumbled career, but something about that fateful outing in New Mexico felt like a flashback of a fun birthday or sleepover from childhood. True, rich nostalgia, because these baseball memories were the only ones I had, and I was starting to realize I wasn't getting any more.

To pass the time, we derived outrageous hypothetical events and decided whether or not they'd ever happened in baseball history.

"Has anyone ever died following a triple play?" I asked.

"Like, someone was dead on the field after a triple play?" Dave asked.

"Yeah."

"I think it's happened," Carl said.

"Sometime in the 1800's when baseball was new and rugged. And everyone was drunk with mustaches. Probably in some exhibition game, a Boston Bean tagged a guy out by pounding the ball into his face. Like, before it was a rule that you couldn't," Dave said.

"Good logic."

"But really, back to what matters, which is. Has anyone ever shit in a Mike and Ike's box?" Dave asked.

"Mmmmm," Carl appreciated.

"Wow. Good one."

"Thanks."

"I'm pretty sure *Charlie's* done that," Carl said.

We ran into a rare stretch of Route 66 with zero gas stations. With all the gas pedal labor Carl had done, the needle deflated down past E. The fuel sign was on for 30 minutes and on the flat highway we felt we could see miles ahead without any gas stations. The van detected the temperature outside to be 98 degrees. It was a bad place to run out of fuel.

"Turn off the AC," Dave said.

"That saves gas?" Carl asked.

"I'm not sure."

Then there was a very slight hill which seemed to descend endlessly to the horizon. We put the car in neutral and coasted down in the slow lane. We slowed to about 20 miles per hour. We waved at passing cars, hysterically laughing with our hands out the window, mimicking children on a rollercoaster. At the bottom of the hill a few miles later was a gas station with one pump that seemed to have been built in the 60s. Our car was actually making those puttering noises when we rolled in to the pump. Carl needed another chew to relax again and we all needed water.

"This gas station saved us, man!" Dave cried in the snack shop, which had things like Cowtails and RC Cola covered in dust among other items which I thought stopped existing after "Leave It to Beaver."

A wrinkly man behind the counter nodded indifferently.

"If I had a nickel for every time someone came in here and said that," he said, then stopped what he was doing, looked up and squinted. All the wrinkles in his face deepened. He looked out the window, seeming to conjure some reflective grandiose notion. Then he looked like he might've been asleep.

"I wouldn't be working at this gas station," he said finally. By this time the car was gassed up. We hopped back on the 10-East for Houston. This meant a few more hours of flat roads and tumbleweeds rolling like pinballs between turnoffs for Hardees and McDonalds and Texacos.

At some point in Texas, Carl achieved a speeding ticket. The silver cop SUV had appeared behind us seemingly out of nowhere, and the paralyzing, surreal feeling of seeing cop lights and sirens go off from behind hit us all. As the engine clicked and cooled on the side of the highway, we waited for the Texan cop to come issue the law. Carl reached for the Skoal tin. The situation necessitated a chew. The car was dead silent until Dave exploded a laugh into his hand.

The cop handed Carl his ticket, then for five more minutes

he reminded Carl that he had just received a ticket. When the cop left we had a photo shoot with a disgruntled Carl and his speeding ticket. Then we text-messaged everyone the news.

Some of the replies were:

"What took him so long?"

"What was his excuse?"

"Wow you'll never hear the end of this."

"I was only setting the cruise control," Carl snarled, unaware of the texts flying in. "You have to accelerate the car to set the cruise control."

Carl obsessively repeated this for two hours. We calmed his nerves with promises of more eating competitions eating competition for him tomorrow.

"We'll find you burgers made of bacon parts sandwiched in chicken cutlets," Dave soothed.

Carl threw the ticket onto the floor of the car with the accumulated trash.

I began to feel anxious about Coach Clark. Last I'd seen him, I'd been in the best shape of my life.

It had been just a year since then, but it felt like a whole era had passed, like I was gearing up for a ten-year reunion, self-conscious about my gray hair. It was clear I hadn't been lifting or doing anything baseball-related and I feared the part of our conversation when he asked: "whatever happened with pro ball?"

On the I-5, Dave, Carl and I were in grease-stained, over-worn wife-beaters, sweating after turning off the AC to eat up less gas. We had half-beards. The floor of the van was indiscernible through empty wrappers of seeds, pork rinds, banana peels, tins of Skoal, and the latest addition, Carl's ticket.

"Emil, did you bring your glove?" Dave asked at some point that afternoon as we neared Houston. I felt a surge of panic, the same kind of panic I felt about seeing Clark. It was akin to claustrophobia.

"Nah. Still resting the arm," I said.

"Yeah?" he asked, puzzled. "When you going to Belgium again?"

"Uh, next month," I said, with no conviction.

"Yeah. Hey," Carl said. "If you need someone to work you out? On this trip? I got plenty of exercises that you can do with just your body that are great for a pitcher. Just let me know."

Carl was finishing up his kinesiology degree at San Diego State, getting ready to become a personal trainer. I'd spent my college off-seasons doing obscure workouts out in his basement because I was too broke for a gym membership. We'd power clean, front squat, take a sledgehammer to a big tire in his backyard. One of his workouts entailed walking 100 pound cinderblocks in circles. We'd pushed his baby-blue Toyota Tercel down the block for exercise. On a few occasions, I puked up a lung. I could still smell the laundry detergent air of his basement. I could still hear Tech N9ne and Wu Tang Clan from his Tercel speakers. I missed those summer mornings. I missed terribly the feeling of being strong.

I texted Kendall.

I miss you.

Really, I was just feeling down, and she was pretty much the only person I allowed to be vulnerable around.

Maybe I can come drive down and see ya'll when you're in Jacksonville, she said.

I'd like that.

We met Clark at a bar in Houston. He now looked like a porn star—sunburnt, sunglass-tan, angular cheek bones, jocular smile. He had the ultra-trim build of someone getting in shape for a triathlon.

We got into baseball stories immediately. What else could we have talked about? Back and forth we went: the dreary Uncle Billy's buffets, the time Wichita State scored 20 against us and then *their* coach gave us a pep talk. How Coach called our utility infielder Christian Stephenson Stephen Christianson for the kid's whole career. How Coach's sign for a pick off was to indiscreetly chirp "Pick 'im! Pick 'im off!" from the dugout. How one time I struck someone out and the batter was so mad he went back to the dugout, and slammed his helmet so hard it bounced fifteen feet high, out of the dugout, and into the stands. How Coach E never cut anyone from our tryouts.

"That's not true," I said. "Remember? Coach E did cut a guy once. He came to tryouts wearing a bucket hat and Teva sandals. The knuckle baller. He raised his hand while Coach E was talking and said 'I have a heart condition, and can drop dead at any minute.'"

"Coach E cut that guy?" Coach Clark asked in disbelief.

"Another pitcher, please!" I ordered.

I kept the conversation where it was because I didn't want it to drift to my pro career. I didn't want him to ask whatever came of the YouTube clips of my bullpen, or why I was so thin. I didn't want to have to say that the stories we were telling were going to be the last baseball stories I would have.

In our periphery the homerun derby was airing on TV. We were lazily attentive as Prince Fielder hit bomb after bomb. Brandon Inge put up a big fat goose egg and we laughed about it. We went through too many pitchers to count. The more I drank, the less I cared about my health, and what I was possibly doing to it by drinking. Then we went to another bar and did rows of shots, served on a ski, which were creatively named "Shot Skis." Carl fanatically overdrank. Dave was observed by staff vomiting in a urinal, then invited to leave. He got behind the wheel and drove us to a taco place. Carl ordered nine tacos. Clark's friend "Rusty" arrived. He wasted no time before laying out to Carl the importance of diversifying his portfolio and stock options. Carl was blacked out and didn't even own a check book. Back at Clark's place, Dave passed out on the carpet before eating a single taco. Carl ate his nine tacos, then ate Dave's. I had the spins. Carl was hiccupping his fifteen tacos. Clark called over a girl and had some needlessly loud sex.

I lay on the couch amidst the taco wrappers. I thought, two years ago this night would have been considered a groundbreaking success—drinking, bros, tacos. But now, not so much. It felt weird. It wasn't that I had *outgrown* nights like this. After all, we were in our early 20s—*the* age for drinking, bros, and tacos. But something felt inauthentic. I was no longer the person from the stories we'd told tonight, but I'd carried myself as though I was. I felt like I'd committed identity theft, of myself, if that was possible.

If Clark knew the *real* me now, the me who couldn't even *grip* a baseball, he'd probably laugh. We'd laugh at me together, just like we'd laughed at Brandon Inge as he failed to hit a single homer in the derby. And it had only been a year ago that Clark was sending me into games, watching my bullpens, calling "Atta babe!" from the dugout, video-recording me pitch to help me get a pro contract. Rheumatoid Arthritis had taken the person I thought I was, and turned me upside down. It had taken my body from me when I needed it most.

I woke up thirsty and swollen, hardly able to turn the faucet or bend my fingers around my phone to check the time. It was eight a.m. and Carl was already trading time between finger pushups and loud sighs, his way of sending us the message that he was ready for us to be awake. In my crippled state, his pushups felt like a form of bullying.

Soon, Coach Clark sauntered out of his room in his boxers. I wanted to get out of there before I blew my cover and he saw my deformed fingers, or my wincing as I lifted my travel bag into the van.

"So down the road there's this place, the Itty Bitty Burger Barn. They got a big burger challenge. It's a mountain of cholesterol with jalapenos."

Carl was eagerly packing his bags. We went out on Coach Clark's lawn barefoot. It was already ninety degrees.

"Come visit us in San Francisco," Dave said. "We'll take care of you."

"Thanks for the burger rec," I said. We clapped hands, hugged. Then we were off, drowsy, relying on the air conditioner as if it were life support, as we closed in on Florida—and Charlie. We never spoke about my career. He never asked. Maybe he saw the writing on the wall. Maybe he'd noted the famished look of my arms. Maybe he'd just forgotten about the career altogether. Maybe he'd moved on. And maybe it was time I did the same.

35
JACKSONVILLE

We'd driven through syrupy sun and thunderstorms for eight hours. We'd passed hundreds of Waffle Houses, and driven alongside thousands of white guys in trucks who sported farmer's tans and Bass Pro Shops hats. At one point, we filled up the tank at a Chevron and Dave was nearly struck by lightning. He leapt like a cat and we all fell over laughing, and then it stormed like hell on us.

Finally, we were in Jacksonville, pulling next to her Jeep Wrangler with the top down.

The first thing that struck me was her smell. She smelled like soft skin and shimmery hair and peach freckles dotting her nose. I hadn't smelled anything like her in months—particularly in the past week in a van with Dave and Carl. Then her smile registered—her set of improbably white teeth—which was like a Disney animal singing a song. My arms hugged her in the parking lot of Jacksonville's Super 8 motel, wrapped around her waist, fingers through her belt loops, and I felt a surge of flu-ish warmth.

"Ha A'm Kimball," she told Dave and Carl. Then she came back to me. Her hand found mine and there was the uncertainty and foreignness of touching a stranger, but also a comfort and yearning. We went to our room to unpack before dinner. The last time we'd been in a hotel was Manteca, when my elbow started to hurt.

Our eye contact was full of the wonder of: *are things the same?* We made immediate love. Carl called in the middle, likely with questions about exactly how *soon* we might be hungry for dinner. I picked up the phone and spiked it down. Kendall clung to me, looked hungrily at my body as though nothing had changed since I was the kid in Hawaii. She held my hand even though our fingers didn't fit.

At the sports bar where we ate dinner, it was "Lady's Night," which meant beer was unlimited for chicks, but served in very small cups. Kendall was the only female in the bar under 50 and not in an XL men's shirt. Carl watched adoringly as she chowed on spicy wings. When she walked away to the bathroom, he said "I need a southern girl."

In the bath after dinner, Kendall asked delicately about my joints, as if my disease was so painful that it hurt to be asked questions.

"I might just coach high school ball," I said, splashing water restlessly.

"Good, baby," she said. "That'd be just fine." Her *fine* sounded like *fan*. She said it so simply, so sincerely, as if to her pro ball in Belgium was a distant second to coaching high school ball with a disease.

"Get out, I'ma give you a massage," she said, and then she told me I looked nice in reference to the weight I'd lost.

"The good news, from this whole mess, is now I can see your abs some."

Abs suhm.

Her massage was tender where I was swollen, near my right wrist, near my left knee, and firm in the places far from brittle joints, like my calves, my shoulders. I wondered why anyone loved me this much. We slept snug and woke up in the same position, glued to each other.

In the morning, everyone hopped in her Jeep. The top was down, and the doors were gone. We drove to the Jacksonville beach, where the crowd was junior college kids on summer break. There were white guys with Eminem hair, and black guys with dreads. The girls were sexy in a repellent way, if that was possible. Their bodies were flawless, and their clothes purposely skanky, but they smoked cigarettes and looked jaded as though they'd already been through numerous custody battles. I couldn't imagine a higher tattoo-per-capita area in America.

"Let's play whiffle ball homerun derby," Kendall suggested.

"Yes!" Dave said, as if he'd been trying to explain a logic that finally made sense to someone.

We devised rules and boundaries. Carl took the game very seriously and ended up tied for last with Kendall.

"I'm too strong," Carl said. "Seriously. It puts too much backspin on the ball."

"Me too," Kendall said, and flexed her muscles.

During my at-bats, I fouled pitches back or squibbed them into a spinning blur mere inches from my feet. Occasionally I hit a homerun, occasionally I outright swung and missed, and I smiled and just kept swinging and kept no tally. It was the first time in over a year I had swung a bat (Unlike Carl, I was not too strong; the ten-ounce bat was the only kind I could swing). I was actually smiling, like the old ladies in the RA commercials. In that moment, I thought, *had there been one RA ad from the Focus Group that I vibed with, it would have shown young buddies and a girlfriend playing whiffle ball on a white sand beach.*

I was flooded with memories.

Dad and me out in a eucalyptus-filled park, bonking jumbo whiffle balls with a red bat, being cheered on by strangers. My one homerun in high school, which was a sharp ground ball on a field without a fence. Playing "The Game" with Charlie in the cage after school every day until the sun was gone and we couldn't see the ball anymore. Hitting a ball to the warning track in Santa Clara when Coach E let the pitchers take batting practice senior year, and begging him to give me a few more so that I might put one out. The lazy, glorious practices in Hawaii, when pitchers spent hours with fungoes, hitting grounders to infielders, grounders in the hole, choppers, slow rollers, double-play balls. I recalled the excitement of being in the on-deck circle during our championships at AT&T Park, swinging the weighted bat me and Charlie made (a normal wooden bat with stones duct-taped to it), thinking *just what if I actually hit a splash hit right now?* There was no way I could even pick that heavy bat up now; I'd been more of a man at 16 than I was now. But in that moment on the beach, I didn't mind.

Kendall lay on the beach tanning, with sunglasses and salt-clumped hair. She was so beautiful. And she still loved me, skinny arms, bony wrists and all. Carl and Dave waded in the mild waves, praying for the tattooed Jacksonville babes to float in their direction. I stood in the sand swinging.

After lunch, a thunderstorm exploded overhead, and we had to pull over and hysterically peel back the roof of the Jeep. By the end we were soaked and shrieking in unfounded delight. Kendall and I said goodbye, kissed with soaked lips in the after-drizzle of the storm, and she cried. The trip felt so short. I hadn't gotten used to her smell. Each time we touched I almost flinched from the heavy sensation it gave me. Watching her cry as we drove off was a devastating thing, like watching a child confused by the newness of pain.

Dave and Carl said little, respecting the moment, perhaps feeling melancholy themselves. They let the music of *40 oz. To Freedom*—an album that depicted so purely the angst and loss and excitement of our early 20s—do the talking as we entered the homestretch.

36
WATCHING CHARLIE

The Cardinals had set Charlie up in a condo in Jupiter with a couple other guys from the team. We coasted the ailing van into his driveway after driving into a handful of wrong cul-de-sacs, waving at strangers in their windows.

Finally, Charlie charged out of his door in a Cardinals tank-top and stained basketball shorts hollering "YEEEEAAAAAAAH!" He set a coal grill on his sidewalk, a cooler of Natty Light, and lawn chairs. The sun fell behind the beige houses as the beers became crushed cans. We (Carl) went through a pack of Hebrew Nationals and a tin of Skoal. It was the kind of dinner that made a human desperate for a cup of water.

"Man," Charlie sighed and smiled. He was happy to see us. Maybe even relieved. No one had visited him since he'd been drafted, not in rookie ball for the Batavia Muckdogs or low A ball for the Quad Cities River Bandits. He'd been on this journey alone for the most part, and I hadn't even considered that until that moment out there on his sidewalk, hearing his sigh. I felt bad to have lost touch with him over the past year, to have stranded a best friend.

"The characters you meet out here, man. I'm telling you. The Bible Belt of America produces people you can't fathom."

"Exactly," Carl said vaguely.

"I played with a pitcher who was so devoted. Dude, we had pregame meetings with the coach talking strategy. Coach would say, 'Ok, how do you wanna pitch this guy or this guy? This guy is a first pitch swinger. This guy chases 'em up high. This guy is a big guesser. He gets jammed later in the count.' And you know what the dude said? He said 'I ain't bitin' my nails. God'll decide. It's his plan.' It's like, bro, this is professional baseball, what the hell is wrong with you?"

"What happens when he gets shelled?" Dave asked.

"He just goes back to the clubhouse and says, 'Whelp? God didn't want me to have it today. Oh well...'"

"I'm like. I *wish* I thought that little about shit," Charlie said. "I might play better. Definitely would sleep better."

He was antsy. Maybe a tad high strung. I saw his neck veins as he talked. Wrinkles creased the sides of his eyes from sun. I wondered what High School Charlie would have said about this. What antidote would he have for the stress? Would he tell him he ought to just Man Up and stop overthinking?

"We have a clownish Dominican lefty that throws legitimately in the 70s," Charlie said. "I know for a fact he's pitched drunk. He straight up has beers in his locker. And he wears women's jeans."

"The good life," Dave said.

"I had a coach who was a downright racist," Charlie continued. "The kind you thought only existed in Mark Twain books. He heard I was Jewish and thought it was the funniest thing ever, like it was a growth on my dick. I'd heard he was going to have a baby boy, so I asked him what he was thinking about naming him. He said 'Oh I dunno, Jimmy, Johnny,' then he looked at me and said '*Adolf.*'"

"Your *coach?*" I asked.

"He made a joke of segregating the buses one time. The nicest fucking kid you've ever met, Jermaine, he told him, no, Jermaine, you're on the black bus. Ha, ha. But, you could tell, he really meant it."

We were captivated, like hearing folk tales of how humans once were.

"These are real people, dude! And the craziest thing? These people I'm around? They think *they're* normal. And even crazier?

They're *good* at baseball. Somehow! They can throw a baseball 95 fucking miles an hour. They can barrel a ball and send it... just. It's like war footage of bazookas, some of the homeruns. And I have to worry that they might take my job. There's guys in the bullpen that look past the left field fence during games and fantasize about taking out their Glock, *which they've brought to the fucking ballpark,* and hunting down a buck."

We sighed dramatically. We didn't really know what to say.

At this point, Charlie's roommate Adron Chambers moseyed out of the house in only tighty-whities. He was a short African-American outfielder from Mississippi State who would go on to get a World Series ring with the Cardinals in 2011 as a pinch runner, but now, he was just standing essentially naked on the sidewalk, scoping out our gathering.

"I'd give anything to go back to high school baseball, dude," Charlie said after a while. We were kind of quiet. The irony of his statement being: dude, you're a pro, you're living every kid's dream.

"Here he go again," Adron said.

"Things were simple," Charlie went on. "We played to win. That was all there is to it."

He spoke of how in pro ball, the innocence of the game— the reason we ever loved it to begin with—was buried under the stress to perform and the hope that nobody came along that was better. Hardly anyone at his level cared about winning the game. There wasn't the brotherhood like in high school. He couldn't help but worry what the coaches and general managers said of him after a bad game.

"Nobody gives a fuck about you out here. I'm not feeling sorry for myself. I know I'm a lucky guy. They just don't care if you're hurt. And if you're slumping, your job is in jeopardy. Especially at this level. Right, Adron?" Charlie asked.

"Amen, reverend," Adron said, then inspected his belly button. He went inside.

"Are they going to bench me?" Charlie continued. "Are they going to release me? Are they going to sign someone better? I'm a .300 hitter, but guys that got drafted higher than me, with bigger signing bonuses, play more than me, even if they're hitting a buck-twenty. They're going to give Brett Wallace more chances to fail. He was their first rounder. I was fourteenth. It's just how it goes. It's partly because they're good and deserve a chance, but mostly because organizations have too much pride. They want to feel like their instincts are sharp and their dicks are huge."

The next night we sat in the stands and watched the Palm Beach Cardinals. Charlie was in the bullpen to start the game. I observed the players, their nuances, their nonchalance in the dugout, their practice swings. I took note of their walkout songs, who chose rap and who chose country. I noticed who chewed tobacco, who chewed gum, who ate seeds one at a time and who ate them by the cheek-full, who seemed out of shape with love handles and double chins, who seemed clumsy with big feet and bow-legs. I noted who insecurely looked in the crowd, and who went about their business as if there weren't a single person watching. I noted who wore a jacket in the heat, and who seemed to daydream. I wondered what their daydreams were.

Suddenly I felt like a kid again, going to minor league games with Dad. Over spring break, my family would always go to Palm Springs to visit my nana, and in the mid-90s, Palm Springs had a minor league team, the A Angels. The sky was forever cotton candy at the time of first pitch. The serenity of the crowd, the closeness of the players and the intimate sound of the *thwack* of the bat—it was all an irreplaceable peace, a lullaby. I always cared more about foul balls and autographs and playing catch in the parking lot and ice cream than watching the game.

"Watch the baseball for two innings, then ice cream," Dad would say.

I remembered middle school with Charlie at our All Star tryouts, when he looked like a trucker with a unibrow. And improbably, that yokel became my catcher and best friend. I pitched to him in suburban night games, in muggy and floral Hilo, at AT&T Park, in cities with names we never cared to learn. Coaches, even our parents, hardly recognized us without the other. Then we went separate ways, me to the islands, him to Cal. We had our separate careers, and we both earned professional careers. Except now, there he was. And here I was.

In those steel bleachers the stadium lights took over, as the sky grayed, and I sipped Coke from a souvenir cup, salivated from the buttered popcorn, malt chocolate, and foaming beer in the air. As I watched the teams with slight envy and concealed amazement—like I had as a child when I fell in love with the game—I realized I had entered a realm of fanhood. And I knew right then that it was permanent.

Charlie was playing.

I was watching.

A smile spread across my face. It was not a coming-to-terms smile, or a congratulating-someone-for-beating-me smile, but something else, like I'd long been the butt of a joke and finally realized the joke was on me, and had been on me all this time. It was a smile that said "Ok, I get it. Good one. I get it now."

37
ALUMNI GAME

In 2010, my first year coaching, I resented my players. Practices conflicted with daily naps. The kids seemed to take the game for granted. During warm-ups their conversation centered around "where the party at?", and who would squash who in video games, and who would trade who in fantasy football. It wasn't much different from when I was in high school, but for some reason now it appalled me. These were kids with young and able bodies: why weren't they overly gracious for the opportunity to play? Why weren't they hanging on my every word of wisdom and begging for more? I expected them all to want to play college ball at all costs, to hate losing with a fiery passion.

I didn't understand that they were kids, busy with their own lives, and that baseball was not their glaring priority. They didn't know me, or care about my past. All they knew was what they had been told, that I was a good ball player in high school and college. And I got the feeling they suspected it was bullshit. Who could blame them? If I was so *good*, why wasn't I still playing? If I was *good*, why was I coming back to coach at my old high school? The only people who did that in their 20s were losers.

I was cranky and short with them. When they took goofy swings in the cages, when they cut corners on team runs, when they came back to the dugout smiling after a strikeout, or whenever I got the sense they could take or leave baseball, I laid into them with deranged sermons that went right over their heads.

"You guys show up and play without *passion*, you'll go onto the field and lose. You play soft, you'll lose. You want to talk about fucking video games? You know what that makes you? Nothing. Life forgets you."

Speeches like that undoubtedly made them want to lose.

I avoided throwing batting practice. They wanted to face my D1 arm but I told them it wouldn't be fair. They smiled naively. I intentionally arrived to games just before the start so I could avoid being asked to hit infield practice because I could hardly swing a bat most days. I couldn't bear the thought of high schoolers putting the pieces together and realizing that their tough jock coach was weaker than most of their grandmothers.

As pitching coach, I called the pitches and assigned hellish postgame runs. I also took the liberty of reminding them that sooner than they thought, the game they'd played their whole lives would be gone, in most cases forever.

We were eliminated in the playoffs that year. Every senior's baseball career ended. No one went on to play college ball; I'd likely spoiled their love for the game. When the year ended, I had this sort of ugly satisfaction knowing they wouldn't have a chance to ever do what I did. It was sick, truly, and it came from a place inside me created by the disease. I knew that I was no longer a baseball player, but I still had trouble being around those who still *could* play. I was having trouble finding my place in the game.

That year I played my first alumni game. I hadn't ever felt more anxiety. My heart drummed as I suited up. I wrapped my wrist in electrical tape, the only kind of tape my dad had in the garage. I took an ace bandage and wound it tightly around my left knee. I lathered my elbow in IcyHot which I'd bought for this occasion, as though it might improve anything.

The anxiety came from the thought of being outed at the game. Having a wrist unable to swing a bat or hold the weight of my glove or withstand the impact of catching the ball, having a knee so blown up that I only hobbled, having people watch and wonder quietly *didn't he just finish college ball?*

I showed up to find 20 or so alumni, each in different gear from the spanning eras they had belonged to the program. I heard the groans of people airing out their first tosses since last year's alumni game. I wore UH Hilo gear instead of Lowell gear as a pathetic badge to commemorate how much better than them I was. Just to make sure they knew.

Those who recognized me came up and said hi. People started with the talk of me throwing a complete game and I shook my head and said, no: this game was for everyone else to play. I was trying to pass myself on as the politician going to a function just to show face.

"You're not going to pitch at all?" someone asked.

"Those guys see my arm all the time in batting practice," I lied, "They need some new looks."

"How was Hawaii?" people asked, and those who were too old to know saw my jacket and asked "You played for Hawaii?"

"Yeah."

"Wow, what years?"

"'04 to '08."

"No way," they said. "So you just finished last year?"

It must have been hard to believe. I was a bit hunched over, almost *skeletal*, while everyone else seemed to be getting wider with age. I already wanted to leave. I grabbed one of the beers from the case resting on the bench which was commonplace at every alumni game.

I sat the bench the majority of the game, allowing people to assume that, having just finished a D1 career, I was here just to catch up and not stoop to taking an alumni game seriously. Really, I would have given anything for an at-bat.

The Lowell players occasionally beckoned me to join the game.

"You're scared, Coach!" they called.

"Shut up before I come in and mow you down," I called back.

We all laughed. I was on my second beer. I was terrified to be near the mound.

After every inning, people modestly came up and asked if I wanted to pitch.

"No, thanks," I said.

"You sure?" they asked. "Not like this would be any fun compared to Hawaii."

"Let Jake go one more," I said of the guy who'd just thrown a wobbly inning.

After my third Sierra Nevada, I didn't care that I hurt. Shit, I *wanted* to hurt. I got in the on-deck circle, buzzed, disoriented in a helmet. I labored a couple slices of the bat through the strike zone. All of the Lowell players shook the fence, talked playful trash.

"Whoa, nice hack, coach!"

I looked like the weak and confused kid at tryouts who slumps up to bat having never swung in his life, the kid who went to tryouts because his mom said "just give it a try."

My players ragged on me from their dugout, yelling the phrases I'd yelled at them all year.

"Don't step in the bucket!"

"Short swing Coach, short swing!"

"Head in the zone from start to finish."

I swung at the first pitch, slow, late and loopy. My players erupted.

"Have another!"

The alumni and parents in the stands chuckled. There was always an assistant coach that had played for Lowell who, at alumni games, got heckled by the current players. It was all harmless fun.

I got back in the box and resolved to swing as hard as I could at the next pitch, wherever it was, however ugly the swing, however much it hurt. It was right down the middle, no movement, probably 65 mph. I stepped in the bucket. My arms were long, not strong enough to keep the swing compact. I was completely sawed off; the ball hit inches up the handle from my hand and it sent a resounding shock through my swollen fingers and wrist and elbow, so bad I actually stood at home and shook my hands instead of running. Everyone laughed. I laughed. The ball dribbled toward the shortstop only somewhat faster than a bunt. I broke into a hobble toward first, and then gave up on even trying, and broke down into a waddle. People assumed I stopped because I didn't want to humor such a pathetic baseball performance with serious hustle. But they were wrong: I couldn't run. I got back to the dugout, hiding there the rest of the game, and insisting others hit in my place.

This was baseball, and now I hated it.

PART V:
A FAN'S NOTES

38
RE-BAPTIZED INTO BASEBALL

In the months following the alumni game, in some form or another, I told people about my disease. It was better than everyone asking, *whatever happened with Belgium,* or worse, not asking and just assuming I'd been making it up. People got the hint that I didn't want their concern, that I didn't want them asking how I was holding up. Sometimes I limped, and they acted like they weren't seeing. At poker, I shuffled cards with difficulty, and my friends just kept watching Sportscenter and talking away, just how I wanted.

I made a couple of life changes. First, I quit Jamba Juice. Because seriously, enough was enough: I was 25, being told to wear an orange visor and prance to 80s pop for minimum wage. I didn't pull the epic *Half-Baked* quitting scene *(fuck you, fuck you, fuck you, you're cool, fuck you)* like I wanted to. I just kept cancelling my shifts, seeing how long I could hold onto my employee discount. For a while I was this huge creeper that called asking for the manager; when she was there, I hung up, and when she wasn't, I went in and ordered unjustifiable numbers of smoothies, until one day I went in, and the discount card was declined. I'd been "let go."

I signed up to be a substitute teacher. All the techie jobs were starting to take over the city, and they provided services I either resented or didn't understand, so I didn't join the start-up culture. (Plus, to be clear, I probably would not have been hired even if I did apply; my skillset did not qualify me for *any* handsome paying job). To become a substitute, all you needed was a college degree and some verification that you weren't a molester or a convicted murderer. The day I was fingerprinted for the job, I felt so grateful that after all my adolescent bullshit, I had not amassed a criminal record, never punched a bouncer when being dealt with, never drunk-driven into a cop car, had never taken a leak in front of an elementary school field trip. Something else that made me grateful was that substitute teaching paid me enough for my next move: out of my parents' house.

My new roommate was Mack. He'd been Lowell's assistant coach my freshman year. He was six years older than me. My rent at his house was so cheap because a) he had rent control, and b) the house was rotting; no one who wasn't homeless would ever agree to live there. (Besides me). It resembled the apocalyptic squat house of *Fight Club*—brown toilet water, dog-clawed wood floors, years of marijuana puffed into the walls, beach sand in the beds, central heating which, if turned on, pushed out a lukewarm fart. Roof access was a perk, but once an overweight visitor walked out to enjoy the sunset and fell through.

Everything about the operation was sketchy, such as: I had no idea what the lease was, no idea what other people in the house paid. I never saw an electric bill, or a water bill. Our water was shut off intermittently, our power too. We got used to candles, and drinking water from our earthquake kit. I had to shower occasionally at my parents'.

One part of the house that *wasn't* decaying was the 40-inch flat screen TV. Mack had once held it as collateral from a "friend" who owed him a few hundred bucks, and decided he wanted to keep it.

If I was hearing someone else talk about Mack, I'd have two questions. One: why is Mack growing weed and running a squat and forcefully, and permanently, borrowing TVs at the age of 31? The other question would be: Why did you move in?

Regarding the first question: Knowing Mack's personal history, I know he's come a long way. He grew up in a drug house—like real drugs. Dad was not there. There were no family dinners, no warm Christmas mornings and presents under the tree. He went nights without food. He went through periods of homelessness, sleeping at friends' or cousins' houses or even outside—anywhere to get away from the people staying in his house. Before he was 13, he had to defend his mom from druggies. He became the man of the house all too soon.

Mack's stepdad was related to Orlando Cepeda, and was a great baseball role model in his own right. Mack's fondest memories were of family picnics. He got to play catch with Orlando. His stepdad would hit him groundballs forever.

"Necesitas bailar con la pelota, hijo," his stepdad would tell him. *"Suave como agua."*

His stepdad told him to watch the Braves games—Maddux, Glavine, and Smoltz—on TBS, and write down what pitches he thought they'd throw, then write down what pitch they actually threw. Mack did this better than any homework for school, and he grew into a great hitter as a result.

Orlando taught him the importance of swinging like a man, and "using a man's bat." "Don't think. See the ball, hit the ball. Jump on fastballs early in the count," he'd tell Mack, "No one's going to throw you junk if you can't hit the heat."

In 1999, a senior at Lowell, he was the best ballplayer in San Francisco. But he also knew he couldn't realistically go away to college, even with a scholarship. He had younger siblings, and his mom still had a drug problem and worked graveyard shifts to accommodate it. So, despite his talent, he worked 20 hours a week at a restaurant, went to school full-time, and played baseball at College of Marin, a junior college, so he could look after his siblings.

Mack's head coach was subsidizing his living situation, providing him some finances so he didn't have to live at a drug house. This gesture was under the radar, and illegal. Mack was hitting .340 for College of Marin and Cal was interested in signing him as a shortstop. That is, until Marin's coach was caught exchanging money with him. Mack fell off after that, hit .200, and Cal lost interest.

After that year, he played junior college ball at San Francisco City College, living at home with his siblings. He also coached Lowell baseball that year. I was a freshman. He was a drill sergeant. He hit rockets at you with the fungo and if they got by you, he hit the next one harder.

"Get off my field if you ain't gonna stay down for a grounder."

I had heart palpitations one day during infield that sidelined me for the rest of the day. His intensity was sheer terror to a 13-year-old, but it made you better.

Mack went on to a short career at a small NAIA school in Indiana. A knee surgery kept him out for the first year and half. Then he was unofficially benched for dating a black girl.

"Hey, you gotta get rid of that girl, man," his teammate told him once. "We need you out there."

"Say what? Half the school is black!" Mack responded

"We see you together, driving her car. You know Coach won't have that."

Mack got into a fight which lead to another benching. A second fight and then he was done. A career destined for greatness, fizzled, done quicker than he could even process.

Now, nearly ten years later, he smoked weed in sweatpants and coddled his pit bull (named Lakota after Mack's fractional affiliation to the Native American tribe). He paid the electric bill in cash. He didn't have a credit card, or a debit card, or a bank account. He hadn't paid back a dime of his student loans, hadn't ever shown up for jury duty. For at least a week, every month, his phone got shut off because he refused to get off the couch and go downtown to pay the bill. He wasn't lazy, but he was stubborn. (This was evidenced by the excess of dog shit in the backyard which, if you put it all together, you could build a hut.)

And he wasn't a druggie. Or an alcoholic either. He didn't have kids running around somewhere. He was big and fearless with anger issues but tried his damndest to use rational thought over impulse.

He was a loyal friend. Whatever he had in the fridge, he offered you, because he knew what it was like to be truly *hungry*. When he spoke of his underwhelming bartending jobs, he said proudly: "I put food on my table." I'd always thought of this as an over-glorified and dated phrase, something coal miners and railroad workers said to their kids to make themselves seem heroic. But really, in Mack's case it was true. He *hadn't* had food growing up, and now he did.

He hosted an annual Thanksgiving at our house with some of his high school buddies, some co-workers, nearly all of them with long histories of bad decisions and worse luck, all scraping by. During football season he'd invite these people and others over for a Monday Night Football potluck. He'd spend all the tips he made bartending on chicken thighs and potato salad and an enormous watermelon and Ruffles and Sierra Nevada and everyone would come and get buzzed and sneak chicken skin to Lakota.

"Good friends and decent food, man," he'd say. "Life is good."

In this sense, Mack *had* come a long way. He *was* the mature one.

Ok, so the second question: why did I move in?

Well, rent was $500 flat (in the most expensive city in the country). And we got along well. Mostly because of baseball. We watched almost exclusively baseball. 20 hours a week, easy. Every night during the season we flipped back and forth between A's and Giants games, then watched the post-games and highlights on MLB Network. I'd sit there on my computer with Lakota at my feet, typing the very first pages of this book. Mack would fall asleep in his chair, barefoot, the coiled burners of the kitchenette stove red-hot to keep the room warm, an empty bowl of ice cream and spoon in his lap, with a blunt put out in it.

Part of what Mack loved about baseball was seeing all the things done wrong that he would do right as a player and manager. Like: he couldn't stand it when managers took the starter out in the sixth for the "lefty matchup."

"That's the *starter's* game. You let *him* give up the go ahead run, not some roast beef FATASS who only has THIRTY pitches in his tank. No offense, Emil."

"None taken," I always said of his ongoing skepticism, and frustration, with relief pitchers.

When analysts like Bob Costas or Tom Verducci—well-respected sports men with no documented history of having ever played a sport—became opinionated about things which they tangibly knew very little about, Mack blew a gasket. Specifically, when they brought up Barry Bonds and his tainted career.

"I cannot listen to these WORMS who have never played a game of baseball in their lives talk about Barry Bonds! Why are people *listening* to them? Why do people care what they say? Have they ever done *anything?* These fucking idiots don't realize that everyone did steroids, not just the good ones. Bud Selig *wanted* steroids, just like the American government *wants* heroin and cocaine. How do these slapdicks not get that? That they have a vote in the Hall of Fame is more treacherous to baseball than fucking STEROIDS!"

He got disgusted when the analysts and journalists over-exposed small mistakes and minor slumps of players just to make a story, and he faulted all of sports talk-radio culture, and the general public, for getting so wrapped up in the minutiae of the game: "in the past thirty games, Aubrey Huff's striking-out-to-end-the-inning percentage is ten percent higher than league average. Is this a concern? Do we move him down in the order?"

"Where do these sexless trolls come from?" Mack would cry.

He understood baseball at a level I didn't. Metaphorically, he knew the game to its rubber core; I only knew the stitches. He was perversely fixated on aspects few paid attention to. The majesty of a stolen base, the walking-lead to steal third. He studied how pitchers held runners, varied their looks, tipped that they were going home—the cat-and-mouse of it all. He spoke of the rhythm of fielding a ground ball and timing its bounces, and the music of a batting stance, the ebb and flow that became the load that became the explosion. He always kept his composite wood bat nearby so that he could stand next to the TV and emulate batting stances, admiring the ingenuity of certain ones, and critiquing the flaws of others. Lakota always rose with him, her tail wagging, her paws getting tripped up with his slippers, thinking it was all a game. Mack's baseball sermons were nightly. They oozed unconditional love and nostalgia for the game, and at times hearing them gave me the feeling of watching the last scene of *Field of Dreams*.

When I moved in with Mack, I never thought about what I stood to learn from him. I hadn't thought there was much *to* learn; I figured he was a perfect example sometimes of how *not* to live. As in, pay your bills on time to avoid living by candlelight and coming home to eviction notices taped to your gate. Have a bank account so that you don't have to hide your money in a Crown Royal bag as a 30-year-old. Pick up your dog's shit so she isn't constantly having to tip-toe across her self-made minefield, and so our neighbors don't leave us notes telling us their quality of life is being depleted.

But I *did* learn a lot from living with him. About baseball.

Not just because he was a walking baseball encyclopedia, not just because of the sexy art of a ground ball: ("Ground balls are music, man. It is all rhythm. If you can't field a ground ball, you can't fuck a girl right," was a Mack-ism.) Mack taught me how baseball figures into your life, how to co-exist with it, how to *love* it still when you're no longer a factor.

What I mean is, with all his baseball talk, his stories, his memories, his screaming at Tom Verducci on TV: he never sulked about his own career, how he'd been screwed. Which had to be hard. I was always meeting people who chose to devote so much energy to explaining how they'd been screwed by the game, how coaches never played them, how injuries plagued them, how they didn't get enough *love* and no one showed them *faith*, when really, they were simply never good enough.

Mack, on the other hand, had *had* a chance. He'd had pro scouts handing him cards in high school, his *tito* was in the Hall of Fame with connections. His baseball future had once been bright. You would think Mack, whose career expired long before it should've, would just *once* have said:

"If it wasn't for that fight, I'd have played more. I would have had a shot at getting drafted."

Or:

"If I didn't have a torn meniscus and MCL, I would have had more at bats. Screw Troy Tulowitzki, I was *better* than him in high school."

Or:

"If I didn't grow up in a meth house, wondering if I would eat that night, I wouldn't have had to put baseball on hold to watch my younger siblings; I would have had a scholarship, and played out my four years, and I would have had a career."

You'd think just *once*, sitting on the couch, smoking a blunt, he'd wallow in his misfortune. Or when we went to the beach at midnight after a few Rolling Rocks, to walk Lakota because she had lots of energy but also fought other dogs, and the beach at midnight was the only place she could go. You'd think, sitting and as the black tide in the distance gush and fizz, he'd sigh and say: *mannnn, if only...*

But nope. Never.

He blamed no one, when it would've been so easy for him to hold a grudge, like I had developed since getting Rheumatoid Arthritis. And so Mack, the guy who allowed his pit bull to chew his socks while they were on his feet, he became someone I admired, someone I learned a lot from. He preached the love of the game, and by living with him, he re-baptized me.

While I was out and he at home on the couch, I'd receive texts from him like: *Does Juan Pierre go to the Hall of Fame? Almost three thousand hits and over six hundred stolen bases...think about it.*

Sometimes, he'd get even more obscure, asking about some phenom from the 70s with an absurd name like Diffy Duncan, or Ross Boss, and I'd respond:

Does Charlie Hayes go to the Hall of Fame? He did catch the last out of a World Series once.

He'd laugh at my ribbing him for his over-obsession, then reply:

Ok, but how about Jimmy Rollins though? Seriously. 2300 hits, almost 500 sb, 4 gold gloves, and he's not even done yet.

We'd continue the dialog, and at seven that night, I'd find space on the couch with him and Lakota, and we'd watch another game. We would both hope—even when the Giants or A's were winning—that the other team would come back and tie it, just for the excitement, for the possibility of a few more innings.

39
THE IN-LAWS

When I visited Kendall for the first time in South Carolina, I was horrified. I'd never spent any time with people from the South, hadn't ever met a real, in-the-flesh George Bush fan. I feared everyone would unfurl their Confederate flags, show me their guns, and ask what the hell my intentions were with their daughter. I cinched my belt so tight it cut off oxygen to my brain. I wore the only polo shirt I owned, every day. They called oatmeal "porridge," dinner "supper." Cooking chicken wasn't a BBQ; it was a "grill out." It was only BBQ if you made BBQ, whatever that meant. Everyone used koozies, the foamy encasements for beer or soda that kept them cold; I had previously thought that only people in trailer parks with crude forearm tattoos used them. In the South, college football was not as big as Jesus, but it was definitely poking its head in the clouds.

With Kendall's family, baseball was the safest conversation topic: our only other options were politics, religion, premarital sex. Not to mention, as I'd learned in Hawaii—Kendall had a baseball family.

"Yelp," her stepdad Denny said. We were driving to get a family meal at Cracker Barrel. "My adult league'll get pretty competitive. There's some players, Emil."

"What's the average age?" I asked.

"Oh, probably forties. We got a sixty-year-old always trying to bunt for hits. He's tore his hammie once or twice. Got a coupla fifty year-olds stealin' bags, sliding head first. We post our stats online."

I was having a hard time not laughing. Did he not think

this was funny?

"Guys'll swing for the fences and wrench their backs. But they refuse to come out of the game."

"Sounds dang serious," I said. I had heard people actually use *dang* since getting to the South, a word that I thought people universally stopped using after fifth grade. I decided to use it to blend in.

"Emil. We had a guy *(gah)* on our team, a prominent banker, solid shortstop. Kept himself in great shape. Played with a lot of pride *(prad)*. He was always padding his stats, looking to stretch singles into doubles. So one Saturday he bloops one over the shortstop. He tries to get himself a double. Well, it was the weirdest thing. On the way to second, his pants just fall down. I guess his belt snapped, in a dead sprint. Well he tripped something bad, fell face down into the dirt. Son of a gun had a compound fracture."

"His leg snapped because his pants fell?" I asked.

"They almost needed a chopper to get him out in one piece," he said somberly.

"Geez," I replied, struggling to keep a straight face.

"Say, how about you tag along and hurl for us this Saturday?"

I flinched. So did Kendall. This was the summer of 2009, when the disease was in its brutal first months. The term Rheumatoid Arthritis was still new to me. I was still getting used to the concept of no more baseball. I still clung to the hope that whatever this was, it might not be a disease. This was before I started the meds. My elbow was lumpy and soft like a bruised banana. My fingers were hard and bulbous like mutant coral, unable to wrap around or even hold a baseball.

"Denny," Kendall jumped in, "He's got a bum elbow, and it wouldn't be any fun to pitch to ya'll. He threw against Oregon State and stuff."

"What ain't fun about striking everybawdy out?" Denny shrugged.

"Emil didn't come whole across the country to get recruited by some *has beyins* and *never wuzzes*," her mom Ginny said. "He's here to be with family." She winked at me in her rearview. My RA winked back.

Denny chuckled.

"Awlright, awlright. But hey, can we just have the boy answer for himself? Emil, ya *wawna* pitch for us this Saturday? We could use ya. And ah can almost guarantee you'll shut em *ayout*, even with a bum elbow."

The funny thing about Denny was, he knew my diagnosis was not "bum elbow." The family knew I had very recently canceled a pro contract, due to something a bit more serious than bum elbow. Kendall had told them, likely so conversations like this could be avoided. I sensed Denny didn't believe it was true, like whatever I had was more of a sensitive thing derived from the touchy-feely West Coast, with all our meditation, and group massages, and green tea.

"No thanks," I said finally. "I don't want to ruin anyone's stats."

"This boy gotta eat!" said Papa, the grandfather of the family. Six months had passed since my first visit, and I was back in the South. It was wet and humid there in the spring. If there was a park nearby, you could smell the grass from blocks away. There was an infestation of polo shirts, pastel-colored shorts, and terrible visors. By this time, I was physically diminished. Gaunt, even. My left knee was the size of a roll of toilet paper.

Kendall and I were in the park with her grandpa. His handshake cracked my wrist like burnt toast. He'd seen pictures of me pitching. That was who he'd expected to meet. So who was this twig with the mushy handshake, dating his favorite granddaughter? He was probably thinking, *I could whup this boy. Shit, Kendall could whup this boy.* And Kendall had to deal with knowing her whole family was likely thinking the same thing.

It should be mentioned that Kendall comes from superhuman genes. Everyone in her family has forearms capable of impressive strangling. Their jawlines are sharp. Her brother and uncle can consume almost exclusively french fries, yet remain trim with muscles that twitch and seem to wrestle *each other* to get stronger. Kendall's mom doesn't lift weights more than five pounds for fear of looking like a steroid abuser. Her family is physically at the top of the food chain, and one needn't look hard to see that, all stems from "Papa."

"You better eat a sandwich, or you might just disappear!" he chuckled, and looked to Kendall, who awarded him a smile. "Those pretty-boy California diets ain't holdin' up here in the Carolinas, are they, sweetheart?"

"No, sir."

After our picnic, during which Papa eyed my sandwich to make sure it contained mayonnaise, we strolled around the pond. I struggled to keep up with him, as his Popeye-forearms propelled him forward like kayak paddles. Kendall stayed behind with me.

"He's just moving slow to take in the pond, Papa. He's touched by it."

"It's a nice pond," he said, as if willing to grant my sissy feelings a pass, as long as they were in reference to something southern. Papa paused at an access point on the shore. He bent down, picked up a rock, and whipped it into the lake for fun. The pebble shredded the water like machinegun bullets.

"Skippin' rocks is nice," he said, not as an observation, but a dare for me to disagree. As I might have expected, Papa tossed me a stone and invited me to skip a rock.

"Let me see that pitcher's arm."

I looked at Kendall, who laughed. Papa meant nothing by it. No one had meant anything by anything. Not Papa's jabs about my starvation, not her stepfather's insistence to pitch in his Extreme Hemorrhoids League. But there I stood with a stone in my hand. It was such a modest request—*here, skip a rock*—that to have declined would have been deranged. I imagined the rumors spreading in her family.

"I met Kendall's boyfriend, and he outright *refused* to skip a rock!"

I flipped the stone. It *ker-plunked* straight to the bottom of the pond. My elbow rang.

"Son of a gun let me win," Papa griped. I worried that sooner or later, these trips to the South might raise a series of red flags to her family that the boy was too soft for their beloved daughter.

In 2010, Kendall moved to San Francisco. We'd survived a year of long distance. She's been here six years. Now, she rarely asks about my disease, and if ever I want to talk about it, which is never, she listens. She resists showing me the pity one might naturally show a significant other with a disease. I'm grateful for that. More so: she's never rolled her eyes or gotten fed up with the limitations my disease has caused us. After all, Kendall loves to backpack, play tennis, do backflips, cartwheels, have tickle-fights. And there have been plenty of times, bad days, bad weeks, bad months, when my condition has taken the wind out of her adventuresome sails.

There has really only been one time that she's called my manhood into question. One time, in seven years. I was on our couch, drinking water after a short, slow jog. Kendall had just gotten home from work, and was about to go for a jog. Her iPod at the time was in a constant state of mutiny, changing songs in the middle, erasing songs at will.

"Can I borrow yours?" she asked.

I tossed it her way. She unwrapped the ear buds and pushed buttons. I was beginning to strip down for a shower when she approached me and held the iPod in front of me the way wives hold foreign lingerie in front of husbands.

I looked at the screen: Madonna.

I shrugged.

"Baby…" she said softly, like a mother addressing her relapsed son.

In seven years, of all the things that could have made her second guess our relationship, Madonna. I'll take it.

40
RUNNING WITH THE DISEASE, NOT FROM IT

In 2013, I came across an ad for The Arthritis Foundation Run/Walk 5k. This was ironic to me, upon first glance: The Arthritis Run/Walk. Was it a cruel joke? To me, it was like The Foundation for the Blind having a Read-a-thon. Had they considered calling it the Arthritis Run/Walk/Limp/Not Move At All?

"You should do it, baby," Kendall said. "You're always jogging now anyhow."

"I'd be paying forty dollars to do something I do for free," I reasoned. "Not to mention, does anyone ever *know* where money for these 5k things go? 'Research' is conveniently vague. I don't want to be padding some big corporation's wallet."

She rolled her eyes.

"Ok, forget it. I just remember a boy a couple years ago who couldn't even push his legs through a pair a' pants. You woulda given anything to be able to go on a jog back then. And now you can."

She was right. I would have done *anything* for pain-free legs a few years back. I would have trumpeted reveille in a salmon costume to a pack of sleeping bears if only to be able to flee from them without arthritic pain. And here I was, functional knees and all, with a chance to run for a very personal cause.

"Haven't I paid enough money for this disease?"

"That's exactly what you said when you did the focus groups," she said. "The disease was 'taking from you,' and 'it owed you.' But you always felt worse after those. I think it's high time you realize that your disease ain't paying you a thing."

My inability to come up with a snappy retort confirmed that once again she was right. If there was one thing I had learned about Rheumatoid Arthritis, it was this: it wasn't the kind of thing that reimbursed you. It wasn't a give and take arrangement. It wasn't *fair*. It wasn't a mooching friend to whom after a few beers you asked for the money he owed. It wasn't even a tax return which gave you a morsel of condolence after killing you for a year. Rheumatoid Arthritis was an enigma. It was alive, and it was moody. It had your whole life in its palm and could crush you if it felt like it. If it was inside of you, it owned you, no matter how you felt about it, no matter how you dealt with it, no matter how much you thought it *owed* you. If you wanted RA to pay you back, you'd be waiting forever.

On the morning of the race, the streets were closed and the air was crisp in downtown San Rafael. There were all kinds of people signing in: kids in strollers, high school kids, people in wheelchairs, and a whole lot of regular looking people. It was a family affair, and oddly, I felt part of the family.

"These people all look normal," I said. "Do you think they all have Rheumatoid Arthritis?"

"Who knows?" Kendall said. "*You* look normal…"

After the first five minutes of the race, Kendall struggled to keep up with me. Aside from a svelte African who was clearly running in preparation for something else, like the Olympics, I was in front. I loved the choo-choo look of breath from my mouth. I remembered the route I'd run in Hilo, from my house up the side street to the waterfall at the top of the hill where I'd run on Sunday nights to sweat out the previous night's booze. Up by the waterfall, away from streetlights, under zillions of stars, with the sound of the water and the smell of flowers, I had the surreal feeling that it was hundreds of years before, and I was the only one on the island.

As I traversed the Arthritis Walk route through the quaint downtown of San Rafael, my iPod played my pump-up songs from college. I was reminded of being at Wong Stadium, running with Saff on the warning track, doing calisthenics before I pitched, sprinting after the game. I began to feel the initial burn and prickle of my body sweating. Soon I was a mile in, and Kendall was far behind.

"I tell you what," she said, catching up, out of breath. She was in great shape, had been a gymnast, a pole-vaulter, and a cheerleader in high school. She could do the splits, could breeze through a P90X video, but jogging for whatever reason killed her. The boredom of it exhausted her. "You run with me the first half, and you run at your pace the rest."

"Deal," I said.

The jog became slow. Kendall heaved for air. Strands of hair fell in her face and she was forever blowing them out. When we reached the halfway marker, she patted my butt.

"Go," she said. I took off, then looked behind at her like a child testing his mom's boundaries.

"*Go,* baby," she said, rosy cheeked.

I nearly sprinted the last mile and a half. My lungs and my legs burned like I was chasing something with the intent to murder.

Having a disease in which my own body attacked itself, and hated itself, had been tough to accept. For years, it made me think less of myself, made me think I'd done something wrong. Which, Lord knows I might have. Nowadays, with the help of the meds, running felt like my one chance to fight back, to show the disease it hadn't completely won. I could still be happy, feel some semblance of normal.

As the race ended, I felt no pain, just a deep gratitude for little things that would otherwise be nuisances: burning lungs, the chilly feeling of sweaty clothes sticking to my body in brisk morning air, the sting of headphones in my ears, calf cramps.

I never thought I'd miss those feelings, but now, I cherished them. It felt nice not to be running from the disease for a change, but to be running with it instead.

41
THE OFF-SEASONS

By 2014, Charlie had played for three different teams. The Cardinals, the Pirates and the Cubs. He was a career .300 hitter with five years in the minors, and still hadn't made it out of Double A. Five years of bus rides from one armpit of America to the next, looking out the windows at oblivion. Five years of catching in triple digit heat in nameless cowtowns where the only thing for dinner was AM/PM or Huddlehouse. Five years of dings and bruises and foul tips off his shoe tops, of texting his girlfriend during a 14-hour bus ride, of watching guys from the Cardinals and Pirates get called up from his team to play in the Bigs—guys that were worse hitters than he.

One time, when he was playing for the Cubs in 2013, he texted: *Some 18-year-old Puerto Rican just came on the bus and asked can I sit here and pointed next to me and I said 'no.' Sorry bro, I haven't been getting bitched down here for four years to share my seat with anyone.*

I understood where he was coming from, mostly. It was a seniority thing. Plus, he was filthy and cramped from catching nine innings in sultry heat and needed legroom. He'd texted me to vent, but also to get something off his chest he possibly felt guilty about.

I replied: *Good. He's gotta learn one way or the other.* It was what he needed to hear, but to myself, I wondered, is it starting to grind you thin out there, brother?

Each off-season was different than the last. Sometimes he came back feeling optimistic. He found the positives in everything. Some years he was resolute, determined to stay the course. He didn't even talk about outcomes, or outside factors like management and trades and draft picks; he just put his work in, trusted the process. And some years he was a grueling realist, psychologically worn down by the odds stacking against him, and the incredible work he was committing without the guarantee of any payoff.

Probably he spent 75% percent of his off-season fishing. All kinds of fishing. He'd drive up north and sit on a pier in China Camp all day with two reels cast, he'd drive hours south and burrow himself into some jetty, he'd freeze his ass off on his boat in the bay and hook tiger sharks and rays. He'd scale cliffs and walk down dizzying switchbacks with his poles and bait and tackle boxes in hand to sit on a perch for eight hours with only the noise of water lapping against rocks below. He'd crab, he'd eel. Up at his folks' property in Clear Lake, he'd set up eight poles, hook up bells to all of them, sit there on the dock with a can of chew and wait all day to hear the ding. He barely ever kept anything he caught; that wasn't what it was about. I'd go out with him and enjoy it for the company and the way the sun or moon reflected off the water, but for Charlie, it was meditative, something deeper, something to take his mind off other things. That was when he'd talk about baseball.

In the 2010 off-season, he said "I like where I'm at right now. I'm hitting .300. They had me at big league camp this year. I was standing there next to La Russa; he was calling me by name. Pujols was giving me hitting tips. I'm sure they'll start me out in big league camp next year. I'm a few strokes of good luck from The Show, man."

And then the next year, in 2011, when they didn't have him in big league camp:

"It's a grind, man. You never know what the front office is thinking. No one does. And they're all that matters. They completely control your future. Nothing else. You can be on a tear, twenty game hit streak, whatever, and they'll demote you or outright release you. I've seen it happen. I'm doing *my* job man, I know I am, but I've been here long enough to know that isn't the half of it. They're going to do what they want, so I don't even try to speculate."

The 2012 off-season was different. He wasn't home until later that fall. After his season with the Pirates, he'd played for Team Israel in the World Baseball Classic qualifying rounds, losing the semifinals to South Africa. Charlie was ejected in the ninth for arguing balls and strikes, as a catcher. The next day, he came home. One night, we drank at Big Rec, Lowell's home field, and Charlie caught me up on his experience:

"It was good, man. I was proud to play for Israel. It reminded me I *love* baseball, dude. It sounds stupid, but I actually *needed* that. I mean, I never loved baseball when I played for the Cardinals, or the Pirates. Is that not fucking crazy? Not only was the World Baseball Classic fun, but you know what? Now I can say I was on a World Baseball Classic team. That's huge on my resume. I realized some things, playing against all those guys, being the catcher of that team. I realized, dude, I am the top one or two Jewish catchers...in the *world*."

He laughed at this, then burped. He was drunk.

"It means something, though. You don't just get to sign up for these teams. You gotta be somebody. They gotta *want* you. It all means something. I'm the top Jewish catcher in the world. I'll have that forever."

"Damn straight," I said, looking at the mound and home plate that we'd thrived on nearly ten years before.

"I mean, listen, dude. I'm a career .300 hitter, blah blah blah. I can sit and bitch about being in Double A. But you know what? *Everybody* gets fucked in this thing. That's something you learn in five years in minors. Everybody gets shafted, it just depends how bad. I'm stuck in Double A, I can't do anything about it. But I'll tell you what I realized, dude. I'm a *good* catcher. I don't care what they think, if they keep me down in Double A. I'm a good catcher. And I'm a *damn* good hitter."

"I know it."

"Fuck. I am. I'm a good catcher."

He seemed to be telling this to himself more than me. After all, *I* never doubted it. But the way he was talking, about being the number one Jew, and a good catcher, he seemed to be identifying lifetime achievements, things to tell his grandchildren someday in the event that he never made it to the majors, something perhaps he was beginning to come to terms with.

It was November, 2014, the beginning of Charlie's seventh off-season. The Giants had just won their third World Series in five years, and now teams were beginning to make off-season moves. Charlie had just finished a year with the Cubs. He was a free agent, able to negotiate his own contract. He was *still* a career .300 hitter, had never *stopped* being one. So while it was somewhat of a surprise that he hadn't ever been called up to The Show, it was *no* surprise that he hadn't been cut. The scouting report on Charlie was that he was a singles guy, a slap-hitter. He lacked the power the big clubs looked for. As a catcher, his pop time to second was a shade under what was desired, also. Literally a hundredth of a second was the difference between a big leaguer and chopped liver. Statistically, at this point, the odds were against Charlie to ever make it to the majors, but if he had ever been a believer in odds, he would've checked out of the game a long ago. Every year, there was that one story, that one guy who'd spent a career in the minors, finally getting his chance. And we all knew that Charlie was the kind of guy who that could happen to.

We were in his Toyota Tacoma headed for the Pacifica Pier; it was crabbing season, and it was one of the few catches that he actually kept. At this time of year, you could hardly find a spot on the pier among the melee, and Charlie was always happy to load his truck up with the gear, put on three jackets, grab a can of chew and hope for a bite. Earlier that day, he'd texted:

Tell Kendall I might be an Atlanta Brave next year.

I told her immediately. She, being a lifetime Braves fan, shrieked like she'd won the lottery, and was promptly making plans to road trip.

"Yeah, man. One of their guys called me this morning," Charlie said. The truck had the unmistakable Charlie smell of Grizzly Wintergreen and fish bait. "He asked me what I'm looking for in a contract."

"That's awesome! So you're going to be a Brave?"

"Not necessarily. Honestly—you know me. I don't care where I play. What that phone call meant was that ball clubs know about me. I'm on their radar. You know? That's all I care about."

"Has anyone else called so far?"

"The Reds. Also the Tigers. The best part about all of these phone calls, dude? Not just that they're happening. But they're happening *right now,* when teams are just starting to make moves for next year. Them calling now is way different than them calling me in three months. It means they *want* me, as opposed to: they're *desperate* for just any catcher to come rot in their bullpen."

"Fuck, yeah they want you," I said. "You're Crash Davis, man."

"You know, I called my Cubs guy? The other day, right after the World Series when I knew all the teams were going to start making moves. I was antsy to find a spot. Because if I didn't? Then I'd be scrambling come spring. I wouldn't be able to enjoy the off-season. I wouldn't sleep. I'd constantly wonder if I was out of a job, if this was it, the end of the road. So I called the Cubs guy Travis and was like, 'Hey man, I wanted to talk about what your guys' needs are next year, wondering if you guys were thinking about resigning me.' And he was all, 'Charlie, great to hear from you. Listen, I'm a little busy right now, let me call you back in an hour or so.' I'm like, no prob

Trav. And you know what? That fucking guy never called me back. I'm like, bro. Fuck you. You're not that busy. Who do you think you are? You're the fucking *Cubs,* bro." (This, of course, was before the Cubs won the World Series in 2016. Charlie did play with Kris Bryant one year in Double A, and he told me repeatedly that Bryant was; the truth. He'd never seen such a natural hitter, never seen the ball jump off a bat like when he hit. This was something Charlie had never said about anyone before.)

Soon we were set up on the Pacifica Pier. Charlie was stuffing sardines into the crab cages, biting fishing line with his teeth and tying knots, getting the poles ready for casting. Surrounding us were Filipino and Vietnamese families. We cracked open our Mickey's tall boys and sat on a bench as the sun nuked the sky. Thin clouds striped the sunset, wavy like bacon strips. The pier went so far off shore that we watched waves start as tiny speed bumps, then gradually gain speed and girth, until eventually they crashed on shore. Charlie reached the reel back and cast the bait hundreds of feet into the Pacific. His cast wasn't dissimilar to his swing—a violent explosion of the hips that ended in an extended-arm pose. He rested the reel on the pier then sighed.

I knew that sigh. It meant he was relaxed, but would feel more relaxed with a chew. He took out a pinch and put it in his upper lip. He was more than a can-a-day kind of guy now. When Tony Gwynn had died earlier in the year, he'd made an effort to cut back. But that lasted only so long. "When I'm trying to grind through these minors, dude, I'm not about to give myself an added challenge. This shit is a challenge enough," he'd said in a phone call. "I got a career to look after. I can quit when I get what I'm after."

"When the ball clubs call, what do they ask?" I asked.

"They ask what I'm looking for in a contract. Just to feel me out, see what kind of info they can get before they have to talk to my agent."

"What do you tell them?"

"Dude. I'm up front. There's no point in trying to tell them what they wanna hear. I learned that from years in the minors. So I tell them, 'listen...' Oh, wait. My phone's vibrating."

He looked at the screen quizzically.

"Hold up."

He got up and walked down the pier.

"Hello?" he asked. "This is him..."

I swigged my beer, watched a sea lion arch its oil-slick back out of the water then disappear. 20 feet away, it did it again. To my left, a dad and his kid had a flashlight on a raw chicken and were hacking it to smithereens with a cleaver. The dad put the chicken in the bait box and cast it over the ledge. Somewhere, a duo of homies was listening to E-40 from their cellphone, smoking a grape Swisher.

Minutes later, Charlie sat next to me. He had his poker face. It was a terrible poker face.

"Who was that?"

"The Angels."

"Yes! What'd they say."

"Same shit."

He was trying to be calm, but I could tell he was thrilled, from the way he was he was biting the sides of his mouth. A habit shared by all three Cutler brothers when excited and trying not to show it. This was Charlie's fourth call in the first week of the offseason. He no longer had to worry *if* he'd play. It was just a matter of where, and for how much, and this was a huge relief. 29 year-olds in Double A were not any ball club's priority, even if they were good hitters, so originally, Charlie had feared it might be over.

"They asked what role I was looking for, what my expectations were."

"And? What'd you say?"

"You know what I said?"

I'll never forget.

"I said I don't care about the money anymore man. I'm old and I'm not in it for the pay. Pay me in chew for all I care. You know what I want? The only thing I want is big league spring training. I want to play in front of Scioscia."

"Yeah?"

"Give me a chance in front of the big boss, that's all I ask. I don't need to be cut any breaks; I haven't gotten any to get where I am. I been here too long. I love the game too much."

"So what did he say?"

"He said that was fair, and that he'd be in touch with my agent."

"Do you think you'll be an Angel?"

"Like I said, I don't care. All I know is, I can't spend another year in minor league spring training. I can't get herded like cattle by some hick in triple digit heat, man. I can't run from station A to station B, getting treated the same as I was seven years ago as a rookie. I can't get in line with a bunch of 19-year-old catchers and do timing drills and 60-yard dashes, and split the batting cages with a pimply 18-year-old from Nebraska. It's dehumanizing. I just want a fucking real chance."

Charlie signed with the Angels a few weeks later. His contract stipulated: big league camp, guaranteed triple A (trips, he called it), and $8,000 a month. Everyone was thrilled. It was the most commitment any team had shown him in all his years of pro ball, at a time when he was most vulnerable. All the stars were aligning for this to be Charlie's year.

About three weeks before he was set to leave for the Cactus League, he texted:

Do you know any doctors willing to write me a fake prescription?

Me:

No. What's up?

Charlie:

Just let me know if you think of anyone.

He wasn't a complainer. But this was his subtle way of telling me his arm was shot. His shoulder. When I asked what happened, he didn't get into specifics, just gave vague answers like "It's just tired, man," or "It's a little dead."

But I knew Charlie. Just mentioning it meant he could hardly lift his arm. And unlike High School Charlie, whose idea of Manning Up was wearing shorts in winter, he couldn't Man Up through this. He also couldn't, under any circumstances, show up to big league camp injured. He'd always told me these exact words: showing up injured is worse than showing up a drug addict, or a murderer.

"I can't ever go on the DL. If I go on the DL, that's my career."

The doctor explained his options: he could take a cortisone shot and rest for a few days and see how it felt and start throwing, or take two cortisone shots—an unhealthy, ill-advised dose of anti-inflammatory that could likely make him able to take shrapnel without pain—and not throw at all until he got to Arizona. The latter was the biggest risk, biggest reward.

Charlie chose the latter. He knew his arm better than anyone else, knew his pain was something fierce, and that he needed it to be in the best shape of his life for big league camp. He knew this could very well be his last ever chance before getting released. So he sat in the chair for 20 minutes in cringing, teeth-gritting pain, as the doctor speared the needle into his rotator cuff to dump the shot.

As I write this, he is road-tripping with his girlfriend to Arizona for his second big league camp, with no idea how his arm will feel when he gets there. He is hoping for the best. He is 29, entering his eighth year in the minors. He's played over 500 professional games. He has crow's feet when he smiles from years in the sun. His voice is permanently hoarse. His shoulder is arthritic and pumped with drugs to stay alive. But in the end, he's still a kid, chasing a dream. He doesn't care about money. He just wants a chance. I'm 30, and I've been away from the game for so long, that his dream is now my dream. I'm pulling for him, as much, if not more, than I ever did for myself.

42
ELIJAH

I've coached for seven years now. I've watched freshmen grow to seniors. I've watched them start as barely five feet and end up taller than me. I've heard their voices drop, listened to their conversations evolve from what Mom gave them for lunch and what movie they snuck into to who hooked up with who and who got drunkest at the dance. Sometimes they get into math or politics, and I tell them to shut up.

Regarding my frequent question: "How's the arm, can you pitch today?"

I've watched freshmen who say "I can't pitch— I pitched six days ago," eventually grow into seniors, who say "I'm going a hundred pitches today, at least," with a look in their eye that says *if you try to pull me out of this game I'll fight you.* I love that look.

I've watched them fight through slumps, try to play through concussions; I've carried broken-ankled players off the field. Players' parents have undergone chemo. Parents have died. And yet the kids return to the ball field. They're just kids, and I'm at the age where I still feel like one of them, but don't remember what it was like to truly be one of them. They help bring me back, or perhaps keep me living, the best time of my life.

I remember sitting with some of my guys once during a lazy summer double header. It was one of those games where people play positions they've never played before, and everyone laughs at everyone sucking.

"I could really go for some Korean barbeque in between games," one of the boys said.

"Yeah that would be ill," Another said.

"Korean barbeque would be Kim Jong *ill*."

"Just kicking back, barbequing during games."

"On a Kim Jong Grill."

Sometimes I think back to when I got diagnosed with Rheumatoid Arthritis, how I tried to cut baseball out of my life. I stopped watching it, didn't care about hot prospects coming up on the Giants or A's; odds were I'd played against some of them. People would talk about Buster Posey and Tim Lincecum and I'd think, *I played Florida State one year before Posey was there, I played University of Washington the year after Lincecum was drafted; I was right there with them. Don't expect me to obsess over them.* During those times, sometimes late at night I would watch the video of my bullpen in Hilo that got me my pro contract. I'd watch the snap of my arm, the elasticity of my legs, the ease of pitch after pitch. I couldn't believe I had been that person just a few months before. After watching I'd have a hard time sleeping.

The period when I was diagnosed was a bad time. I was in pain, depressed from graduating college, gut-punched with the reality of moving back home and having to work dumb jobs. That was the worst kind of college hangover there was. But really, I'm pretty sure, what made that time as bad as it was, worse than those aforementioned things, was the fact that I'd cut baseball out of my life.

Elijah was a kid I coached at Lowell. He pitched a complete game and had three hits in the championship his senior year, but he hadn't always been a stud, and we hadn't always gotten along.

His sophomore year, during a tournament in Orlando, he called me out to the mound in the second inning after giving up an astounding homerun.

"I'm done," he said.

"What do you mean you're done?"

"It's my elbow," he said dismissively. He was too young and dumb to authentically pull off the injury lie. He was giving up in the face of failure. "My elbow hurts."

"Bullshit," I said. "Don't tell me about elbows, man."

"I'm done."

"Tell me one more time, and look me in the eye when you say it."

"I'm done," he said.

After the game, I told the two pitchers from that game—Elijah, and our last-string pitcher who'd come in for mop-up duty until we inevitably got mercy-ruled—to meet me in the hotel fitness center in ten minutes. I had both of them get on the treadmill and told them to run until I told them stop. After ten minutes, I tapped the benchwarmer and told him good job, goodnight. Elijah started powering down his treadmill as well.

"What are you doing?" I asked.

"You said we're done."

"I said he's done. You're done in 40 minutes."

Elijah shot a look at me that was so dramatic he tripped and face-planted on the track, like something out of "America's Funniest Home Videos."

"I need my inhaler," he said.

"Good, go get it."

That summer, the team was running after a game, and I told Elijah he better start giving the sprints his all, or mark my word, we were going to sprint until someone fell. Elijah discreetly flipped me off. I saw it. Elijah ran that day until he collapsed.

That year, Lowell made it to the championship for the first time since I'd started coaching. Before the game, a feature article was done on Elijah in the *San Francisco Examiner* which read:

Saunders credited coaches for his success, particularly Lowell pitching coach Emil DeAndreis, who has helped Saunders on and off the field. Saunders admits he had plenty of growing up to do. "No doubt about it, Emil gave me all the lessons I needed," Saunders said. "I was always a quiet kid growing up, but I could get mad real quick on the baseball field. Whenever I stepped out of line, Emil would take me to the side, talked to me about it and let me know how he felt. The greatest challenge in my career has been adjusting my attitude and realizing that it's an honor to be able to play baseball. I look at the game now and see it as a privilege."

Reading that article, I felt how Mack felt about baseball. Baseball was bigger than me. Much, much bigger. And that made it more beautiful than I'd ever imagined it to be as a player.

After Lowell, Elijah went down to Cal State LA and walked on as a pitcher. His ego was somewhat inflated due to his success in San Francisco's Clownball league, and he thought he would be able to go down to LA and play shortstop in addition to pitch, just like he had for us. I told him his glove and bat weren't good enough for college, but he didn't take my word for it. And what can you do when an 18-year-old is determined? Why crush his dreams just to crush them? I figured he'd find out on his own and that's the best way anyhow.

When he got down there he got a pretty righteous dose of college ball and learned that his days at shortstop were numbered. As predicted, he made the team as a pitcher only, and he was fine with that. One night, that December, as his fall workouts started to wind down, he sent me a text, likely after a couple of drinks:

Coach I want to play baseball the rest of my life. Fuck everything else.

I stared at the text for a while, feeling weird and tingly in my chest, sneezy in my nose. I was caught off guard. When I started coaching years ago, if a kid had sent me this text, it probably would have pissed me off. I would have thought it was a dumb grandiose statement from someone who's watched a lot of movies. I probably would have replied something like:

First of all, talk is cheap. If you want it, work for it, go do some sprints. Secondly, so what? Who doesn't want that? Get real kid, it just doesn't work out that way. Take it from me.

But the text didn't make me feel that way. It warmed me. And this was a big indicator of where I was with baseball now. I felt it was worth it to stay around this game if only to receive texts just like this one.

So I wrote:

How many beers deep are you, chump?

But what I meant was:

Thanks, kid. You brought tears to my eyes. You make me thankful for keeping the game in my life.

43
EPILOGUE:
THE THRILL OF VICTORY,
THE AGONY OF DEFEAT

I have baseball dreams now more than I ever did as a player. They are somewhat irregular, but common enough to know that there will always be another one. When I was a player, they used to be anxiety dreams, like I'd show up to the park without my glove, or I'd be on the mound having to throw watermelons, or whole chickens, for strikes. These days, they're not anxiety dreams. They aren't haunting or tragic or even complex. In them, I always do the same thing, and they end the same way.

Rarely do I know any of my teammates in the dreams. Sometimes they have the names of old teammates and friends but they look like no one I've ever met. Mostly, my jerseys are colors I've never worn. The fields are sometimes places I've never been, places that may not even exist.

Once I dreamt I was pitching at AT&T for our high school championship. Except, in the dream I was 27 years old, and aware that I had already done it ten years before. I threw my warm ups, and in doing so was reacquainted with the perfection of that mound, the flatness of the infield, the crunch of metal cleats in the dirt. I re-experienced throwing harder from adrenalin. I enjoyed the hollow, acoustic pop of Charlie's glove. I knew it was Charlie from the way I talked to him, trusted him, except he was black, with dreadlocks. Scouts were there. So were my parents. I took things seriously and warmed up as though it were perfectly normal to pitch in a high school championship as a 27-year-old. Then it ended. When I woke up and thought about it, the whole thing felt staged, like a charity event from Make A Wish Foundation. Like, "it's been Emil DeAndreis's dream since his diagnosis to pitch again at AT&T, and here he is doing it. Put your hands together, ladies and gentlemen!"

In another dream, I warmed up down the foul line in a different stadium. I was 27 again. This time, I was a big leaguer, about to make my debut. I don't know what team I was on. The backstory of the dream was, I had once been a budding prospect whose career was sidelined by RA, but the disease had gone into such deep remission I tried to make a comeback, got signed as a free agent, and climbed through the minor leagues. There was a lot of press about it. It was a big feel-good-story-in-the-making for ESPN. The stadium was filling up as I tossed. Kids were gathering near the bullpen and chatting. My adrenalin was electric. The sky was an endless, majestic blue. I wasn't throwing flames, probably high 70s and low 80s like always. I woke up before I ever threw my first pitch.

I had one pitching dream that didn't even involve pitching. I dreamt I had woken to an email from Dr. Sherry saying that after recent tests, she concluded I no longer had the disease: *Go outside with a baseball and throw it around to be sure, but the tests are very conclusive, I'm pleased to say, Emil.*

In the dream I sat up in bed, straightened my elbow and realized I could extend it for the first time in years. Dr. Sherry was right. I sprung out of bed in my pajamas and woke people up in my house like it was Christmas morning. I looked at my fingers, and the knuckles shrunk back to normal. I gripped a baseball, mimicked a throw. Pain-free. Like the email said to do, I took a friend to West Sunset Park and long tossed. I threw to the 200-foot sign, like I'd do with Charlie in our college off-seasons. The disease was gone, and I could play again.

When I woke up from the dream, I was groggy. In bed, I

straightened my elbow, just like the dream. I actually walked into the living room, paced around for a while, wondering *was that real? Did I really just get an email saying the disease is gone?* Then I picked up a baseball, looked at the knuckles pressed against the seams, fat and mangled.

My dreams always end before the game begins. I never record an out, never record a pitch. The disease is gone, and I'm cleared to pitch, but I wake up somewhere in the bullpen, somewhere off the mound, warming up in pain-free, delirious excitement for a game that never ends up happening. Maybe my experience with Belgium left me psychologically in "almost made it" mode, and it is reflected in my subconscious. Some might think I resent these dreams, of being in a hallucinatory land of endless possibility, and *still* not being able to pitch. You'd think my mind would create vivid and thorough pitching triumphs whenever possible, you'd think my dream would last long enough to get on the mound.

I don't resent the dreams, though. On the contrary, I find myself looking forward to the next one, thinking about where my mind will put me, what color my jersey will be, who my teammates will be, under what circumstance I'll be warming up, and how close I'll get to going into the game before waking up. I like thinking that one of these days I'll make it long enough in one of those dreams, whether it's set in high school or the minors or the World Series, for the game to start. At that point, I can give up grand slams for all I care.

My dreams, as they are now, emphasize the things easily lost or forgotten in the melee of competition, the little things: the gravelly sound of sliding into second, the feeling of the field beneath my metal spikes, the humidity of a fresh watered field in spring air, the redundant music between innings, the clank of aluminum bats when one is tossed in the pile, the glorious chatter and waiting around for something to happen, the message under the bill of any hat I ever played in—*the thrill of victory, the agony of defeat*—blurring and distorting from rings of sweat.

People ask me what it's like not to play baseball anymore, and I tell them coaching helps. When I coach, my players ask me the same thing, and I tell them how it really is, because someday they'll experience it too. I don't say it in a tone meant to scare. Really it's not that scary of a concept, not any more, at least. And I think they get it. They're smart kids. I tell them it's like a disease you learn to live with.

ABOUT THE AUTHOR

Emil DeAndreis teaches writing at San Mateo College in California, where he also coaches baseball. In addition, he is the coach of his alma mater Lowell High School Cardinals in San Francisco—City champions for four years in a row under his guidance. He lives in San Francisco with his wife Kendall and is at work on a novel.